Socialism and the
English Working Class

Socialism and the English Working Class

A History of English Labour
1883–1939

James D. Young
Lecturer in History
University of Stirling

HARVESTER WHEATSHEAF
NEW YORK LONDON TORONTO SYDNEY TOKYO

First published 1989 by
Harvester Wheatsheaf
66 Wood Lane End, Hemel Hempstead
Hertfordshire HP2 4RG
A division of
Simon & Schuster International Group

Printed and bound in Great Britain by
Billing & Sons Ltd, Worcester

British Library Cataloguing in Publication Data

Young, D. James
Socialism and the English working class:
a history of English labour, 1883–1939.
1. Great Britain. Labour movements.
Ca. 1870–1950
I. Title
335'.1'0941
ISBN 0-7108-1205-1

1 2 3 4 5   92 91 90 89 88

0000507

335.00942
you

Dedicated to George Shepperson

GENTLEMAN, SCHOLAR AND HUMANIST

Professor Emeritus of History
University of Edinburgh

Contents

Acknowledgements

My debts as a labour historian are numerous but belong
mostly to the larger study of European capitalism and socialist
movements of which this book is a byproduct. As someone
who adheres to the materialist conception of history (as
distinct from crude 'economism'), I want to thank the now
defunct Social Science Research Council for giving me a
generous research grant in 1974 to allow me to investigate
British working-class culture and attitudes to state intervention between 1883 and 1914. However, as I got caught up in
the passionate debate about the Scottish national question in
the late 1970s, I decided to produce separate studies of the
distinctive histories of the Scottish and English working
classes since the nineteenth century. The Carnegie Trust for
the Universities of Scotland gave me grants to complete the
research for this study of *Socialism and the English Working
Class*. The imaginative, generous and supportive socialists in
the Institute for Policy Studies in Washington, DC also gave
me a grant to work in the archives of the Socialist Party of
America. The archives of this forgotten organisation contain
much information on the history of the English working class.

On the practical level Margaret Dickson, a secretary in the
Department of History in the University of Stirling, typed the
manuscript of *Socialism and the English Working Class* with
great efficiency, patience and good humour. Moreover, in the
early 1970s George Shepperson and Royden Harrison
stimulated my interest in the distinctive features of the history
of the English workers. Since then – and in the more difficult
and less sympathetic conditions in British universities in the

ix

1980s – they have prodded me in critical ways that proved invaluable.

My greatest debts are to Lorna, Alison and David (or in my non-hierarchical socialist alphabet, Alison, David and Lorna). They know why, and that is what matters. I also owe a great deal to Eddie Boyd, Cathie Thomson, Freddy Anderson and the other rebels with whom I put the world to rights in the pubs of Glasgow and Falkirk.

Polmont, Falkirk,
Stirlingshire
June 1988

Introduction

Half-a-century ago, Karl Kautsky remarked that the gulf between the
classes in modern society had grown so great that the ruling-class, in
order to obtain information about working-class life, had to send out
fact-finding expeditions into territory every bit as unknown as Central
Africa. The gap has hardly narrowed.

Peter Worsley

With the exception of transitory phases in the late nineteenth
century, the period of the 'labour unrest' between 1910 and
1914 and the period of the General Strike in 1926, the
educated elites in the English labour movement were often
very hostile to the workers' autonomous culture and way of
life. Socialist criticism of English working-class life was harsh,
constant and often insensitive. In a society where the working
classes were seemingly so indifferent to the things the
socialists regarded as important, and where trade unionism
and socialism were often associated in the popular mind with
bloody revolution and incendiarism, the socialists considered
it necessary to project a collective image of responsible, if not
actually licensed, protest and revolt.

A major feature of the often tortuous relationship between
socialist intellectuals and English working-class movements
was the *social distance* between the majority of unorganised
workers and the labour movement. Despite the socialists'
denigration of the majority of working-class men and women,
the workers evolved a distinctive *culture* of their own. It was,
moreover, reinforced by a value system and way of life in
which 'unconscious socialism' played an important role in
motivating working people's struggles against the capitalist

1

system. In portraying the social history of the English working class between 1883 and 1939, it is essential to illuminate the hidden, though tangible, conflicts between the *ouvrierisme* (or rejection of 'outside experts') and socialist intellectuals' hostility towards the workers' distinctive way of life as an important factor in preserving the established social order.

Although socialism played a major role in the history of the English working class between 1883, when the nominally Marxist Social Democratic Federation (SDF) was formed, and the outbreak of the Second World War in 1939, the labour movement represented only a minority of the working class. While the socialists' presence in the history of the English working class was often important, the place of educated elites and spontaneous working-class feeling in English socialism and socialist history have been far too often ignored in the dominant labour historiography.

Within the hidden history of the English working class, the elitism and condescension of socialist intellectuals towards working men and women were prominent and endemic. Although the *class* composition and personalities of the dominant educated elite changed over time, the socialist intellectuals' elitist condescension was both constant and detrimental to the realisation of the socialist goal of creating a classless society. But just as these social tensions within the English working class did not force themselves into the dominant labour historiography, so many labour historians still assume an identity of interests between the organised minority and the unorganised majority.

In most historical studies of the history of English working-class culture, the emphasis, since the publication of Richard Hoggart's book, *The Uses of Literacy* in 1957, has usually been on studying the organised minority rather than its relationship to the unorganised majority. Far from attempting to reconstruct a *social picture* of the elements of 'primitive rebellion' within the English working class, the stress has been on the supposedly 'working-class' party, the trade union and socialist intellectual traditions. Yet it is more than thirty years since Hoggart criticised 'historians of the working-class movement' for producing histories of the organised minority and not histories of the English working class.

In savaging the English workers in the late nineteenth century, Karl Kautsky, the 'Pope of Marxism', wrote:

> Their highest ideal consists in aping their masters and in maintaining their hypocritical respectability, their admiration for wealth, however it may be obtained, and their spiritless manner of killing their leisure time. The emancipation of their class appears to them as a foolish dream. Consequently, it is football, boxing, horse-racing and opportunities for gambling which move them the deepest and to which their entire leisure time, their individual powers, and their material means are devoted.[1]

Furthermore, socialist criticism of working-class life and behaviour was not only abstract, it was also part of a living struggle between conflicting social and moral values. Already remote from the mass of the workers in the 1880s, most socialist intellectuals were still further alienated from working-class life and sub-culture. But since vast numbers of working men and women, who were sometimes indifferent or even opposed to socialism, were less literate and articulate than their critics, we know much less about them and must often depend on evidence which is both oblique and diffuse.[2]

In 'explaining' the reasons for English socialist intellectuals' hostility to working-class culture, one historian has argued that 'The contempt for social amusements was the resentment of things which distracted the workers' attention.' Yet in making the specific criticisms of working-class culture, the socialists were saying exactly the same as middle-class critics of working people. Thus Arnold Freeman cited the workers' interest in 'the Picture Palace, Music Hall and Football Match' as evidence of the absence of any 'elevating influences' in their lives; and, James A. Little and Charles Watney condemned the English workers' involvement in the 'picture palaces and football' as being 'very baneful to habits of thrift'.[3]

A major turning-point came with the outbreak of the First World War. From then onwards, the English workers' general anti-capitalist outlook merged with a Labourism which was somewhat more sensitive to workers' attitudes and values – at least in some spheres of working-class social life. What made it easier for the Labour Party to adopt a relatively more sympathetic attitude to the workers' way of life was the mass process of radicalisation engendered by the war. Without this process the Labour Party would not have attracted a mass vote in the general elections of 1918 and 1922.

In arguing that the First World War was important in producing 'a significant transformation in the quality of life of the lower classes', John Stevenson asserts that 'Habits such as cigarette smoking, the cinema, gambling, the use of contraceptives and the decline of organised religion could all be in part attributed to the war.' But although the Labour Party was relatively more tolerant of the workers' gambling and attendance at football matches and the cinema than socialist intellectuals had been before the First World War, English working-class socialism had become more aggressive and articulate by the early 1920s. And despite the election of two 'minority' Labour Governments in 1924 and 1929, workers' culture remained autonomous.

Moreover, the tensions between the socialist intellectuals' socialism and the socialism of working-class men and women were sometimes sharpened by self-taught working-class intellectuals. Thus in a review of Ellen Wilkinson's novel, *Clash*, in 1929, Fenner Brockway wrote: 'Three conflicts are developed in the story, any of which might have provided the title. There is the conflict of the general strike itself. There is the conflict between the claims of the comfortable "arty" socialism of Bloomsbury, and the hard, rugged socialism of the coalfields. And there is conflict between the masculine appeal of a lover with whom marriage would mean the end of personal expression in public work and independence'. By 1939 the Left's relatively greater appreciation of English working-class culture was seen in their belated response to the advent of the dance known as the 'Lambeth Walk'. As one observer explained: 'It was partly due to a long discussion between a leader of Mass Observation and the Transport House propaganda experts, who could not see the faintest connection between the Lambeth Walk and politics until the whole history of dancing and jazz had been gone into.'[4]

I

Throughout the period between 1883 and 1939, the English

working class resented the successive members of the socialist intelligentsia not because they were 'socialists' but because they were middle class. The independent culture of the working class as well as workers' rejection of middle-class values helped to shape the peculiarities of the labour movement. The English labour movement's 'peculiarities' were generally thought both to reflect and impinge upon the distinctiveness of the English working class. The latter, it was usually argued, stood in sharp contrast to the socialist working classes in Western Europe. Writing in 1929, Egon Wertheimer, the German labour journalist and scholar, argued:

> This close affinity of the Labour Party with traditions of national culture has been especially favoured by the circumstances of its tardy birth, the lack of class-struggle ideology, and a historical period of conflict with State and Society. Separated by no class barriers from the mental and spiritual concepts of capitalism, which would otherwise have given birth to an exclusively proletarian way of life and morality, and deep-rooted in national religious tradition, the Labour Party has never been able to make a clean breakaway from capitalist culture.[5]

Although this assessment of the Labour Party was accurate enough so far as it went, Wertheimer tended to ignore the oppositional culture of many working-class men and women.

The English socialist intelligentsia often made the mistake of assuming that they, and they alone, accurately articulated, explained and codified the workers' 'socialism' – or rather lack of it – to the wider society outside the labour movement. Yet a distinctive feature of this socialist intelligentsia was its elitism and aloofness from the majority of working people. In discussing the role of such intellectuals in the working-class movement, Ralph Miliband wrote:

> From the eighties onwards, a growing number of intellectuals came to 'adopt' the world of labour, and to feel themselves as in some way part of it, even though the world of labour might not reciprocate the feeling. What had been a trickle in the eighties became a flood in subsequent decades, and was greatly strengthened with the emergence and consolidation of the Labour Party as a major political force. This connection of reforming intellectuals with the Labour Party and labour movement had a strongly pedagogic impulse, with educated and competent professional

people seeking to guide untutored trade-union leaders and others. One of the early Fabians, Graham Wallas, noted that the British labour movement did not have 'a socialist clergy, such as the German social democrats had created, charged with the *duty of thinking for* the working class'.[6]

Miliband might have added that the English workers insisted on thinking for themselves, particularly during the labour unrest between 1910 and 1914. While a small number of democratic socialist intellectuals from William Morris to R.H. Tawney constantly fought for real enlightenment and dialogue within the labour movement, they were not typical. From the foundation of the Social Democratic Federation in 1883 through to the emergence of the Socialist League in the 1930s, the majority of socialist intellectuals often adopted very elitist attitudes towards Henry Dubb,[7] the legendary member of the rank and file. The elitism of the intellectuals in the Social Democratic Federation found its classic expression in Tressell's authentic 'Marxist' novel. As Ross McKibbin puts it:

In Robert Tressell's *Ragged Trousered Philanthropists*, the socialist hero and Tressell figure 'Owen' (notoriously speaks standard English while his non-socialist workmates communicate in various forms of a debased demotic). It is plain, furthermore, that Tressell regarded such speech as a sign of political incompetence. It seems to me one of the few Leninist tracts in British socialist literature and is so unsympathetic to the working class that the novel's popularity is almost inexplicable.[8]

The Fabian and Labour intellectuals too were just as elitist and contemptuous of English working-class culture as the Marxists in the Social Democratic Federation. The Fabians were committed to the tactic of 'permeating' the Conservative and Liberal Parties with the doctrine of collectivism from their foundation in 1885 until the early 1890s, and hence were more closely identified with an elitist minority than with working-class culture. But with the growing trade union agitation for independent labour representation in Parliament in the late 1880s and early 1890s, the local branches of the Fabian Society in the provinces forced the London leadership to play an important role in the formation of the Independent Labour Party in 1893.

The Fabians' recognition of the place and significance of the music halls in English working-class culture did not, as Ian Britain argues, imply sympathy. Indeed, in an extended discussion of Fabian attitudes to working-class culture, he says that they felt distaste for the workers' inherent 'coarseness'. In a carefully considered and well-documented assessment of their elitism in relation to working people, he says:

> The tendency to judge Victorian working-class culture by the standard of high culture was not a peculiarly Fabian one, and for contemporary observers, whose early social and educational background had afforded them little exposure to anything but the products of high culture, it would have been one that was impossible to avoid. While the Fabians' ingrained prejudices are readily understandable, it is less easy to justify the attempts of some of them to make these prejudices, in the name of socialism, a basis of their general social and political – as well as cultural – policies.[9]

Yet the Fabian intellectuals played a less decisive role in the history of the English labour movement than did Philip Snowden and Ramsay MacDonald.

There were nevertheless important differences between the socialist intelligentsia in Britain and on the Continent. The dominant intellectuals in the English labour movement appear to have been more elitist than their Continental socialist counterparts. A major reason for this was that the really influential intellectuals in the English working-class political movement were Labour rather than Marxist intellectuals, though an independent *workerist* intelligentsia managed to function in English communities at various times between 1883 and 1939.[10] In commenting on these differences, Julius Braunthal wrote:

> I observed also the absence of that socialist passion which was such a dynamic force in the Continental labour movements, especially in Austria and Germany. . . . When I knew the English working-class people better, it appeared to me as though they were less politically minded than Continental workers. They seemed to be accessible to the socialist idea; indeed, their natural sense of fairness and justice invites its acceptance.[11]

Yet the Labourism of the dominant English socialist intelligentsia was not always compatible with the 'socialism' of the working class; and the militancy and disaffection of the latter from the established social order were often more durable and permanent.[12]

But despite the tangible distinctiveness of the 'socialism' of the English working class, Egon Wertheimer was already unusually perceptive in 1929 when he insisted that 'the close connection of British Labour with British national culture and tradition' was the key factor in understanding the peculiarities of the English. And it was certainly true that the peculiarity of the socialist intelligentsia in England shaped the subsequent perceptions in labour historians' chronicles of working-class life. Furthermore, the intellectuals who represented the Labour Party between 1883 and 1939 did not always faithfully express the 'socialism' of the working class.

Ross McKibbin has made some very interesting points on this subject and therefore deserves to be quoted at length:

> Nevertheless, the sort of men who were so prominent in European socialist parties – marginal bourgeois, journalists, theoreticians, professional orators – were comparatively rare in Britain. In the Parliamentary Labour Party the two who came closest to the type were MacDonald and Snowden. Both were autodidacts, both were theoreticians of an eclectic kind . . . both were very hostile to the old-fashioned Lib-Labism which, in one form or another, was still at the base of working-class politics. . . . But the attitudes of men on the margin are essentially ambiguous. MacDonald and Snowden, for example, spectacularly deserted their class in 1931 when the old Lib-Labism (using the term generically) held firm. It is only a short step from journalism and oratory to middle-class styles of life and from that to a contempt (scarcely concealed in MacDonald's case) for working-class narrowness and stupidity.[13]

Yet despite the setbacks experienced by the labour movement in 1926 and 1931, an independent working-class culture survived and preserved its potential for socialist agitation later on.

II

Despite the enormous changes in working-class life between

1883 and 1914 and from the end of the First World War to the beginning of the Second, English working-class culture was not, in Ross McKibbin's words 'an apolitical or inert culture'. In making the point that the English workers' culture existed independently of the dominant culture, he insists:

> It is true that those who had enough surplus income frequented the music-hall and increasingly the cinema. Who, however, was deceiving whom in commercialised entertainment is unclear: working men and women clearly enjoyed it and many found it intellectually stimulating as well. Yet going to the cinema does not eliminate other activities: a comparatively rich associational culture simply scattered and localised political ambitions.[14]

Moreover, although a sizeable minority of the English working class were Conservatives with a capital 'C', and some aspects of working-class culture were conservative with a small 'c', many working men and women frequently expressed fierce anti-capitalist sentiments. Because the dominant labour historiography has focused almost exclusively on socialist intellectuals and working-class movements at the expense of portraying the lives and culture of the unorganised majority, the anti-capitalism of the latter has been largely ignored by labour historians. Throughout the period between 1883 and 1939 there were, for example, strikes of schoolchildren, and strong *class feeling* of the sort expressed by miners' poaching, as well as resistance to changes in the labour process at the point of production.

In state schools a class war was fought against the culture of the English working class down to 1939. As Stephen Humphries argues: 'The fundamental cultural contradiction experienced by working-class children was that state schools were essentially middle-class institutions, which embodied official values, and that commitment to schooling required a rejection of the distinctive styles of speech, thought and behaviour characteristic of working-class culture. The process of class-cultural conflict in which schools were involved is forcibly expressed in the influential Newbolt Report of 1921, which became the standard text for the teaching of English during the interwar period.'[15] This class-cultural conflict produced the strikes of schoolchildren between 1883 and 1914

– a phenomenon rediscovered by Dave Marson in the early 1970s. In his powerful autobiography, *Fighting Through Life*, Joseph Toole described the conditions which produced the children's strikes: 'Schools in my day were not designed for the education of children, as today.'[16]

At the beginning of the present century, R.E. Hughes described the class-cultural conflict identified by Stephen Humphries. As Hughes put it: 'The English parent, too, often instinctively feels that the influence of the school is decidedly opposed to that of the working-class family . . . and the whole attitude of the school is strongly antagonistic to the home and the world outside.'[17] This was the milieu in which the strikes of working-class children in the state schools erupted again and again before the First World War.[18]

But although children's strikes did not occur in the interwar years, working-class children often attempted, in Stephen Humphries phrase, 'to subvert the school syllabus'. In summing up the diverse responses of workers' children to compulsory schooling in capitalist England, he says: 'It was only a minority of working-class children who felt angry and resentful when their schooling ceased at an early age. The hostility that was generally directed against working-class boys and girls who succeeded in entering grammar schools was motivated not so much by envy as by contempt for those 'snobs' and 'poshoes' who appeared to have rejected their own culture in exchange for social advancement.[19]

But just as working-class children resented the teacher as the representative of an alien culture, so were they also antagonistic to the policeman. In an account of working-class life in Manchester in the 1890s, Joseph Toole depicted the ways in which the police disrupted children's games.[20] Nevertheless, the more 'respectful' and better-off elements in the working class were probably less hostile to the police. As Michael Blanch argues: 'There is some evidence to suggest that better-off workers and petty property holders viewed policemen more sympathetically. The conflicts between police and youth were certainly sharpest in the central working-class districts where unskilled and semi-skilled workers lived.'[21]

Although working-class dislike of the police was not quite so intense after the First World War, it persisted.[22] Moreover, worker's notions of 'respectability' often inhibited the better-off elements from expressing hostility to the police. This 'respectability' also functioned before 1914 to prevent many workers from joining trade unions. As Ben Tillet explained: 'A poor, consumptive, doss-house victim, once in a good position, well educated, would carry the complex of "respectability" to his grave. No matter how low he might sink in the social scale – to be a trade unionist was to him an unthinkable disgrace.'[23] Yet despite the decline of this sort of 'respectability' after the war, the tensions between working-class culture and middle-class values continued to be a major factor shaping the politics of the labour movement.

The role of football matches, the music-hall and the cinema in working-class life was, in the view of many historians, one of socialising working people into an acceptance of ruling-class attitudes and values. In a study of the cinema in the years before 1914, David Robinson asserts that:

Before the war the great audience was the poorer working class, and the films they apparently preferred were those of high moral value and didactic tone; and the taste was a heritage of Victorian times. The films of the pre-war era favoured bible stories, morality dramas and melodramas in which virtue was rewarded and vice suitably punished.[24]

In analysing the role of the cinema in Rochdale after the war, Paul Wild is concerned with its essentially conservative role. As he puts it: 'The next time social considerations or messages were to permeate a definite grouping of films was when Warner Brothers began a series of films, including "I am a Fugitive" and "Cabin in the Cotton", during the depression. But very few of these films were successful as social documents or as box office attractions.'[25]

Moreover, when Allen Hutt, the communist intellectual and writer, published an account of *The Condition of the Working Class in Britain* in 1933, he identified the crucial role of the cinema in allegedly imposing bourgeois cultural dominance on the working class:

London affords excellent examples of the perversion of powerful cultural instruments by the bourgeoisie to its own class ends. Here the cinema, as everywhere, has undergone a meteoric expansion while the number of theatres and music-halls has declined. And the whole purpose of the cinema under capitalism is expressed in the cynical comment of the *New Survey* on the report that unemployed men were seen visiting cinemas – 'there is no reason to regard the time or money as necessarily wasted or ill-spent.' With all their defects the cinemas at least serve to divert the thoughts for a time from dark forebodings. As one of the London unemployed observed: 'They make you think for a little while that life is all right.'[26]

But although socialists adopted the same attitudes to the cinema before 1914, official opinion actually portrayed the role of the cinema as a basically anti-capitalist one. Indeed, Charles Watney and James A. Little attributed the 'labour unrest' and 'industrial warfare' from 1910 onwards to the influence of the silent cinema:

> These men from our poorer cities read glowing accounts of the displays of wealth, not necessarily ostentatious, but of everyday occurrence. They know it exists, for they have often caught a fleeting glimpse of it themselves and in their ignorance interpreted ordinary everyday methods of life as vulgar show. They read of costly menus, and know their own outlay on bread and dripping – if that – for their children. They see the pictures in the papers, which love, both from interest and inclination, to chronicle the doings of the famous. They even witness the actual portrayal of it in the cinematograph shows which are springing up – in legions. People do not always appreciate the influence of these two factors in moulding popular thought.[27]

Because working-class attitudes towards English society were *influenced* by such mediating cultural instruments as the cinema, it is important to emphasise that the ruling class never gained an unquestioning acceptance of their values and attitudes. Indeed, in an unorthodox communist account of the role of the cinema in the 1930s, Noreen Branson and Margot Heinemann assert: 'American domination of the screen dream-world was thus one factor which indirectly helped to weaken respect for the old British ruling-class values – titles, hereditary wealth, Oxford accents, public-school manners – among the working class.'[28]

But although English working-class cultural attitudes were influenced by the cinema and bourgeois newspapers, the stubborn resistance to capitalist values in the factories and state schools did not depend on the existence of educated socialist elites. Like the trade union leaders, many socialist intellectuals tried to integrate working people into the established social order.

III

Although many labour historians have assumed that trade unions represented the more militant and anti-capitalist members of the English working class, this was not always the case. Certainly, the engineers and other organised workers in the craft unions remained a part of what Lord Snell described in his autobiography as 'this respectable and carefully deferential movement'.[29] The trade unions, and particularly those formed amongst the unskilled workers from the 1880s onwards, may have played a positive role in working-class life, but they did not always articulate an anti-capitalist philosophy. Those closest to the trade union struggles could, as David Craig argues, 'see time and again how the militancy despised and feared as barbarous by the middle and upper classes was in fact a civilising force',[30] but it was not always a socialist or anti-capitalist force in politics.

The 'new unionism' was most certainly a civilising force. In the London, Liverpool and other English docks the 'new unions' imposed essentially middle-class values on working people. As James Sexton observed: 'In one instance, it was forbidden, under penalty of a fine, to indulge in abusive language to any other member.'[31] In rejecting the 'friendly benefits activities' of the 'old unions', the 'new unions' refused to 'spend most of our union money on burying our members' instead of attempting to 'improve the material conditions of the living'.[32] But by the 1890s they were forced into what they regarded as the pro-capitalist posture of introducing friendly benefits as a 'method of attracting and holding members'.[33] It was, moreover, significant that during the peaks of the labour unrest between 1910 and 1926 new attempts were made by the most militant trade unions to reject 'the goose and coffin approach' of the 'old unionism' by making unions instruments of class warfare.

The trade unions old and new were frequently responsible

for *policing* the social behaviour of working people; in Bradford 'the [Pressers] union was responsible for discipline, levying fines for lateness or for defective work'.[34] In acknowledging the positive role of the 'new unions' in the 1880s, R.A. Woods said: 'To see labourers who a few years ago were deemed almost below being helped now, for the sake of seeing justice done, divide their scanty earnings with the confectioner girls, the seamstresses, the farm hands or with the working men at the other end of the earth, is calculated to give one a fresh sense of what the brotherhood of humanity is.'[35] But the disciplinary role of the 'new unions' was often resented. In explaining this antagonism amongst farm labourers, Frederick Verinder said: 'Not only must this unfortunate "hired servant" show sufficient self-control "not to use profane language" under circumstances of great provocation, he must also exhibit the virtues of punctuality.'[36] This clearly inhibited many workers from joining the 'new unions', except at moments of extreme social tension and class conflict, and contributed to the instability of the unskilled workers' trade unions. But although the instability of the membership of the farm labourers' trade union was crucially due to their antipathy to union discipline, other factors were at work, too. The farm labourers' poor wages in comparison with other workers, their relative isolation on small farms, the farm-owners hatred of them and the decline in the agricultural sector of the English economy all combined to rob them of the industrial 'muscle' possessed by coal miners, engineers or even dockers. Consequently, the protests and revolts of the farm labourers were inevitably individualistic.

During the 'historical' moments between 1883 and 1939, when the militancy of working-class minorities was most obviously a civilising force in working-class life, the majority of English working people were often quiescent in the political sphere. Conversely, when comparatively large numbers of the working class rejected the values of orthodox trade unionism and Labourist politics, workers' militancy was usually immune to the indoctrination of the traditional educated elites such as the 'Marxist', Labour and Fabian intellectuals. Though they probably underestimated the break in the continuity of mass working-class disaffection after 1922, Dan

Finn, Neil Grant and Richard Johnson described the period between 1910 and 1926 as a prolonged moment of considerable working-class resistance to capitalism:

> Throughout this period, forms of working-class politics arose that differed markedly from what became the dominant Labourist adaptation: a trade unionism which united industrial action and political aims; rank and file movements, suspicious of officialdom and challenging the wartime State, the evolution of communism and a tradition of industrial direct action and mass sympathy strikes. Without these legacies the General Strike would not have taken place; its defeat was one of the ways in which tendencies like these were educated out of the class's repertoire.[37]

Yet a constant feature of English working-class life in the factories, mills and coal mines throughout this period was what Ralph Miliband calls 'the process of de-subordination'. In identifying the specific features of de-subordination, he argues that:

> In relation to work, de-subordination is of course a very old phenomenon, and has assumed a wide variety of expression, from 'Luddism' and sabotage to go-slow, strike action, sit-ins, work-ins and different forms of protest, engagement and action. It also involves – and this is one of its most common forms – a refusal to do more than the minimum required, or less.[38]

What it also involved was a rejection of the representatives as well as the ideology of temperance advocacy at the work place.[39]

This rejection of the ideology of English capitalist society, though always taking different forms, and less intense at some historical moments than at others was ever-present. Thus in Jarrow in the 1930s the middle-class 'social-service workers' could not understand the hostility of unemployed men towards their do-gooding activities. In explaining the source of this class hostility in her book, *The Town That Was Murdered*, Ellen Wilkinson wrote: 'I discussed the problems with a few of the men in the unemployed club at the Labour Rooms. They hated everything connected with "social service". Their attitude was that they wanted to organise themselves in their own way. The very word "recreation", they said, had a sort of stigma in Jarrow.' Furthermore, 'The old Labour rooms, nearly falling around our heads, were the centre of vivid, intense communal life, which no social service organisation or welfare worker can ever arouse . . . or for that matter understand its passionate independence.'[40]

IV

English working-class culture and the labour movement were often separate spheres, though the gap between them narrowed considerably between 1910 and 1926. Just as working men were engaged in a cultural class struggle with the middle and upper classes, so working women engaged in a struggle against their slave status within labour organisations. By questioning their status, the women who were employed in industry waged their own distinctive fight against the values of a patriarchal capitalism.

From 1883 onwards there was increasing tension between the dominant social values of the ruling classes and those of many working men and women. But the blurring between the 'underground' cultural class struggle and the distinctive open social struggle over wages and working conditions have obscured the historian's view of what happened and distorted the social picture of working people's overall experience and response to exploitation and inequality.

PART ONE

1

The Labour Movement and 'the Poor', 1883–1914

The voice of the poor themselves does not come to our ears.

John and Barbara Hammond

The idea that outstanding political acts and State actions are the decisive acts in history is as old as written history itself, and is the main reason why so little material has been preserved in regard to the really progressive evolution of the peoples which has taken place quietly in the background behind these noisy scenes of the 'stage'.

Frederick Engels.

The dominant socialist groups in the English labour movement between 1883 and 1914 were more interested in socialism from above than in socialism from below. By 1883, when modern English socialism was born, the classical Marxist view of a mass *socialist consciousness* developing in a 'practical movement' and leading to the 'alteration of man on a mass scale', had been replaced by the concept of the decisive role of the 'vanguard' party in the struggle to create a new society.[1]

But although there were repeated outbursts of English workers' aggressive adherence to authentic socialism between 1883 and 1914, expressions of working-class sympathy for socialist ideas were circumscribed by a bureaucratised labour movement. Furthermore, the bureaucratisation of socialism was, as Carl Levy put it, 'accelerated by the emergence of a stratum of ex-worker officials'. However, in confronting the argument that either a socialist intelligentsia or a 'labour aristocracy' deradicalised the working class, Levy questions 'the existence of a golden age of unsullied socialism before "alien" social groups or conditions' diverted English workers

19

from their inherent egalitarian goals.[2]
Nevertheless a detailed account of English socialism will illustrate how socialists, whether they belonged to the Social Democratic Federation (SDF), the Socialist League, the Fabian Society, the Independent Labour Party (ILP) or the Labour Party, alienated themselves from the poor and helped to integrate working people into capitalist society. As this happened, socialists both began to despair of the emergence of a mass socialist consciousness and contributed to the process which stifled it.

Many English socialists believed in the ultimate collapse of capitalism, and, in 1889, J. Hunter Watts predicted that the existing social and economic system 'would die of self-immolat[ion]'.[3] Although there was a very real working-class hostility to 'socialism', the SDF saw this as irrelevant to their aims. Whilst Harry Quelch, a very talented working-class intellectual and leader of the SDF, asserted that the English workers were most 'backward' in contrast to elsewhere in Europe',[4] he did not lack hope in socialism from above. Such pessimism, together with the importance socialists already attached to orthodox science and raising the general culture level of the working classes, increasingly led most socialists into an elitist posture.

Although skilled workers played a major role in the English branches of the SDF, they were often contemptuous of the poorer workers. When he surveyed the officers in the English branches of the SDF in 1895, R.A. Woods concluded that they were 'skilled workers having good positions, tasteful in their appearance, and modest and agreeable in their bearing'.[5] In depicting the English working class more than a decade-and-a-half later, Fred Henderson noted that there was as yet 'very little socialism' amongst the poor in 'the worst slums, in the most sweated industries or in the world of underpaid rural labour'. Sympathy for socialism as 'a new social order' was, in Henderson's opinion, restricted to 'the better-paid and better-conditioned artisans'.[6]

Robert Blatchford and the Clarion Clubs were very critical of the working-class poor. As Carl Levy argues: 'The Clarion Clubs with their mixture of entertainment, culture and Bohemianism nurtured the "intelligent reader" that Blatchford appealed to. Traditional working-class culture was slighted.'[7] And in the late nineteenth century, many English workers articulated actual hostility towards socialist ideas and representatives. During the general election of 1892, for example, the Labour candidate and his supporters in Jarrow were 'showered with flour, eggs, and anything handy'.[8] Paul Thompson attributed the weakness of the labour movement in Bethnal Green, Stepney and Camberwell to 'the chronic poverty typical of inner working-class districts, breeding a political apathy which made a labour or socialist movement peculiarly hard to establish'.[9]

And yet the existence of labour organisations was not an essential precondition for what Marx and Engels depicted as the workers' 'unconscious socialism'.[10] Mutual aid amongst the poor often existed independently of the labour movement. As Robert Roberts observed in his now famous book about Salford, *The Classic Slum*: 'The poor certainly helped the poor. Many kindly families better off than most came to the aid of neighbours in need without thought of reward, here or thereafter.'[11]

Moreover, the poorer workers were hostile to state interference and social reforms because they did not appreciate 'the value of all benevolent effort working from above'. Despite the 'excessive thrift and prudence of the better-class poor', they did not hesitate to help 'the poorer' working-class families.[12] Commenting on English working-class life before the outbreak of the First World War, Margaret Eyles asserted that 'The communism of the old days, for mutual protection, has given place to an unnatural individualisation.'[13]

But such Marxists as Ernest Belford Bax, Harry Quelch and H.M. Hyndman did not recognise the 'unconscious socialism' of the English workers. Appalled by the illiteracy and ignorance of the working class, and profoundly convinced of the utility of science and education, Hyndman wrote: 'Nowhere more than in England do we need the help of the class which has absorbed all the higher education.'[14] Then, in an editorial entitled 'Ignorance and Education', *Justice*, the organ of the SDF, put the socialist case for more and better education and criticised those establishment figures who were opposed to educating the working classes: 'No doubt they think that if the "lower orders" were educated they would not be such subservient slaves as they are today. Well, we are inclined to agree with them, and it is precisely the reason why we want better education.'[15] This commitment to raise the educational level of the workers was quite compatible with the elitist outlook of most socialists. Working-class cadres were just as elitist as their middle-class counterparts and were, in their own estimation, culturally superior.

A decisive circumstance in deepening the socialists' initial elitism and hostility to working people was their isolation from mainstream working-class social life.[16] From 1883, when the SDF became committed to socialist principles,[17] down to 1914, most members of the SDF adopted an elitist posture which was out of step with Marx's fundamentalist thesis that the workers had to emancipate themselves. The members of the SDF broadly identified themselves with Marxism, but they also distanced themselves from some of the basic assumptions Marx repeatedly expounded about the complex relationship between politics, education and economics. H.M. Hyndman wrote: 'That, as Marx said, the emancipation of the workers must be brought about by the workers themselves is true in the sense that we cannot have socialism without socialists. But a slave class cannot be freed by the slaves themselves. The leadership, the initiative, the teaching, the organisation, must come from those who are born into a different position, and are trained to use their faculties in early life.'[18]

For the SDF the relationship between the laws of history which would ultimately create the supreme revolutionary moment and the political role of their cadres was complementary and not dichotomous.[19] Democracy and authoritarianism, like voluntarism and determinism, coexisted within the same individual socialist heads. In 1885 the English working classes were being gradually 'stampeded towards socialism' and 'a compact minority' of revolutionary socialists were waiting to 'take advantage of some opportune accident that will surely come'.[20] From this perspective the middle-class intelligentsia and the working-class intellectuals had an indispensable role to play in creating a class-conscious working class.[21] In the face of formidable difficulties and mass working-class apathy, if not hostility, to elitist socialists and often socialism, too, the SDF held firmly to the concept of the vital role their compact minority would play in making the socialist revolution when the time arrived for decisive action. What some workers disliked was not socialism, but the representatives of 'socialism' in the English labour movement. In 1899 one worker wrote to the editor of *The Clarion* objecting to the development of a 'cultural, intellectual elite in socialism . . . withdrawing into select coteries where only subjects of philosophy and higher education are talked over'.[22] Unaware of the exact nature of English working-class culture, most socialists saw workers' thrift, self-help and 'respectability' as inherently anti-socialist. However, in explaining the poor's repugnance for a pauper's funeral, Eugene D. Genovese recognised that 'an English worker who, say, gave his child a pauper's funeral would thereby pauperise himself – that is, would diminish his credibility as a "respectable" working man – in the eyes of prospective employers.'[23] Workers' 'respectability' was not, therefore, inherently anti-socialist, though it sometimes inhibited working men and women from joining trade unions.

As working-class antipathy to socialism was seemingly intensified, the socialists, whatever their particular political affiliations, persisted for nearly four decades in prosecuting their original approaches to the working classes.[24] Everything that socialists valued most – knowledge, learning and high culture as well as *dignified* protest – was ignored or dismissed by many working people. For example, a semi-literate worker, in a letter to the secretary of the Socialist League in London in 1886, mentioned in passing that socialism, though discussed by working people, was often 'a butt for ridicule'.[25] When asked what would happen to the workers under socialism, a rather didactic, though idealistic member of the SDF who was lecturing his fellow artisans on the need for a socialist society, replied: 'When we get socialism, there won't be any people like us, we shall all be civilised.'[26]

Alongside what was only a thinly concealed contempt for the working class as it actually existed, socialists in the SDF, the Socialist League, the Fabian Society and the ILP soon discovered a strong, if not always acknowledged, emotional identity with the educated elements in the middle class.[27]

This, coupled with a burgeoning middle-class sympathy for some socialist ideas in the 1890s, made most English socialists increasingly sensitive to the possibility of the riotous unemployed and striking workers alienating middle-class opinion. Moreover, if the working classes were 'cussed' and indifferent to their atrocious conditions and fate, the same could not be said of the leaders of the middle class. The latter were fighting for improved working-class social conditions and were displaying sympathy for socialism as they understood it.[28] Since patience was a cardinal virtue in the individual cadres who made up the compact minority, their resolution was of prime importance.[29] As early as 1888 their commitment to wait for the 'opportune accident' that would destroy capitalism had been stiffened by their belief that socialist ideas had 'permeated the thought of the age'.[30] Such reformism and palliatives as the agitation for effective compulsory education and a legal eight-hour day were not therefore ends in themselves;[31] they were the primary means of raising the cultural level and class consciousness of the working class.[32] Besides, in a society where workers were seemingly so indifferent to the things the socialists regarded as important, even the Marxian socialists in the SDF considered it necessary to project a collective image of responsibility, if not actually licensed, protest and revolt.

I

The young Engels was the first 'Marxist' to criticise the workers' intemperance, improvidence, sexual licence and 'general inability to sacrifice the pleasure of the moment to a remoter advantage'.[33] Nevertheless he praised and identified with 'the humanity of the workers', who, having experienced 'hard times themselves', were friendly and able to 'feel for those in trouble'.[34] A similar theme runs through Marx's *Capital*.[35] Far from seeking 'reformist' socialism to integrate the workers into the existing social system, Marx and Engels wanted an independently educated and class-conscious working class who would 'conquer the brutal element of the revolution and prevent a Ninth Thermidor'.[36] Victims of their own elitist middle-class prejudices, and lacking the conviction of Marx and Engels that working people could sometimes 'feel for those in trouble', the SDF consistently worked to create an academically educated elite of proletarian and middle-class cadres. They also systematically proceeded to criticise almost every aspect of working-class life.

In *The Ragged Trousered Philanthropists*, Robert Tressell articulated the anti-working-class prejudices of the SDF with great brilliance. What is frequently overlooked in discussions of the SDF's Marxism and Tressell's socialism is their shared belief in the imposition of the socialist revolution from above. The pages of *Justice* were full of observations that socialism would ultimately be imposed on a hostile working-class population by a 'compact minority' of revolutionary socialists.[37] But perhaps the best exposition of how socialism would come in the midst of working-class ignorance and 'stupidity' was offered by Ernest Belford Bax:

> The majority, therefore, under a capitalist system will necessarily for the most part vote for the maintenance of that system under one guise or another, not because they love it, but out of sheer ignorance and stupidity. It is by the active minority from out of the stagnant inert mass that the revolution will be accomplished. It is to this socialist minority that individuals, acting during the revolutionary period, are alone accountable.[38]

It was this commitment to socialism from above that permeated the world-view of most members of the SDF between 1883 and 1914. Also, because they rejected the potential creativity and ability of English working people to make their own history, they did not find it at all difficult to ridicule and denounce them. In a letter he sent to Margaret Harkness, the author of the novel, *City Girl*, in 1887, Engels said:

> In the *City Girl* the working class figure as a passive mass, unable to help itself and not even making any attempt at striving to help itself. All attempts to drag it out of its torpid misery come from without, from above. Now if this was a correct description about 1800 or 1810, in the days of Saint Simon and Robert Owen, it cannot appear so in 1887 to a man who for nearly fifty years has had the honour in sharing in most of the fights of the militant proletariat. The rebellious reaction of the

working class against the oppressive medium which surrounds them, their attempts – convulsive, half-conscious – at recovering their status as human being, belong to history and must therefore lay claim to a place in the domain of realism.[39]

In rejecting the agency of democratic working-class struggle, the members of the SDF were forced into a pessimistic stance. However, the pessimism of H.M. Hyndman, Belford Bax and Robert Tressell was not idiosyncratic. It was at the very heart of the elitist and socialism-from-above orientation of the SDF. There was actually an innate dialectical relationship between their rejection of working-class struggle and their deep pessimism. Although he does not seem to grasp the symbiotic relationship between pre-1914 'Marxist' antagonism to the English working class and pessimism about *when* the inevitable English socialism would come, Stuart Macintyre makes some interesting comments:

> The air of gloomy antagonism to the bone-headed working man was extremely prevalent among pre-war Marxists and emerges with particular clarity in Harry Quelch's own sub-Dickensian short stories about working-class life which were collected in *Literary Remains* (1914). Indeed, *The Ragged Trousered Philanthropists* only elaborated and improved the literary quality of an established genre of such pessimistic proletarian fiction.

In asserting that 'contempt for the unregenerate [English] worker' declined after the formation of the Communist Party, Macintyre had to ignore the evidence to the contrary.[40]

Moreover, there was a minority of English Marxists in the Socialist Labour Party – a small group founded in 1904 in the wake of their protracted fight with Hyndman and Quelch - who did not attack working-class culture. Just as Marx and Engels had spoken of the 'unconscious socialism' of working men and women, so John Carstairs Matheson, a leading thinker in the Socialist Labour Party, approved of the workers' 'untutored discontent'. For insisting that the working class could become an agency of fundamental social change, the members of the Socialist Labour Party were dubbed 'the impossibilists'.[41]

The English labour movement before 1914 was not monolithic – and the Socialist Labour Party, particularly influenced

by Daniel De Leon, the American theorist, always waged war
on pessimism, the belief in historical inevitability and the
denial and denigration of the socialist potential of the working
class. A qualified optimism, a belief in working people's
socialist potential, and an emphasis on the agency of the class
struggle constituted the guts of their socialism-from-below
orientation. But other Marxists – and, indeed, non-Marxists
– were less tolerant of the English workers' culture and way
of life.

Most English Marxists did not approve of football matches,
sport or gambling. In a typical comment a member of the
British Socialist Party said: 'Your recreation and amusements
today are not credible to your knowledge and intelligence and
energy. You crowd to football matches and cinemas, you
spread yourself over Antonio's bar and the fried-fish counters,
you tell silly, soppy jokes and dirty stories, and loaf and horse-
play about the street-corners in a way that you think is manly,
but is not.'[42] Socialists and establishment figures alike
condemned workers' gambling, though police officers' cor-
ruption and 'interference with popular habits' was a source of
class antagonism amongst the poor.[43]

Although 'unskilled working-class culture became more
self-contained and increasingly segregated from middle-class
life' from the 1890s, the establishment became exceptionally
critical of the behaviour of the poor.[44] In an important book,
How the English Workman Lives, a German social reformer,
noted that 'Many, even miners, bet on the racecourse among
themselves by tossing a coin, and this is the most honest way.'
At the same time, he lamented the fact that the poor were
always interested in sport and gambling rather than politics.
As he summed up: 'But all is sport in England. It is sucked
in with the mother's milk.'[45]

Just as the middle-class social reformers were hostile
towards 'poor working-class girls' who shared 'the craze for
betting', so the *Lancet*, the voice of the medical profession,
deplored 'the existing craze for watching football matches' as
an unhealthy sign.[46] But it was left to Karl Kautsky to argue
that the growth of football and gambling amongst the English
poor was the major reason for the weakness of the labour and
socialist movements.[47] Moreover, non-Marxian socialists were

just as critical of working-class culture as their fellow socialists in the SDF and the British Socialist Party.

Workers' lives were haunted by unemployment, hunger and fear of the workhouse. Working people feared the workhouse for the simple reason that paupers were treated as sub-humans – able-bodied men from 'some Northern poorhouses' were humiliated by the authorities as a deterrent to others. In every city and town a permanent pool of unemployed workers threatened the security of those in employment, and General Booth, the leader of the Salvation Army, spoke about deaths from starvation.[48] Moreover, unemployment and irregularity of employment fashioned the behaviour of the poor and the artisans alike, and in the 1890s miners in the Rhondda valley dreaded the possibility of 'being buried by the Poor Law in a pauper's grave'.[49]

A quarter of all English workers over sixty-five years of age were paupers. Only in Scotland, where different traditions of poor relief existed, did the number of paupers decline in British towns and cities.[50] In London older workers preferred the brutality they sometimes met with from their own families rather than enter the prisons they described as 'the Big House'; and in St Helens and Widnes some of 'the wasted alkali workers' who were 'toothless, asthmatic and half-blind' became 'stone-knobblers in a last, desperate attempt to stave off the Workhouse'. This was not simply the fate of the poor; for in London 'prosperous artisans and working men' told middle-class social reformers that there was not 'a week between any of us and the Workhouse'.[51]

Just as the shadow of the workhouse loomed over the lives of the poor, so working people placed a high value on self-respect and relative independence from official scrutiny. The labouring poor were very aware of social control from above and experience led them to distinguish between 'them' and 'us'. Nevertheless the behaviour of the labouring poor was governed by what Charles Booth described as 'strict rules of propriety'; and one consequence of the cultural class struggle was workers' reluctance to accept help from the Poor Law authorities.[52]

Thrift, mutual aid and recourse to the pawnshop were undertaken to keep the labouring poor independent of official society, and contrary to the assertions of the *Lancet* and middle-class opinion, the unorganised poor did not murder their children for the 'insurance money' or keep burial money for other purposes. In the words of one of Charles Booth's informants: 'There is a feeling among the poor, that when a man dies if he has money, it is his: "He made the money, poor fellow, and he shall have it".'[53]

Nevertheless the tangible differences between the subcultures of the organised and the unorganised workers obscured the fact that few workers had any real contact with middle-class life. But all male workers had a common attitude to clothes. Furthermore, a common feature of workers' culture was a presentable Sunday suit. Fred Willis put the point in his description of the labouring poor in London:

> Sunday clothes were absolutely essential. Anyone who appeared on Sunday in workaday clothes was beyond the pale. The ritual of Sunday clothes was sacrosanct, to the labourer in his respectable black suit, black choker and bowler hat, as much to the Balham bank clerk in his silk hat and frock coat.

In the poorer working-class districts working people took their clothes out of pawn as soon as they collected their pay on Saturday. Poorer workers often told middle-class social investigators, 'I am a respectable person.'[54]

The hunger and starvation suffered by the labouring poor fashioned the culture and way of life of the unskilled and unorganised workers. In Leeds the poverty of women workers was exploited by employers and foremen. Yet this did not destroy the women workers' solidarity with each other. The poorer workers survived in very difficult circumstances and they displayed 'great kindness to each other, even to those who [were] strangers'. Thus when the 'new unionism' developed and called for sacrifices, a tradition of collective self-help already existed.[55]

II

The existence of a workers' culture of mutual aid did not, however, inhibit socialists from criticising workers' respectability, attitudes and values as being inherently anti-socialist. However, if SDF criticism of the labouring poor was concrete as well as abstract, a major source of their blistering criticism was the assumption that working people had little enthusiasm for social reforms. Moreover, SDF and Fabian contempt for working men and women was a motif of their practical and literary activity. Thus George Bernard Shaw, who contributed articles and short stories to diverse socialist newspapers and journals, found the authentic note of English socialism before 1914 when, in his short story 'The Death of an Old Revolutionary Hero', he wrote: 'The governing class keep the mass of the people enslaved by taking advantage of their sloth, their stupidity, their ignorance, their poverty, their narrowness, their superstition, and their vices.'[56]

In the world of everyday capitalism, and far away from the left-wing novelist's literary workshop, Robert Tressell, who had ironically abandoned his trade union activity to win his fellow artisans to the SDF, lambasted the labouring poor. The artisans Tressell hated and poured contempt upon were 'the real enemy' and this was why his novel was popular with the SDF and later on with the Communist Party. The artisans as well as the labouring poor not only defended capitalism, but 'opposed and ridiculed any suggestion of reform'.[57]

In reality the labour movement, of whom the orthodox trade unionists rather than the socialists were the most important elements, had succeeded in compelling the Tories and Liberals 'to vie with each other in presenting programmes of social reform between 1883 and 1914.' Nevertheless attitudes of hostility to working people and the poor were expressed by socialists and employers, and both groups voiced their own notions of social and cultural superiority. A strike of engineering workers – a strike of elite artisans – provoked one engineering employer in Birmingham to reply to the engineering trade union's demand for shorter hours thus: 'It has pleased God that the masses of the inhabitants of the world should be hewers of wood and drawers of water. . . . You want reduced working hours, the men don't. They want more money for drink.' Similarly, in the midst of a struggle to extend the 'new unionism', John Burns, a leader of the SDF, told a mass meeting of cab drivers in London: 'Now do make

a reasonable use of the higher wages which you have fought
for. . . . Don't drink, but give the money to the missus.'
Faced with indignant interruptions and objections, he replied.
'Oh, I know you; you can't take me in. Your wives are worth
more than you are.' And he had just previously written that
he had done his 'best as an artisan to educate his unskilled
fellow workmen'. In the communities, where the socialists
gained influence, such elitist attitudes had to be modified.[58]

Though there were communities where authentically mass
militant socialist movements existed down to 1914, they were
seldom typical of English communities as a whole. In a
controversial essay on the concept of the labour aristocracy,
Henry Pelling has argued that the skilled workers were more
militant and socialistically inclined than most labourers. But
while many of the organised skilled workers were sometimes
more militant than the organised poor, the Lib-Labs were
more in touch with the realities of working-class life and more
sympathetic to the poor than such socialists as John Burns,
Dan Irving, Harry Quelch, Tom Mann, Robert Tressell, A.P.
Hazell and J. Hunter Watts.[59]

The Lib-Labs, though moving towards the Left, were
aware of the ruling class's new social attitudes; and, while
supporting some of the SDF demands within the trade unions,
nevertheless identified with the working-class values and subcultures which had crystallised in the mid-Victorian period.
Harry Quelch savagely criticised the artisan as well as the poor
worker for talking 'of his home as not bad for a working man',
his set of books as 'quite credible to a working man' and his
children as a 'good-looking lot of kids for a working man'. In
contrast, George Howell, a traditional Lib-Lab trade union
leader, who lacked Quelch's colossal intelligence and devotion
to principle, had a much better understanding of prevailing
conceptions of workers' respectability when he wrote: 'In the
industrial world of England there is perhaps no point so tender
as the idea of being buried by the parish. A pauper's grave
and funeral are more repugnant to the sensibilities of the
working class than any other social degradation.'[60] Even so,
many socialists criticised the labouring poor for their
adherence to thrift and insurance.

In these circumstances the Lib-Labs within the trade

unions including the 'new unions' during the immediate period of the 'labour unrest' before the First World War got the edge on the socialists when both groups were fighting for conflicting aims and social and moral values. In theory Tom Mann, a young engineer and member of the SDF, had some justification in the 1880s for arguing that 'in fact the average trade unionist of today is a man with a fossilised intellect, either hopelessly apathetic, or supporting a policy that plays directly into the hands of the capitalist exploiter.' On the other hand, the Lib-Labs, in spite of their 'fossilised' intellects, and their deeper ideological influence among the labouring poor, owed much of their influence to their sympathetic respect for working-class life and sensibilities.[61]

As the SDF and other socialist groups denounced the ignorance and stupidity of the labouring poor, Lib-Labs like T.R. Threlfall, who had, in 1885, drawn attention to 'a stronger moral activity amongst the masses' and 'a searching desire to get to the primary causes of our troubles' and the urgent need to initiate domestic reforms, had little difficulty in subsequently intensifying their ideological influence within the trade unions. By contrast, John Burns said: 'We are not going to tell them [the poor] how much power they have until they become sufficiently educated to be worthy of it.' And the riotous activity of workers, whether they were 'the poor', the semi-skilled or the elite artisans, was seen by the SDF, the Fabians and the ILP as hindering the creation of a politically educated working class. By their contempt for the real working class as it existed, they were unwittingly stifling the forces which were capable of creating the socialist society they all wanted to build.[62]

Moreover, newcomers to industrial life in the large towns and cities were often bawdy, rumbustuous and unruly. They were not going to be attracted immediately by the self-conscious, self-righteous socialists who were preaching and lecturing on what were essentially middle-class values. At a time when Saturday night drunken riots in English towns and cities were commonplace, one leader of the SDF wrote: 'Socialism is not to be won by riots, but by the steady combined movement of an educated social democracy.' A sign of the SDF's intense support for law and order beyond their understandable concern not to alienate middle-class public opinion was seen in their criticism of the spontaneous workers' food riots in Italy in 1898, because they were 'individualistic' and not an expression of an educated working class.[63]

Being prisoners of a social vision in which they saw working people as nasty, violent, riotous and brutal, many English socialists sometimes put themselves to the right of middle-class Liberals and other establishment elements. An outbreak of looting by unemployed workers in London in 1886 provoked H.H. Champion to tell one Liberal journalist: 'If I had a revolver and I saw the mob looting a shop, I would shoot the fellows down right and left with my own hand.' Such attitudes were commonplace in the socialist movement; yet Gareth Stedman Jones has argued that the reason for Champion's attitude was simply that the SDF drew 'a certain distinction between the working class and the "residuum"'. In fact, many socialists were terrified by the very existence of the working class, and, by displaying attitudes of cultural superiority, they were crushing the emergence of the latent forces of militant socialism-from-below.[64]

Certainly, the English workers' culture was hostile to 'this social reform stuff'. The hostility arose from the belief that social reform was forcing them into 'useless imitations of middle-class virtues'. This antipathy towards social reform was particularly visible during the two main phases of the 'new unionism' in the 1880s and in the 1910s. One consequence was that the 'poorer workers' accepted the 'inevitability' of unemployment, though it often led them into chronic debt.[65]

Until 1885 English trade unions had, in the opinion of Sidney and Beatrice Webb, been 'an impenetrable barrier against socialist projects'. Then in 1890 William Graham, the socialist leader, said that 'the English working classes are not socialists, nor are they very promising materials out of which to make socialists, if we may judge by the proceedings of recent trade union congresses.' But in refuting these judgements by insisting that 'a "new unionism", definitely and aggressively socialistic, deployed its forces' and 'all but succeeded in capturing the trade-union citadel', F.J.C. Hearnshaw, a left-wing journalist, failed to realise that the distinctive culture of the labouring poor was responsible for working-class antipathy towards 'socialism'. In rejecting the insurance aspect of trade unionism – the infamous goose-and-coffin approach – in order to wage class war, the 'new unionists' alienated themselves from the very members they had been recruited during spontaneous strikes. Consequently, they had to restore the goose-and-coffin aspect of trade unionism. In doing so, however, they allowed their members to reject what would later be regarded as a harbinger of the Welfare State.[66]

From the perspective of Ernest Belford Bax, socialism 'did not signify everything *by* the people, but everything *for* the people.' Although many members of the ILP were also very elitist and condescending towards the labouring poor, they were not always as anti-democratic as most of the Fabians. The Fabians were not only unsympathetic to the working classes, they were sometimes hostile to the democratic process itself. In 1895 Sidney and Beatrice Webb objected when the editor of the *Clarion* asserted that democracy meant that 'the people would rule themselves'. What the Fabians wanted, as H.G. Wells put it, was 'the compulsory regimentation of the workers and the complete State control of labour under a new plutocracy'.[67] As early as 1888, Sidney Webb had articulated his loathing of working people when he wrote:

> But if the conscious intelligence of the natural leaders of the community lags behind the swelling tide beneath them, if we ignore the vast social forces now rapidly organising into conscious action, if we leave poverty and repression and injustice to go on breeding their inevitable births of angry brutality and savage ferocity of revenge – then indeed social evolution will necessarily be once more accomplished by a social cataclysm. From the catastrophe, the progress of socialism is the path of escape.

But the path of escape did not depend on the labouring poor. Writing about the crucial role of the socialist intelligentsia in inducing a movement for socialism-from-above in 1914, Sidney Webb observed that: 'The landslide in England towards social democracy proceeds steadily, but it is the whole nation that is sliding, not the one class of manual workers.'[68] Far from having a positive role to play in the struggle for socialism, the Fabians saw working-class self-activity as detrimental to what the socialist intelligentsia was trying to bring about in the midst of 'stupid and ignorant workers'.

III

Many English Labour historians are so trapped in their images of the working classes and the relationships between workers and 'vanguard' groups that they have failed to develop a critical awareness of a certain 'socialist' vision of working people which, with other factors, contributed to the present cumulative crisis of the Left. They have also ahistorically attributed the SDF, ILP and Fabian opposition to the suffragettes' agitation to a narrow sectarianism. What such historians depicted as sectarianism was really an elitist fear of a mass, popular movement. This can be seen in an editorial in *Justice* in 1912 entitled 'Votes for Women', where it was asserted that 'socialists everywhere have always deprecated and condemned riotous violence by whomsoever committed'.[69]

The least educated sections of the working classes were sometimes the most radical and militant; and underneath the social world occupied by most activists in the SDF, the Fabian Society and the ILP, class consciousness was, under the growing socialist agitation for the enforcement of compulsory education, manifesting itself in totally new and unforeseen ways. But the 'explosion' of class conflict at various *moments* between 1883 and 1914 illuminated the social distance that existed between the labouring poor and many English socialists.

2

Racism, the Working Class and English Socialism, 1883–1914

Pride in their port, defiance in their eye. I see the lords of human kind pass by.

Goldsmith, *The Traveller*

During the three decades between the foundation of the Social Democratic Federation (SDF) in 1883 and the outbreak of the First World War the extensive and widespread anti-black racism of the English working class was *covert* rather than overt. In the novel, *The Ragged Trousered Philanthropists*, Robert Tressell captured and portrayed the dominant covert racism and imperialism of the English working class with insight and accuracy. But although the importance of this widespread covert racism was emphasised in the title of the opening chapter, 'An Imperial Banquet', Tressell did not suggest that it was a major ingredient of working-class consciousness.[1]

By 1906 the National Sailors' and Firemen's Union was insisting that 'one lascar sailor in every five should be able to speak English'. But it is arguable whether this was really evidence of the racist attitudes of some English trade unionists. In fact the English trade unionists' anti-black *covert* racism before the war was much less aggressive and assertive than the *overt* anti-black racism which was seen in the 'race riots' in British towns and cities in 1919. Despite the racist prejudices encountered by Indian and African students in the late nineteenth century, there was no 'colour bar' in hotels or restaurants before the First World War. Also, in insisting on the organised seamen's 'hostile attitude to lascar employment', Rozina Visram overlooks the positive role played by men like Edward Tupper.[2]

With a somewhat excessive emphasis on the racist aggression of the English working class between 1883 and 1914, Perry Anderson and Tom Nairn have repeatedly ignored English socialists' anti-racism.[3] In a direct critique of the writings of Anderson and Nairn dealing with the racism and pro-imperialist sympathies of the English workers, E.P. Thompson said: 'But an examination of the very examples which Anderson cites – the suspicion with which the suppressed jingoism of Hyndman and Blatchford was regarded by a substantial part of their following, and the rapidity with which they lost this following when it became fully exposed – would reveal a very much more complex picture.'[4] Furthermore, in 1911 the National Sailors' and Firemen's Union fought for the rights of black seamen. As Edward Tupper put it: 'The victory of 1911 had enthused the men of all races and colours who manned the British Mercantile Marine; 1912 had opened with visions of high membership, sufficiency of funds, efficient local organisations everywhere.'[5]

On the surface, English working-class patriotism seemed to be extensive, intense and widespread. Writing in 1883 Jules Vallés, a French writer, depicted the patriotism of English working men and women: 'They are proud of being English; that's enough. Without a shirt on their backs they find consolation in seeing a scrap of bunting on the wind – a Union Jack; shoeless, they are happy to see the British lion with the globe beneath its paw.'[6] In an article originally published during the Boer War, Ernest Belford Bax wrote that he had 'seen one slum vying with another more squalid than itself in the number of Union Jacks and royal ensigns it could display.[7] English imperialism reached its zenith between 1883 and 1914, and racist theories and doctrines enjoyed their greatest popularity in the British universities as well as in scientific circles.

In this milieu, racism and racist attitudes were inevitable. In sketching the overall ethos in English schools, Robert Roberts observed:

Teachers fed on Seeley's imperialistic work *The Expansion of Empire,* and often great readers of Kipling, spelled out patriotism among us with a fervour that with some edged on the religious. Empire Day of course had special significance. We drew Union Jacks, hung classrooms with flags of the Dominions and gazed with pride as they pointed out those massed areas on the world map. 'This, and this, and this', they said 'belong to us.'[8]

This imperialistic world-view quite obviously impinged on workers' consciousness to some extent. In reporting the dialogue between a group of house-painters in Hastings, Robert Tressell wrote: 'Why, even "here in Mugsborough", chimed in Sawkins – who though still lying on the dresser had been awakened by the shouting – "We're overrun with 'em! Nearly all the waiters and the Cook at the Grand Hotel where we was working last month is foreigners".'

British imperialism was at its zenith; the working class simply could not escape the virus of imperialist propaganda. This was the era of the 'Imperial Idea'. As François Bédarida put it: 'The basic idea was quite simple: the English were a chosen race entrusted with a mission that was both human and divine, and which it was their duty to discharge.' In 1894 Curzon dedicated a book 'to those who believe that the British Empire is, under Providence, the greatest instrument for good that the world has seen'. At the same time Rosebery declared: 'We have to remember that it is part of our heritage to take care that the world, so far as it can be moulded by us, shall receive an English-speaking complexion, and not that of other nations.' In other words, every inch gained by the British flag meant the advance of civilisation.[9] This was *the* era of '"scientific" racism' and social Darwinism.

The 'Imperial Idea' was carried into the state schools. As Robert Roberts explained: 'Compulsory State education had been introduced with overt propagation of the imperialistic idea: especially was this so after 1880. Schools – and none more than those belonging to the Church of England – set out to instil in their charges a stronger sense of national identity and a deeper pride in the expanding Empire, an exercise stimulated by a whole series of events that demonstrated Britain's might and glory, from the Ashanti wars of 1873, through Victoria's dazzling jubilee to the crowning of George V.'[10]

English workers' patriotism existed in many communities, but it was not identical with the patriotism fostered by the ruling class. There was an important distinction between the two. As Hugh Cunningham has argued:

> There can be little doubt, however, that patriotism had distinctive meanings for the working class, even if these are difficult now to recapture. In 1908 a middle-class resident at Toynbee Hall had been struck by the fact that 'certain words which had always to him signified clear and worthy ideas, such as honour, patriotism, justice, either form no part of the working-man's vocabulary or are grossly and indignantly perverted from their true sense'.[11]

While such an extreme sentiment as jingoism existed in many working-class communities before 1914, Francois Bédarida argues that 'the *jingoism* of the masses has been *grossly exaggerated*'.[12]

Peter Stearns, the American labour historian who has made a major contribution to English labour history, although very aware of workers' right-wing sympathies, found only one example of racist violence between 1883 and 1914: 'Sailors in Cardiff attacked Chinese laundries suspected of white [i.e. slave] trading. Their leader noted, "They knew for themselves that these ships of growing white womenhood became the body slaves of the laundry lords".'[13] Working-class racism did not, in short, 'explode' into violence until 1919 by which time the 'Imperial Idea' was beginning to go into decline.

Despite the displays of Union flags in the slums of English towns and cities, patriotic nationalism and jingoism did not enjoy mass working-class support. In the late nineteenth century the English working class remained, in Hugh Cunningham's idiom, 'largely immune from appeals to nationalism'. In the social reality of a class-divided society, English patriotism 'proved incapable of surmounting the barriers of class'.[14] Although there was some working-class support for British imperialism in the late nineteenth and early twentieth centuries, it was not representative of working-class attitudes as a whole. As Henry Pelling has argued:

> Obviously the 'little England' attitude was unpopular among workers of certain occupations which benefitted from a strong foreign and defence

policy, as for instance shipbuilding and the Birmingham metal trades. There was also a good deal of long-term sympathy for Unionism among working-class electors in Glasgow and Liverpool, where the rivalry of the Orange and the Green was strong. Frank Bealey's study of popular reactions to the South African War suggests that in Scotland, there was a marked contrast between Glasgow and the other cities. . . . Yet among the organised workers, these manifestations of support for the war were exceptional. Obviously, once war had broken out, there were those who thought that it was wrong to provide comfort for the enemy or embarrassment for British troops. There were also those who thought that too emphatic a political participation by the [English] unions at a time when people's views were sharply divided would be bad for the unions' industrial functions, which after all deserved first place in their deliberations.[15]

If war provided an acid-test of working-class attitudes to imperialism, there was little popular support for the Boer War. As François Bédarida argues: 'Even during the Boer War, at the high tide of imperialism, many of the working class and most country folk remained uninfected by the colonial fever.'[16]

The English workers were not touched in any significant way by either colonial fever or the racism being fostered by the ruling class. When Robert Roberts' argument about the racist doctrines taught in the state schools is taken into account, there was something of 'a generation gap' before workers' racism became overt. At the time of the Boer War *mass* workers' support for the war simply did not exist. In a wide-ranging survey of English working-class attitudes to the Boer War between 1899 and 1902, Richard Price made two very important discoveries. In the first place, he found that 'imperialism as a concept was too tenuous for working-class society to react to it in any clearly identifiable manner.' Secondly, he chronicled and documented the hard fact that 'working-class dissent represented an opposition far exceeding the handful of doctrinally committed socialists who often acted as the hard-core of local anti-war committees'.[17]

Nevertheless, racist doctrines permeated English political thought between 1883 and 1914; and parliamentary democracy and representative institutions were to be confined to the English, and not extended to the 'backward' subject peoples within the Empire. As P.D. Curtis has explained: 'For

British racists of all brands, the Empire was their Empire, and the idea of a multi-racial commonwealth was a contradiction in terms.'[18] Because '"scientific" racism' had such a strong impact on English intellectual thought, it is useful to quote Curtis's assessment of its diverse influence and characteristics:

The missionaries' image of the non-Europeans blended with the existing cultural arrogance and with the pseudo-scientific arguments for racial superiority. The result was the complex attitudes now known under Kipling's phrase, 'White Man's Burden'. . . . By the later nineteenth century, this attitude was not confined to the missionaries. It was taken up by some who were rather the opponents of the missionaries than otherwise. Mary Kingsley was one of these. Herself a field ethnologist, she held that in West Africa . . . 'the Protestant English missionaries have had most to do with rendering the African useless because they missed the point of racial difference and were trying to bring about racial equality through education. This was the wrong approach because "a black man is no more an undeveloped white man than a rabbit is an undeveloped hare: and the mental differences between the two races is similar to that between men and women between ourselves." Therefore the Africans should be encouraged to develop in their own way, rather than to climb the Europeans' "own particular summit in the mountain range of civilisation".'[19]

Moreover, pride of race had a strong impact on English radical-democratic thought and historiography. As Raphael Samuel puts it: 'One of the more ambiguous legacies of radical-democratic history is that of English nationalism – the notion that the English people have been somehow singled out for a special place in history, that the English language is superior to others, and that the liberty of the individual is more secure in England than it is abroad.'[20] But English nationalism did not produce mass chauvinism among working-class men and women. In addressing the question of how much influence imperialism exerted in working-class communities, François Bédarida concluded that: 'Pride of race, pride in British achievement at home and abroad was enough, without having recourse to abstract theory.' Such theory did have its effect, but not as widely as had been made out. 'What should they know of England who only England know?' remarked Kipling, with a hint of arrogance. All the same many of his compatriots, whose horizon was confined to

England alone, might have replied that they were 'well aware of the nation's dynamic urge to expand, and full of feeling for their brethren abroad'.[21]

However, if there was no mass working-class support for English imperialism before the First World War, this was at least partly due to the traditional policy of nineteenth-century Liberal-Radicalism. With the advent of the 'new imperialism' in the 1880s, traditional anti-imperialist Liberalism began to decline. Indeed, A.L. Morton and George Tate argued that 'the last really serious Liberal campaign against war and imperialism was during the South African War, 1899–1902'.[22] But this, of course, raises the bigger question of the English labour movement's attitude to imperialism and racism.

In opposition to Perry Anderson and Tom Nairn, E.P. Thompson emphasises the importance of the anti-racist and anti-imperialist currents in the English labour movement. As he sums up:

> This Left, both working-class and intellectual, with its crude and no doubt 'moralistic' refusal to compromise with imperialism does not appear in the Nairn–Anderson canon. Indeed, at points the record is plainly falsified . . . Anderson can do this only by ignoring the acute tensions within Liberalism; by confusing the socialist tradition with the small elitist Fabian group; and by trimming his examples – William Morris, Tom Mann and Keir Hardie would have offered a different interpretation. (Similarly, Nairn offers Tillett's notorious outburst of chauvinism at the first annual conference of the Independent Labour Party (ILP) as if it were the authentic article; he does not mention that Tillett was immediately rebuked.) It is certainly true that imperialism penetrated deeply into the labour movement and even into socialist groups; this is the tragedy of European socialism in this century.[23]

Furthermore, one of the legacies of the Liberalism of the 'Little England' mentality in working-class communities was the existence of widespread *pacifist* attitudes. Until at least the Boer War many Liberals were sympathetic to pacifism.

In acknowledging that imperialism penetrated deeply into the English labour movement before the First World War, E.P. Thompson insists on focusing on working-class opposition to imperialism. The opposition was often solid and vociferous, despite the often ambiguous attitudes of H.M. Hyndman towards the role of English imperialism overseas.

In discussing the ambiguity of Hyndman's attitudes, Frederick J. Gould argues thus: 'He continued to oppose the South African War, but he thought of the Coloured Races as well as the Dutch. Both Boer and British, he said, crushed the Black Man. In any case, he added "I do not believe we are acting worse than the other European powers would have acted in the circumstances".'[24] Ernest Belford Bax made similar statements, though he detested racism as he defined and understood it.

But although E.P. Thompson's strictures against the unhistoric condescension of Perry Anderson and Tom Nairn are fully justified, the protagonists in the debate about 'the peculiarities of the English' both tend to ignore the covert racism of working-class men and women before 1914. Certainly, overt racist antagonism towards the Africans in England scarcely existed before the First World War, perhaps because the black population was, in James Walvin's phrase, 'a depressed people, eking out a living on the poverty-stricken fringes of society'.[25] But although the most progressive Liberals and Marxists in the English labour movement were often sympathetic to the blacks in Africa, India and England, they were almost always motivated by a sort of paternalism influenced and shaped by the stereotypes of '"scientific" racism'.

In an article originally written for the *Commonweal* in 1885, Ernest Belford Bax expressed a fierce opposition to the role of British imperialism. As he summed up: 'The foreign policy of the great international Socialist Party must be to break up these hideous *race monopolies* called Empires, beginning in each case at home. Hence everything which makes for the disruption and disintegration of the Empire to which he belongs must be welcomed by the socialist as an ally.'[26] Even so, the anti-imperialist attitudes of the most progressive socialists were often indistinguishable from those of the left-wing Liberals.

In a very detailed study of the attitudes of Labour, Lib-Lab and socialist Members of Parliament towards English imperialism between 1880 and 1920, Tingfu F. Tsiang, an American historian, was struck by their common paternalistic attitudes towards the black Africans: 'As regards the African natives, they objected to forced labour in the mines and demanded *for* them political power. The sympathy shown by British Labour for the trade unionists in South Africa was especially noteworthy. One of the stimuli of imperialism in South Africa was cheap labour. British Labour's reactions on all these questions was anti-imperialistic.'[27] On the other hand, when he examined their attitude towards English imperialism in the House of Commons during those same years, he concluded that 'The predominant characteristic of the reaction of British Labour to imperialism in Africa is acquiescence.'[28]

II

Though workers' anti-black racism was not overt in England before the outbreak of the First World War, English socialists often reinforced the existing covert racism by popularising the dominant stereotypes of the Africans and Asians as 'backward' and 'childlike' from 1883 onwards. While Ernest Belford Bax paid lip-service to the Africans' struggle against English imperialism, he was, in practice, influenced by the doctrine of '"scientific" racism'. As even the most progressive socialists saw the Asians and particularly the Africans as 'backward', 'childlike' and 'uncivilised', they could not identify with the uprisings and revolts of the blacks in Africa. At best they protested against the ill-treatment of the Africans in the same paternalistic tones as the left-wing Liberals.

Although H.M. Hyndman, Ernest Belford Bax and other English socialists usually used an 'enlightened' rhetoric about Asians and Africans, they did not challenge racism. Most English socialists did not break away from the Liberals' racist stereotypes of the Africans' inherent 'backwardness', and this was why they did not identify with the Africans' revolts and uprisings. They were no more sympathetic to the black Africans than the Lib-Labs. In many specific ways, the Lib-Labs, and particularly the Lib-Lab Members of Parliament, protested against the black Africans' ill-treatment in a more consistent way than the socialists.

Ernest Belford Bax refused to recognise national frontiers.

He therefore argued that the way to create a truly international community was to 'favour all disruptive tendencies within the British Empire'. Yet this abstract objection to English imperialism did not persuade him to reject the theories of the imperialists' 'progressive' role in African countries. Other English socialists were even more supportive of imperialism and '"scientific" racism'.

J.R. Widdup, a prominent member of the SDF, defended the 'progressive' and 'civilising' role of English imperialism in Africa by arguing that when socialism came the English would be the first to 'drop the thought of any superior racial characteristics'.[29] When the Boer War broke out in South Africa, George Bernard Shaw and the Fabians criticised those unpatriotic international socialists who were aiding and abetting 'the disruption of the Empire from within by Declarations of Independence'. As the gold mines belonged to South Africa, Shaw declared that, 'The elector who does not ask his candidate [in the general election] whether he means the Rand gold to remain the public property of the South African provinence of the Empire is not fit to exercise the franchise.'[30]

The Boer War provided English socialists with an opportunity to exonerate themselves from complicity in the crimes of English imperialism in Africa. With assistance from the brilliant pen of Daniel De Leon, the American socialist thinker, English socialists denounced the 'new imperialism' in Africa at a time when the metropolitan press was whipping up racial hatred between the Boers and the English. Even J.A. Hobson, who was at bottom pro-English, expressed amazement over what he characterised as 'the race-lust' of the English in Bloemfontein.[31] An outspoken critic of the war blamed the British press for the behaviour of Englishmen who 'were demonical in their animosity, gloried in revenge, and gloated over carnage'.[32] But although English socialists often protested against English imperialism, they generally accepted many of the underlying assumptions of the imperialist culture.

In contrast to the Americans, the English socialists were not confronted with an internal 'Negro question' before the First World War. The critics and defenders of English imperialism did not, however, distinguish between the blacks in Africa and those in England and France. They were all regarded as being 'inferior' to white Europeans. The black Africans within the British Empire were assumed to be 'racially unfitted for "advanced" institutions such as representative democracy. For English racists – including many in the socialist movement – the Empire was British, and it could not be shared with 'backward' peoples.[33] At the peak of its popularity in English scientific circles in 1914,[34] racism permeated the thought and the writings of the most progressive socialists.[35]

The English imperialist's image of the Empire was very paternalistic. When Alexander Davis published a study of *The Native Problem in South Africa* in 1903, he projected a paternalistic image of the black Africans who were in need of English protection: 'The South African native is frequently compared with a child. This mental estimation inspires the mode of treatment almost universally recommended in dealing with him.'[36] But the paternalism could be quickly changed into unbridled hatred when the Africans even tentatively challenged their white masters. This was seen when Davis was forced to face the political challenge presented by the Aborigines' Protection Society.

English imperialism was experiencing its heyday. The Union Flag flew over 800,000 miles of British territory in Africa alone. The land belonging to the black Africans was usually annexed by rape, pillage and plunder. When the Mashouland rebellion broke out in Southern Rhodesia in 1896, the Aborigines' Protection Society protested against 'the indiscriminate and merciless slaughter of thousands' of black Africans.[37] As the Mashouland rebellion had proved the folly of 'reliance on the apparent submission of a savage and warlike tribe', the British military authorities were determined to impose 'absolute submission'.[38]

In a series of well-documented pamphlets and appeals to the Houses of Parliament, the Aborigines' Protection Society exposed English imperialism's polity of brutality and rapine on behalf of the South African company. With the connivance of Cecil Rhodes, the Chartered Company of South Africa had played a major role in engendering the Boer War. For exposing the South Africa company's policy of robbing the black Africans of their land and subjecting them to forced labour, the Aborigines' Protection Society was denounced by such defenders of English imperialism as Alexander Davis. The Society's exposés were countered by the absurd comment that 'While the Aborigines' Protection Society was filling its adherents, and trying to imbue the Government and the public, with dire tidings of native slavery, the residents at their wits' end for labour, were memorialising their government to initiate some measure of order to induce the native to offer his labour for a liberal wage.'[39]

The Europeans' scramble for Africa got underway in 1883 at the same time as the SDF was founded in London. The birth of modern socialism in England coincided with the advent of the 'new imperialism', the doctrine of 'trusteeship', the intensification of racist propaganda about the 'backward', 'child-like' Africans and the anti-imperialist agitations of the labour movement. From 1883 onwards, the English ruling class (including the schools, pulpits, newspapers, magazines and political parties) developed and fostered imperialist and jingoist propaganda about the racial 'inferiority' of the child-races of Africa, and blacks in general.

The advent of the 'new imperialism' and the sense of white superiority led the English ruling class to develop the doctrine of trusteeship. In a powerful, perceptive and well-documented book, *The Image of Africa*, P.D. Curtis explained the significance of trusteeship:

> If it were assumed that the Africans were racially inferior, and yet spiritually equal and capable of receiving the Christian message, the moral duty of the superior race was clear. It was to take up the 'white man's burden' and exercise a trust over the spiritual and material welfare of people whose racial status was equivalent to that of minors.[40]

Despite the benevolent colours in which it draped itself, English imperialism became increasingly predatory. Trusteeship always implied the annexation of colonies. Further, in a world where different European powers were scrambling for Africa, the English ruling class saw the Empire as the only effective antidote to socialist revolution at home. But although the 'new imperialism' perceived the British Empire as a 'bread and butter question', the relationship between imperialist ideology and the exploitation of the Empire was very complex.

Moreover, English imperialist ideology preceded the advent of the 'new imperialism'. Racism, jingoism, imperialism and the sense of an innate white 'superiority' were already powerful ideological currents in English society; and the new doctrine of trusteeship fitted into existing imperialist and racist attitudes in England and throughout the British Empire. In *Staying Power: The History of Black People in Britain*, Peter Fryer identifies the coalescence of the doctrines of ' "scientific" racism' and trusteeship:

> The trusteeship plank in British imperialistic policy had two main components. Essentially it was a blend of the missionaries' view that the Africans 'represented unregenerate mankind, sinful and unwashed' and the pseudo-scientific arguments for racial superiority. Britain marched across Africa with a clerical boot on one foot and a 'scientific' boot on the other. Since Africans were inferior, said the trustee theory, the British who ruled them owed a special obligation, not unlike the obligation that decent Englishmen owned to women, children and dumb animals.[41]

The transformation of the Tory Party into the *Party* of English imperialism began in the 1880s. As George Lichtheim has explained:

> At the same time Toryism was reconstituted upon a new social and ideological foundation: no longer merely the bulwark of the landed gentry and the Church, but increasingly the Party of the Empire and the fountainhead of the English (as distinct from British) nationalism. The nationalism, that is to say, of the dominant majority within a multinational society; for the Scots, Welsh and Irish all had their own forms of national sentiment: not to mention India, the White-settler 'Dominions', and the African colonies – all garrisoned by British-officered armies and navies who looked to the Conservative Party to uphold their status.[42]

Also the 'new imperialism' played an important role in the split in the Liberal Party in 1886 and the creation of the breakaway Liberal-Unionist Party, although the Irish question provided the initial motivation.

The Liberals remained divided in their attitude to imperialism until their decline after the First World War. Furthermore, even the most progressive Liberals were extremely condescending towards the 'inferior' black Africans within

England and the Empire, and many of them approved of the 'colour bar' in Africa. Indeed, the Liberal-Unionists became the most vociferace advocates of the 'new imperialism' at the same time as they were engaged in almost hysterical criticism of socialism and the socialists' criticisms of English imperialism. In outlining the character of British imperialism from 1883, A.L. Morton and George Tate argue that:

It was hoped that imperialism would smooth over class antagonism by winning over the mass of the population to a belief in the exploitation of the Empire, by providing an 'outlet' for 'surplus' population and markets which would give stable employment. Cecil Rhodes said in 1895 that, after attending a meeting of the unemployed in the East End of London and listening to the 'wild speeches which were just a cry for "bread, bread, bread"', he became more than ever convinced of the importance of imperialism as a solution for "the social problem". "The Empire," he said, "is a bread-and-butter question. If you want to avoid civil war, you must become imperialists." Thus imperialism, both in the sense of an economic policy and of a system of ideas, became in this period an integral part of the British social structure, which is affected throughout. The old Liberal-Radical anti-imperialism which had been the traditional policy of the industrial bourgeoisie and its working-class allies in the nineteenth century did not at once die away, but it was losing strength and was forced on the defensive.[43]

The British Empire was increasingly seen as a bulwark against the encroachment of socialist ideology.

But although the ideology of British imperialism was rooted in earlier national history, the 'new imperialism' was of enormous economic importance for the survival of capitalism. At the beginning of the twentieth century, Joseph Chamberlain said:

Today no-one contests any longer the enormous advantage of a unified Empire, keeping for ourselves the benefit of trade which at the present time is actually a benefit to foreigners. Believe me, the loss of our domination would weigh first of all on the working classes of this country. England would no longer be able to feed her enormous population.[44]

Yet despite the great economic importance of English imperialism between 1883 and 1914, the working class did not articulate an aggressive racism towards black people in England.

In this overall context covert racism in working-class communities was inevitable. It was, in fact, environmentally engendered; and in contrast to those socialists like Ben Tillet and Robert Blatchford who constantly expressed racist ideas and attitudes, others opposed racism. Keir Hardie did not just oppose racism, however; he also attacked imperialism and identified with the anti-imperialist agitations in every part of the Empire. In a letter addressed to Henry Sylvester Williams, the advocate of Pan-Africanism and founder of the newspaper, *The Pan-African*, he wrote:

> I am much interested in your proposed new venture, *The Pan-African*, and cordially wish it success. I know that apart from a few interested parties of the South African millionaire type, the wrongs done to your people under British rule are more due to ignorance than to any desire to act unjustly. Such an organ as *The Pan-African* will do much to remove this ignorance; and this, if backed by strenuous action on the part of your own people, will, in the course of time, lead to a redress of those wrongs, the continuation of which is a disgrace and a source of weakness to the British Empire. Again I wish the venture success.[45]

A.R. Orage, the founder of Guild socialism, encouraged Duse Mohamed Ali, another advocate of Pan-Africanism, and published many of his articles. From 1907 onwards, when A.R. Orage became associated with the socialist movement, the *New Age* was always hostile to British imperialism. During the two years when Duse Mohamed Ali was a frequent contributor to the *New Age*, Orage was sympathetic to the aspirations of the militant Asians and black Africans. The *New Age* consistently published articles attacking imperialism and racism by W.F. Hutchison and Theodore Rothstein, an exiled Russian Marxist. But the major theme of Ali's articles in both *The African Times and Oriental Review* and the *New Age* was colour prejudice in England and the Empire. In an article published in the *New Age* in February 1911, Ali asked:

> Why will Anglo-Saxons cultivate this insane and irrational policy of unwarranted colour prejudice in the interest of a false ideal? Repression, of whatever kind, has never yet been successful in establishing prestige. The duty of England is to treat her dark races in such a manner as to let them feel that they are members of the Empire in fact; by respecting their liberties, protecting them from aggression and abolishing a

pernicious system of repression. The time is now. The writing is on the wall.[46]

Racism and racist prejudice against black people aroused the ire of Duse Mohamed Ali more than anything else. He was very annoyed, too, by the frequent slurs in the British press about black men's sexual relations with white women.[47] In taking up the cause of black Africans and Asians in England and the Empire, Duse Mohamed Ali played an important role in raising the question of colonial 'emancipation' in the progressive press.

When W.E.B. Du Bois visited London in 1911, he was appalled by the racism he encountered in London. Writing in *The Crisis*, he focused on the important fact that racism could not remain for ever:

> The Empire is a *coloured* Empire. Most of its subjects – a vast majority of its subjects – are coloured people. And more and more the streets of London are showing this fact. I seldom step into its streets without meeting a half-dozen East Indians, a Chinaman, a Japanese or a Malay, and here and there a Negro. There must be thousands of people of colour in this city . . . one senses continually the darker world.

III

As a result of the few hundred strong black population in London, Hull and Cardiff before 1914, working-class racism remained covert and the trade unions did not discriminate against black workers in the same way that they would later. Although such black intellectuals in England as Henry Sylvester Williams and Duse Mohamed Ali felt threatened by racist doctrines and ideas in books and newspapers, working-class racism was not yet aggressive.

By 1907 the Second International had formulated a new colonial policy in which the emphasis was now on asking Parliamentary groups to 'protect the rights of colonial peoples' and to 'do everything possible to educate them for independence'.[48] But English socialists were influenced by paternalistic Liberals, not the policy of the Second International, and English imperialist culture impinged on the consciousness of such socialist organisations as the SDF, the ILP and the infant Labour Party.

H.R. Fox Bourne, the secretary of the Aborigines' Protection Society, was the leading authority on racism and imperialism. An important figure standing within the English Liberal tradition of anti-imperialism, he contributed a great deal to influencing the thought of leading members of the SDF, ILP and the early Labour Party. Ernest Belford Bax and H.M. Hyndman were particularly close to Bourne, both personally and ideologically. Fox Bourne not only cooperated with leading British socialists, but was given extensive space in socialist publications (including Marxist theoretical journals) in which he developed and popularised paternalistic Liberal ideas and concepts about the 'inferiority' of black people.

As an advocate of 'the separate development' of the black Africans on 'native reservations', he contributed an important article to the Marxist theoretical journal, *The Social Democrat*, on the 'Bechuana Rebellion', in which he denounced the crimes of English imperialism. In a blistering attack on the South African company, he said: 'Of the numberless crimes committed upon black communities by white usurpers in Africa, the most recent, on a large scale, and one of the meanest, is that of which several thousand Bechuana are the victims.[49] Elsewhere he described the so-called Bechuana rebellion as 'a small disturbance provoked by the intruders' as 'a pretext for a formidable attack on the rebels with the avowed purpose of depriving them of their lands'.[50]

The British imperialists' image of Africa though blended in with the economic needs of metropolitan capitalism. As the white European had 'a greater brain capacity' and 'a higher degree of intellectual development' than the black Africans,[51] the whites were obviously entitled to rob and exploit them with impunity. Not surprisingly, the defenders of English imperialism were very critical of Fox Bourne's activities. As Alexander Davis put it:

> Dismissing from consideration the personal aspects of the case – whether the Aborigines' Protection Society is properly equipped or otherwise to pose as an arbiter of the fate of the natives and attitudinise as censor of colonial morals – the native question in South Africa is so closely bound

up with its political, social, and industrial life that what a small sect in England consider a matter of mild employment and a subject of amiable endeavour is a problem of deepest importance to the communities in the colonies. It is the one burning question which, if handled without prudence and moderation by the imperial Government, will unite Briton and Boer, administrator and people, against the interloping outsider.[52]

Clearly, interference with the imperialists' policy in Africa was inimical to the material interests of British capitalism.

H.R. Fox Bourne also chronicled what he regarded as the 'progressive' role of imperialism in Africa alongside a withering critique of the injustices inflicted on the black Africans. After depicting the activities of the Boer farmers in South Africa in selling and exchanging their black African victims 'among themselves', he concluded:

They can never hope to be their own masters, and are subordinate members of households in which they rank rather with the dogs and cattle than with the white-skinned human beings; but, if they obey orders and behave well, they have opportunities of enjoying life in their own ways.

What was really important in Africa was the 'civilising' mission of English imperialism. Although the assumption of the *progressive* 'civilising' mission of the British within the Empire was a major characteristic of the *official mind* of English imperialism, the unofficial mind of left-wing anti-imperialism shared the same basic assumption. In articulating this 'unofficial mind' Fox Bourne said: 'Though the white usurpers have killed off many thousands of blacks, their rule has almost entirely put an end to the inter-tribal wars by which the natives formerly killed off one another in great numbers. though the advent of "civilisation" has imposed on them many hardships, it has conferred upon them, or brought within their reach, many advantages.'[53] He did not, however, enumerate any of the alleged 'advantages'.

An insight into the unofficial mind of English imperialism can be seen in the writings of J.A. Hobson, a major anti-imperialist thinker and writer. Like the Tory jingo, Alexander Davis, Hobson opposed the notion of granting the vote to the black Africans who were 'still steeped in the darkness of savagery'.[54] What upset him was the role at the turn of the century of the 'new imperialists' in weakening English hegemony by welding 'Afrikanerdom' into a 'strong dangerous nationalism'. A defender of the older English colonialism in Africa, he wanted 'a "sane" imperialism devoted to the protection, education and self-development of a "lower race" rather than the "insane" imperialism' he witnessed in Southern Africa. As he also wanted to see 'the separate development' of the black Africans instead of allowing their lands to become 'repositories of mining or other profitable treasure', he sympathised with the Aborigines' Protection Society.[55]

The official mind of English imperialism was obsessed with the impending threat of mass uprisings and revolts in the colonies. There was an ever-present fear of unwittingly letting 'loose vast forces of discontent' induced by contemplating a 'native franchise'; and the Boer War was seen as something which had already awakened 'excitement' in a 'primitive' people.[56] A few Afro-American pastors already had their own Churches in Southern Africa; and critical imperialists like Alexander Davis saw the black Africans' quasi-religious movements as being potentially subversive. Articulating the profound fears of official English imperialism, he anticipated a time when the Zulu, Basuto, Swazi, Xosa and Bechuana tribes might unite to overthrow the white man:

> Occasions arise in the case of great populations of African aborigines when a movement once initiated, either through its inherent adaptability to native conditions and native thought or the genius of the founder, obtains sufficient momentum at the outset to increase its ratio to the extent of cohering a large section of the native tribes.[57]

Because J.A. Hobson was in favour of the older English colonial policy, he blamed the 'new imperialists' for the Boer War:

> That which appears to us an achievement of British imperialism, viz. the acquisition of the two Dutch republics and the great North, is and always has appeared something quite different to a powerful group of business politicians in South Africa.[58]

Moreover, in a critique of *The War in South Africa* published in 1900, he revealed the exact nature of the unofficial mind of the older English imperialism when he insisted that:

If the present conflict is concluded without a native rising the danger will still continue, for no-one save an ignoramus believes that any other than a surface settlement is possible between the Dutch and the British for at least a generation. The prospect is indeed a dark one. Hitherto the white races, however they might bicker among themselves, readily united to present a single front against the Kaffirs, and the moral influence of race harmony was even more potent in repressing native agitation than actual co-operation. The sudden, complete break-up of this harmony into a fierce, palpable, and lasting discord is nothing less than an upheaval of the very foundations of white civilisation in South Africa.[59]

Far from Hobson's defence of the role of foreign capital in 'backward' counties in 1911 being 'uncharacteristic of the views for which he is celebrated',[60] he had always championed British investment in Africa.

As an increasing number of black Africans were 'wrenched from their previous mode of production' and 'constrained to place their labour power at the disposal of alien forces of production', revolts and uprisings were increasingly likely.[61] European settlers were, for example, beginning to arrive in Kenya in large numbers at a time when 'the idea of organised labour' was 'utterly foreign to the tribesmen'.[62] By dispossessing the black Africans from their land in traditional societies, where the means of life were held in 'collective ownership',[63] a series of revolts was the consequence.[64] But many of the revolts, such as the Chilembwe rising in Nyasaland, were cloaked in the religious and millenial language of the Watch Tower movement.[65] Instead of attempting to develop an independent critique of English imperialism, most English socialists – and particularly the leading members of the Social Democratic Federation – identified with the analyses and ideas of H.R. Fox Bourne both before and after the Boer War. Although the Boer War provided them with the opportunity to make some criticisms of J.A. Hobson's analysis of English imperialism, H.M. Hyndman and Ernest Belford Bax did not develop an independent Marxist analysis of either English imperialism or '"scientific" racism'. And because the revolts of the black

Africans were cloaked in what Victor Kiernan characterises as a 'negative form' of religious protest,[66] the English socialists were usually unsure about how to respond to them.

The SDF's policy towards the struggles of the black Africans was characterised by ambiguity, inconsistency and paradox. Although he defended the 'progressive' role of English imperialism in Africa and India, H.M. Hyndman nevertheless looked forward to the day of the black Africans' emancipation: 'The future of Africa is', he predicted, 'with the black man.'[67] The SDF also encouraged F. Colebrook, a socialist frequently described in the pages of their newspaper, *Justice*, as a 'black Englishman'. In a review of J.A. Hobson's book, *The War in South Africa*, Colebrook, who was probably an Indian, criticised Hobson and the Liberal critics of the Boer War for dreaming of a return to 'the conditions of things which prevailed' before the war began.[68] In contrast to Colebrook's sharp critique of British imperialism in Africa from the viewpoint of 'a black man', Hobson was more lenient in assessing the role of the Europeans in 'backward' countries. In fact he 'explicitly denied that any backward people has the right to refuse to other peoples the use of natural resources located in their territories.' Interference on 'the part of civilised white nations with backward races' was, as he put it in one word, 'legitimate'.[69]

The tragedy of English socialism was that the leaders and rank-and-file of such organisations as the ILP and the SDF accepted racist stereotypes of the 'backward', 'child-like' black Africans. Therefore they accepted the racists' evaluations of 'backward' peoples and 'backward' countries; and they could not – and did not – identify with the struggles of the black people in Africa and India. The leading and most influential English socialist thinkers were influenced by the ideas and analyses of men like H.R. Fox Bourne and the Aborigines' Protection Society. Though anti-imperialist in a formal, theoretical sense, they did not challenge any of the assumptions of '"scientific" racism'.

Although such leading Marxian socialists as H.M. Hyndman and Ernest Belford Bax believed in the ultimate emancipation of the black peoples in the 'backward' under-developed countries, they did not transcend the thinking of the paternalistic anti-imperialism of the older Liberalism. Thus they both argued that it was best to let 'a tribe develop by itself its own special character and type.'[70] Seen within the context of Southern Africa, where Alexander Davis suggested the creation of large 'native, and perhaps tribal, reserves within the vicinity of the Rand, instead of the existing 'confined compounds near the shaft',[71] the SDF did not engage in any independent thinking about colonialism. Similarly, the SDF, the ILP and the Labour Party did not challenge the doctrine of '"scientific" racism'; and they did not create the climate of opinion in which an anti-colonial working-class movement could develop in any part of England.

Black people, whether in Africa, India or England, hardly existed for English socialists before 1914, except during such exceptional events as the Boer War. The best index of English socialist attitudes towards black people can be deduced from how they behaved in Africa. Whether the English socialists in South Africa had been trained in the English branches of SDF, the ILP or the Socialist Labour Party (SLP), they did not conceive of the black Africans as being capable of playing any role in political struggles. Edward Roux, the son of a member of the SLP, described the typical attitude of white socialists in South Africa when he said: 'My father and his socialist friends were glib with their talk of the workers. But by the workers they meant the white workers and did not at all consider that in South Africa the majority of workers were black.'[72]

On the surface, the socialists in England sometimes appeared to be more sympathetic to the black people in the Empire than their counterparts in South Africa. But because the white socialists in South Africa constituted an 'aristocracy of Labour', they could not be too sympathetic – or even sensitive to – the aspirations of the black Africans for freedom and national autonomy. In England the most progressive socialists did not even begin to develop an independent critique of imperialism or racism.

Despite the racist climate of opinion in schools, universities, pulpits and scientific circles, and despite the English socialists' failure to confront imperialist and racist doctrines head-on, the English working class was not very influenced by the 'new' imperialism'. Most English workers, though often parochial, were not convinced by imperialist doctrines. Furthermore, the black population in England was minute; and English workers did not have a vested interest in racism. With the outbreak of the First World War, however, the workers' covert racism would 'explode' into an aggressive, overt, imperialistic racism.

3

English Working-Class Women and the Labour Movement, 1883–1914

> Socialism and the socialist movement have always stood for equality of opportunity to the men and women in every department of human activity where sex does not impose an unconquerable barrier.
>
> Ethel Snowden

In late Victorian England working-class women were oppressed by their menfolk as well as by the wider society of ruling-class institutions and networks. Nevertheless the advent of modern socialism in 1883 introduced a new factor into working-class relationships, and the English ruling class was forced to respond to the socialists' critique. However, many socialists did not always practise their own principles in relation to women, and the patriarchal culture of the working-class movement remained strong.

What modern socialism did, however, was to provide working-class women with the stimulus and encouragement to participate in strikes, industrial militancy and cultural revolts against inherited attitudes. Unfortunately, many historians who have chronicled the history of working-class struggle have often ignored the women's role in strikes.

Yet the match-girls' strike occupies a major place in English working-class history because the match-girls were among the first women 'in the lower ranks of labour' to engage in struggle with their employers. Isolation was not so big a problem among the match-girls as it was for other working women, and they had a long tradition of 'sticking up' for themselves long before their spontaneous strike for better conditions. As one historian put it: 'Though they had never had anything to do with the trade unions, they had already got into the habit of getting together either to discuss their grievances and stick up for each other when the charge-hands, who were usually men, had a "down" on them, or for the purpose of buying finery.' Their strike, in fact, simply 'exploded' when the manager adopted a condescending attitude towards the militant minority of match-girls who had protested against the victimisation of their main spokeswomen.[1]

The militancy of women workers was encouraged by the development of the 'new unionism'. Although the Women's Protective and Provident League had been trying since the 1870s to organise women workers, the leaders of the League were just as surprised as the employers when the match-girls' strike erupted in 1888. But the leaders of the League blamed the public's 'insatiable demand for the lowest price' for the economic pressures that led to the employers' ruthless exploitation of the match-girls. Yet some working-class women were not convinced by such arguments, and thousands of them engaged in spontaneous sympathy strikes.[2]

Moreover, women played a major role in the strike for the 'dockers' tanner' in 1889. As two historians of the dockers' strike put it: 'They used to obtain admission by coming to the entrance at dinner time carrying with them the mid-day meal. At Tilbury, where the blacklegs were especially plentiful, the womenfolk of the dockers came to the gates and with a shrill voice exclaimed, "Tell the men to rest, we'll get them out".' Then in the national miners' strike of 1894, the miners' wives became self-appointed pickets.[3]

Yet despite the beginning of real progress, social change was very gradual. Already committed to the exclusion of 'women from paid work', the 'labour aristocracy' of artisans and skilled workers argued that the 'woman's place was in the home'. Therefore the education and training of working-class girls in industrial skills was detrimental to their domestic role in the home; and artisans' wives, too, were 'drudges'.[4]

Nevertheless the working-class movement played an important role in breaking down the social attitudes engendered by a capitalist social structure, and the pioneering women of the cooperative movement initiated the slow process of changing working men's views on women's role. When a few advanced working women began to organise women at the community level, they were opposed by artisans and labourers alike. As one writer explained: 'It was the custom in those days for men to think, and to say, that "the woman's place is at home".' This opinion found expression in remarks such as "Let my wife stay at home and wash my moleskin trousers", and less polite phrases.' As early as 1883 the leaders of the women's cooperative movement were forced to confront such attitudes. In an interview in the *Women's Outlook* much later, Ms Acland explained their experiences at that time: 'People charged me with stirring up unrest and discontent amongst the women, but one knows now that one only voices the unrest – the desire for a wider outlook – that was rising in the minds of women.'[5]

Hostility to women's rights remained a very real problem within the English working class. Thus the United Society of Brushmakers and other trade unions incorporated their male chauvinism into their trade union rules. Members of such trade unions were forbidden to 'teach, help or work with women'; and in another trade union the male painters of pottery formed a combination to 'prevent the use by women of the arm-rests required in the work'. Furthermore, working men in London formed a combination to 'prevent women workers from using the low-priced trains'.[6]

Even so, important changes in working-class life were already underway. Male trade unionists who discriminated against women workers were beginning to be challenged within their trade unions. New social relationships began to crystallise in working-class families; in a minority of families wives became partners on 'equal terms with a free voice', and it was only in the poorer families that the wife could say, 'Oh! I don't know what 'e gets; I only know what 'e gives me.'[7]

Traditionalism was seen in a very few of the poorer families' toleration of wife-sales. In fact a very small minority of working-class men still believed in their 'innate right' to sell their wives. The 'marriage tie lay lightly' on some of the poorer working men, and 'a rough and summary method was sometimes used to dissolve it'. In 1888 the House of Commons was informed of the case of a working man who had recently sold his wife for a quart of beer; and at Alfreton in the same year a man sold his wife in a public house for a glass of ale.

The traditions of the past were indeed pressing upon and enslaving the living, though wife-sales were rare.[8] But wife-beating remained a major social problem.

Indeed, the need for working people to change society by changing themselves expressed itself in the new 'dialectic' introduced by the socialists; and this was why John Burns, socialist and leader of one of the 'new unions', addressed the London dockers in 1889 thus: 'I want to see some of your wives bear less evidence on their faces and bodies of your brutal ill-treatment. I want to see you men use this strike as a new era in your personal and domestic lives.' As the socialist counter-culture represented by Burns began to impinge on working-class consciousness, the labour movement had to confront the question of women's oppression by men, including working-class men.[9]

Just as the 'new unionism' of the male workers, who were unskilled or semi-skilled, at least initially involved a commitment to socialist values, so the 'new unions' challenged the cultural hegemony of capitalism. Employers and foremen had, according to the reports of women factory inspectors, long been in the habit of raping working-class women; and in the 1880s and 1890s women's trade unions were formed 'for the purpose of moral protection'.[10] Certainly, sexual assaults on domestic servants were widespread, and women who worked in factories were subjected to a whole range of indignities. Isabella Ford, who was engaged in forming women's trade unions, explained some of the problems: 'A premium is sometimes put on impropriety of conduct on the women's part by a foreman. That is, a woman who will submit or respond to his coarse jokes and language and evil behaviour, receives more work than the woman who feels and shows herself insulted by such conduct, and wishes to preserve her self-respect.' Far from restricting their agitations to bread-and-butter questions, the early women's trade unions were also interested in social and cultural questions.[11]

Within the Trade Union Congress (TUC) male chauvinism was commonplace, and the male trade union leaders often tried to drive women out of industry altogether. This led to constant conflict within the TUC between male trade unions and the Women's Protective and Provident League (later renamed the Women's Trade Union League). As a result of this conflict a compromise resolution on equal pay for men and women who did the same work was adopted. Even so, the motives of many of the male trade unionists who supported this compromise were somewhat suspect. In the discussion in 1888, a delegate who supported the successful resolution on equal pay made it clear that he was supporting the agitation because it would encourage employers to drive women out of the industry rather than result in their gaining equal pay.[12]

A vociferous group of self-taught workers and intellectuals within the Social Democratic Federation (SDF) criticised the agitation for women's liberation; and instead of challenging ruling-class cultural hegemony head-on, they helped to reinforce it. Furthermore, hostility to women's equality was widespread in the broad socialist movement as well as in the trade unions; and the 'preaching of female suffrage' had yet to become 'a thing of the street corners'.[13]

Often unaware of women's potential militancy as an agency for social change, socialists sometimes excluded women from the labour movement altogether. One example of their total exclusion was cited by Samson Bryher: 'Robert Giliard had been asked to draft a "manifesto" for publication, explaining the aims and objects of the [Bristol] Labour League, which he submitted to "a special assembly of members", and one sentence declaring that female workers might become members was voted out after considerable discussion.' Many branches of the SDF did nothing to raise the condition of women; and the task of arguing the case for women's liberation was left to the Socialist League.[14]

Ernest Belford Bax was the strongest critic of the agitation for women's rights, and he frequently tried to argue that women were actually enslaving men. In an editorial entitled, 'the Cult or Abstractions', *Justice*, the SDF newspaper, criticised the agitation for women's rights. This editorial opened up an internal Party debate about the relationship between socialist theory and sexual morality.

The views of the libertarian socialists were expounded by the Scot, James Leatham, in an article titled 'the Cleanliness of the Sexes'. In a reply justifying the theoretical position of the leaders of the SDF, the editor argued that there was no 'socialist theory as to sexual morality'. Leatham's assumption of 'sex-subjection' was criticised, and Eleanor Marx entered the controversy to support the views of the minority of libertarian socialists. Moreover, rank-and-file women members participated in the debate in the pages of *Justice*, and Mary E. Boyd, one of the correspondents, wrote: 'Another fetish is destined to go – worship of the male principle.'[15]

However, if worship of the male principle was doomed, it was still very strong. Yet in 1891 a Mr Jackson, whose wife had left him, ultimately lost a long legal battle for the restoration of conjugal rights. This famous legal battle led Thomas Higginson to say: 'But the worst of the old abuses were extinguished, and by 1900 English women were, in the main, both free in their persons and their properties, their minds and their consciences, their bodies and their souls. they were still politically outcast and economically oppressed.' Though this was a reasonably accurate description of middle-class women, it did not apply to working-class women to anything like the same extent.[16]

I

As a distinctive workers' culture crystallised during the years between 1900 and 1914, some working-class women transcended the subordinate role that had been imposed on them by a patriarchal, capitalist society. In those years a significant and growing number of working-class women began to struggle for control over their own lives; and by joining trade unions, initiating strikes, practising birth control, resisting reforms that interfered with their social life and by protesting against sexual assaults in factories and textile mills, they attained a higher status for working-class women as a whole.

Workers' culture was predominantly a male culture, and the mass, multi-dimensional revolt of working-class women in those years occurred within the context of a patriarchal society in which hostility to women determined women's low status and subordinate role within the working-class family. Just as the possessing classes took it for granted that the woman's place was in the home, so, in turn, did working men assume that their wives, daughters and sisters were – and ought to be – their subordinate dependants. This basic social attitude – a social attitude consistently inculcated by the possessing classes from at least the beginning of the Industrial Revolution – was what shaped the culture of the working-class family.[17]

An important concomitant of this new workers' culture was that the self-images of many working-class women were undergoing a fundamental change, and in a whole host of ways many of them challenged traditional assumptions, social values and social attitudes. Nevertheless there was, in the language of Robert Roberts, an 'undermass' of working-class women who were not dramatically influenced by the new social attitudes; and survival was the most ambitious social goal to which they could aspire. One working-class woman, who, as a professional street singer, belonged to the lowest strata of the labouring poor, gave Olive Malvery, a middle-class investigator, a graphic description of how the 'undermass' of working-class women saw themselves: 'True enough', the woman said. 'We ain't much count – still we manage to live.' In any case, for the women who belonged to the lowest strata of the labouring poor, life was not only very harsh, it also induced apathy, pessimism and fatalism.[18]

Most working-class women were still oppressed and subjected to a wide range of social controls, and the explosive growth of women's consciousness highlighted the narrowness of traditional notions of the working-class women's role in the home. What was new was that a significant number of working-class women began to reshape the pattern of their social life without the aid of the middle-class women's movement. Other social factors were at work undermining the social values and attitudes that had crystallised in the mid-Victorian period, and working people generally began to reject the older social values and attitudes. The notion of working-class 'respectability' which had hitherto inhibited membership of trade unions among men and women was gradually being rejected; and the most enlightened elements in the socialist movement were evolving a critique of women's subordinate role in labour organisations.[19]

This persistent subordination of working-class women was a very real phenomenon, yet it must be seen within its historical context in which traditional social attitudes were beginning to change as an increasing number of working-class women became a conscious group of conscious personalities. Their subordination was, moreover, inseparable from their self-struggle for emancipation; they were locked together in a dialectical relationship; and the historian cannot emphasise meaningfully one aspect of this relationship without at the same time emphasising the other.

However, in contrast to the past when the drudgery of working-class women was taken for granted, libertarian socialists and working-class activists in the labour movement protested against women's subordinate role in the home. Those women who were active in the women's cooperative guilds protested against 'the incessant drudgery of domestic labour'. Not only were such social criticisms unprecedented, but they also led to radical critiques and proposals to ameliorate the plight of married working-class women. This was why Dora B. Montefiore advocated the introduction of 'a legal minimum wage of not less than sixpence an hour' for married working-class women whose sole job was domestic labour within the home.[20]

A new feature of those years was that working-class women now criticised traditional assumptions abut their role in society. Most working men as well as the possessing classes still regarded 'the care of the household, the satisfaction of man's desires and the bearing of children' as women's role; but some working-class women were gradually beginning to adopt a new mode of social behaviour. None the less the older ideas of women's role survived in most working-class communities; they were encouraged by the possessing classes; and they were sanctified by the law.[21]

Besides, where the law actually impinged on the lives of working-class women, the oppression of women was most apparent. However, in contrast to the past, women's oppression was not only exposed by middle-class Liberals but also opposed by working women themselves. While the historian could easily emphasise the brutality that was inflicted on working-class women as well as their low status in society, it ought to be stressed that the abundance of material relating to women's subordinate status was the outcome of their multidimensional resistance to their traditional role.

The persistent oppression of women was reinforced by the Church as well as the law, and one contemporary described the 'obedience on the part of the woman' as 'being in strict accordance with Church teaching'. Furthermore, the law still discriminated against women *per se*, a wife did not even have the right to invite someone into the matrimonial home 'without the husband's permission'. A working man was legally entitled to regulate his wife's 'mode of life, her domicile and her domestic arrangements'; and the man's control of his children' was 'one of the most sacred of rights'.[22]

As social attitudes changed, working-class women were no longer prepared to 'meekly and literally obey the clench-fisted demands of her autocratic spouse'. Just as working-class women were beginning to demand control over their bodies, so they were also struggling for a new dignity in the factories, mills and workshops as well as in the home. Moreover, if the 'undermass' of working-class women were still inclined to sum up their own position in the phrase 'we ain't much count', they were nevertheless increasingly prepared to join trade unions and initiate strikes.[23]

Though some observers thought that patriarchal attitudes about the women's place were losing much of their traditional significance, the statistics of women's employment tell a different story. In Leeds male trade unionists in the textile mills came out on strike against the employment of women and in Newcastle married women who were employed in industry were forced to conceal the fact from their husbands. As Annie Abram put it: 'So effectively do they hide themselves that the general idea among trade unionists is that there are no married women wage-earners except char-women.'[24]

Opposition to the employment of married women was a fundamental ingredient of a patriarchal working-class culture, and working-class girls were trained for motherhood from the time they left the cradle. The employment of unmarried women and girls was seen as a transitional phase before marriage, and the working-class girl who was employed in industry or domestic service knew that 'she was a fairly cheap article'. It was therefore only in such 'she-towns' as Dundee and Norwich that a very large proportion of the labour force consisted of married women.[25]

In 1901 there were 13,189,585 females of ten years of age and over of whom 4,171,751 were engaged in industry and 1,829,035 in domestic service. Of the total number who were engaged in industry only 917,509 were either married or widowed. By 1913 there were 14,671,048 women over ten years of age and over of whom 5,309,000 were employed in industry. Though the statistics are in dispute there is no evidence to suggest that the percentage of married women gainfully employed was any higher in 1913 than it had been in 1901. Furthermore, the expansion of women's industrial employment was due solely to the opening up of 'new fields of employment'.[26]

By general consensus the woman's place was still in the home, and a whole complex of working-class social values kept most married women out of industry altogether. In Liverpool, females who required to earn a living were in 'disgrace', and the married women who worked in jam factories, tin-box factories and fur-sewing houses in London were of 'a very rough class'. The employment of married women often conflicted with notions of what constituted working-class respectability, and there was 'a strong taboo' against the employment of married middle-class women, too.[27]

Those women who were employed in industry were still subjected to incredible brutality, and in a London factory several girls were burnt to death as a result of the appalling conditions in the factories. In most factories and workshops hours were long, discipline was harsh, and fines were imposed for singing, carelessness, unpunctuality, bad language and untidy appearance. The exploding consciousness of the militant women was seen in their choice of working in the smaller factories where the discipline was not as strict and singing and talking were permitted. Nevertheless, there was 'a real sense of community in many factories, and the prosecution of 'a firm for employing women in the dinner hour gave publicity, during the hearing to the details of how women and girls supplied gratis the labour, clothes and buckets to keep their factory clean.' This sense of community within the factories and mills contributed to a new mood of increased expectations.[28]

As the self-confidence of a growing minority of working-class women within the factories and mills developed, so, too, did they challenge practices that had previously been accepted. With the aid of the newly appointed women Factory Inspectors, working-class women attempted to prosecute foremen and employers who had sexually assaulted them. In 1904 four foremen or employers were formally accused of sexual assaults on factory women; and in 1910, 1911 and 1912 there were twelve, twenty-two and nineteen similar complaints. However, convictions were difficult to secure in the courts, and 'the tradition of sex oppression and sex servitude survive[d] in the power exercised by the foremen'.[29]

The power of the foremen was not only enormous, but it was also buttressed by the failure of the courts to convict those who were often guilty of sexual assaults on factory women. In one case where the evidence was clear-cut, the female Inspector of Factories described the outcome: 'In one case in which criminal proceedings were instituted by the police and the magistrate taking a serious view sent the case to trial; the facts were fully admitted by the employer, and a defence of consent on the part of the girl put forward. He was set free to continue his malign use of his position of authority towards young girls in his employment.' Bearing in mind, too, that it took great courage to make such charges in the first place, it is clear that new social attitudes were transmuting the traditional, fatalistic assumptions of working-class women.[30]

Yet it ought to be emphasised that the new social climate and the greater readiness to question traditional ideas about women's subordinate role in society was the work of a minority of working-class women, middle-class women, Factory Inspectors who were sympathetic to the labour movement, and the middle-class women's movement. In the case of sexual assaults on factory women, the attitudes of working-class women themselves proved to be crucial. This point was summed up by Adelaide Anderson: 'These appeals [against sexual assaults] were never numerous, though markedly increasing in the last few years before the War, when women workers were growing bolder in self-expression and self-help. The relative smallness of their number was balanced by their intensity.'[31]

Outside the factories and domestic service altogether, rape and indecent assault were, according to the women's movement, increasing; and artisans, miners and labourers were involved in sexual and 'aggravated assaults' on women. While drink sometimes played a role in rape and aggravated assault, the general ill-treatment of women was largely a result of their low status. Nevertheless working-class women's new readiness to seek redress against sexual assault probably influenced some of the provisions of the Children's Act 1908 under which indecent assaults on females under sixteen years of age could be punished in the courts of summary jurisdiction.[32]

In contrast to factory women, domestic servants could do little to prevent the sexual assaults to which they were subjected, though their mistresses were said to view them with more sympathy than hitherto. Sexual assaults on domestic servants were seen by Lady McLaren as inevitable: 'These young girls live in a house where obedience is one of the first duties, and are thrown constantly into the society of the master, who is of a higher social status, and possesses a certain glamour as a gentleman.'[33]

Such differences of experience, attitudes and responses to their treatment by the 'masters' influenced the antagonism that existed between domestic servants and factory women. There was really nothing but 'contempt' between the domestic servants and the factory women, and a young woman whose relations worked in a factory lost 'caste' if she became a domestic servant. Already fully aware of the tensions that existed between distinct groups of working-class women, the advocates of female emancipation concentrated on accentuating the positive features of women's resistance to the traditions of the past.[34]

II

As the most serious social problems of the time, wife-beating preoccupied the attention of magistrates and lawyers. Nevertheless wife-beating and obstacles to divorce were a reflection of patriarchal traditions and attitudes to women. Moreover, if the obstacles in the way of upper- and middle-class women who wanted a divorce were formidable, divorce was beyond the reach of working-class women altogether. Indeed, under the Matrimonial Causes Act 1878 working-class women were sometimes getting separation orders because the expense of divorce was 'prohibitory'.[35]

A few legal experts were of the opinion that the divorce laws were 'notoriously unfair to women'; and the difficulties involved in acquiring a divorce were attributed to patriarchal customs. As C.G. Hartley put it: 'Whenever divorce is difficult, there woman's lot is hard and her position low. It is part of the patriarchal custom which regards women as property.' Moreover, some magistrates would only grant separation orders if they thought that a woman's life was in real danger; and separation orders were exceptionally difficult to obtain. The difficulties were explained by Lady McLaren: 'Great numbers of separations under this Act have been granted, notwithstanding the fact that serious assaults or wilful dissertion must be proved in evidence. One magistrate did not think much of a black eye, and another recently compelled a wife of only sixteen to return to her husband even though violence had been proved against him.'[36]

Nevertheless the divorce rate was increasing dramatically, and so were separation orders. In 1900 6661 separation orders were made in the courts of summary jurisdiction in England and Wales; by 1914 the annual figure had jumped to 14,000. These statistics bore eloquent testimony to women's new consciousness and challenge to traditional ideas about their role in society; the separation orders provided crucial evidence of the revolt of working-class women.[37]

However, just as the available statistics of wife-beating were an inadequate guide to the extent of the problem, so were the statistics of separation an inadequate index to the new social attitudes of working-class women. Side-by-side with the newer attitudes of working-class women, older working-class values inhibited the separation of unhappily married working-class couples. On the one hand, there was 'an overwhelming demand amongst married women belonging to the artisan class for a drastic reform in the divorce laws'; but on the other hand, separation conflicted with notions of working-class respectability.[38]

The desire or application for separation was motivated by the problem of wife-beating, though many working-class wives were prepared to put up with ill-treatment because they could see no way out of their predicament. Those women who belonged to the working classes were well aware of the practical consequences of separation: 'They do suffer from public opinion when separated. "The disgrace" is dreaded, and we were told it would go against you at the works and be a hindrance in looking for employment.' There was, moreover, an 'instinctive dislike for the separation allowed by law', and many working women preferred to put up with ill-treatment rather than go before a magistrate. In other cases many working people separated of 'their own accord'.[39]

However not only was the law itself ambiguous in relation to the problem of wife-beating; but magistrates also interpreted the law in the light of their own prejudices and attitudes to women. In a study entitled *Marriage and Divorce*, Cecil Chapman argued that, though the law no longer recognised 'the right to correction', bad customs were still surviving the bad laws which had given rise to them. Wife-beating was, moreover, 'a flagrantly common offence in England', and it arose from and impinged on working-class culture and conjured up the figure of the mother-in-law as an ogre who interfered with wife-beaters. An oft-quoted rhyme – 'Of all the old women that ever I saw, Sweet bad luck to my mother-in-law' – was said to sum up a major obstacle to married happiness. In reality, however, the wife's mother frequently provided the only real protection she had 'from starvation and violence'.[40]

As in the mid-Victorian period, the middle-class women's movement took up the issue of wife-beating. One important consequence of the debate they opened about the whole issue of wife-beating as a serious social problem was the introduction of the Assault on Wives (Outdoor Relief) Bill in 1910. This important Bill was described in the language of the Edwardian period: 'The object of this Bill is to enable a court to order outdoor relief, at a rate not exceeding ten shillings a week, to be given to a wife whose husband is sentenced to more than one month's imprisonment for an aggravated assault upon her. The receipt of such relief is not to constitute the wife a pauper.' It is interesting that this Bill focused on the aggravated assault (that is, kicking or standing on a woman, setting her hair on fire, etc.) rather than the ordinary assault, and in any case it did not complete its passage through Parliament.[41]

In working-class communities women were 'the property of the men they married', and even a right-wing woman opponent of the movement for women's liberation attributed wife-beating to the 'old view' of a husband's right to correct his wife by physically punishing her. Crimes against property were viewed much more seriously than assaults on wives – wife-beating was a crime which met with 'very lenient treatment when compared with an offence against property'. Patriarchal attitudes were so deeply ingrained in British culture that wife-beaters were treated less harshly by the law than poachers, and the law was described as 'the concrete expression of man's attitude towards women in the mass'. The difference in attitudes to poachers and wife-beaters was summed up by C.W. Saleeby: 'Woe to the poacher, but the wife beater has only strained a right and may be leniently dealt with; woe to the destroyer of pheasants, but the destruction of wives is only a detail.'[42]

A crucial factor contributing to the high incidence of wife-beating was police magistrates' lack of sympathy for women who were brutally beaten by their husbands. In his auto-biography entitled *Grain of Chaff*, Alfred C. Plowden, a police magistrate, observed that it was 'wonderful how many black eyes' they tolerated before they sought the protection of the law. His own patriarchal view of women was only thinly disguised, and he articulated the inherent ambiguities of the many police magistrates who sat in judgment on wife-beaters when he wrote: 'Very often a man looks upon his wife as a fit subject for a kick or a blow whenever she fails to rise to the full height of her domestic duties, and unless the dose is repeated too often, I am not sure that the husband sinks much in the estimation of his wife for taking this view of their relative positions.' This police magistrate, a Liberal-Unionist, had his counterpart in James Johnston, a Fabian, who described the black eye that a working-class woman had acquired on a Saturday evening as a 'love tap'.[43]

While such views of women were commonplace among the rulers of society, it is not surprising that there was so much brutality among the working classes. Patriarchal attitudes came down from on high, and the ideas of women's subordination that had crystallised in the dark decades of the mid-Victorian period were still strong among men irrespective of the particular strata to which they belonged. At the heart of the problem of wife-beating was the common assumption of working men that they actually *owned* their wives. This was why one working man indignantly told a police magistrate that: 'Things have come to a pretty pass in this country when a man can't thrash his own wife in his own kitchen.'[44]

Since such views and attitudes permeated all sections of society, it was not surprising that wife-beating was so brutal and widespread. Indeed no country had 'such a reputation for wife-beating as England', where women were 'freely kicked, stamped on, thrown down stairs and their eyes gouged out'. As it was 'a bold thing for a wife to come forward and charge her husband with assault', the cases that came into court were only a small fraction of the actual assaults on wives. Besides, the latitude allowed 'by the law in the matter of the personal chastisement of the wife' inhibited many working-class women from going to court at all.[45]

If the middle-class women's movement developed illusions about the efficacy of the law in minimising, if not eradicating, the problem of wife-beating, there were even more right-wing thinkers, politicians and writers who blamed the whole problem on women themselves. As one such right-wing, anti-women writer put it: 'Sometimes a woman, whose face has been beaten almost to a jelly by her burly brute of a husband in the dock, will plead ardently to the magistrate not to be "hard on him"; adding, perhaps, that he has always been a good husband, and never lays hands on her when he is sober. Which, perhaps is not very often! This sort of marital advocacy altogether baffles male reasoning, and under the circumstances the magistrate usually considers it necessary to be cruel to be kind, and so, in spite of wifely intercession, to give the inhuman husband a spell of imprisonment.' This analysis ignored the evidence of what actually happened in most cases of wife-beating, just as it glossed over the environmental factors that triggered assaults on wives in working-class communities.[46]

Working-class culture was still predominantly a male culture and the male worker was 'the master'. As 'the master' who took the ownership of his wife for granted, the working-class man felt that he had an innate right to beat her. Working men who used violence on their wives were usually fined ten shillings; and a fairly typical outbreak of violence was described as follows: 'There is a sudden quarrel, a man lurches violently against the mother, and the edge of the spoon is pushed hard against the infant's gums, and blood comes into the mouth.' Moreover, it was already established practice that no one interfered with such family violence. 'In the middle of the night dreadful shrieks arose from the next house, where a woman was being beaten, and although she screamed "Murder" and her cries filled the neighbourhood, no one seemed to interfere.' In the objective conditions of the time, there was little incentive for anyone to interfere with the wife-beater.[47]

The patriarchal culture of the possessing classes, the distinctive workers' culture of the artisans, miners, agricultural labourers, factory workers and labourers, the attitudes of police magistrates and the social attitudes of working women themselves created a climate in which wife-beating became difficult to eradicate. The social attitudes and responses of working men were explained by Cecil Chapman:

A husband is brought before me for violently assaulting his wife, and when I ask him whether it is true, he replies: 'Yes, it's true enough, but she kept nagging me first about money and boots for the children, which she knew well enough I could not give her. I am sorry I hurt her, but what else could I do with her?' Another woman complains that her husband has thrashed her with his belt, and on inquiry the husband explains: 'She whacked the child because he called her out of her name, and I told her if she did that I would whack her; and she defied me, so I beat her.'

Yet even this perceptive Liberal lawyer, who understood the social attitudes surrounding the problem of wife-beating, tended to ignore the importance of environmental factors.[48]

Socialists themselves often offered conflicting interpre-
tations of the problem of wife-beating. Far from thinking
about social problems either deeply or independently, there
were many middle-class socialists who were influenced by the
most superficial bourgeois magazines such as *Punch*. In
discussing the problem of wife-beating, Ethel Snowden
reflected the sick humour of the most supercilious of the
middle-class commentators and observers:

> *Punch* put the matter in popular but forceful style in a cartoon which
> appeared in its pages some little time ago, when 'Liza' is made to say to
> ''arry, why don't 'ee knock us about a bit?' A sad experience came into
> the life of the writer a few months ago. An acquaintance of hers was
> passing the door of a working-class house in a Lancashire town, when
> he heard a noise, and a frightened scream from a woman inside the
> house. 'Murder! help' she shouted in such terrified tones that he burst
> open the door and rushed to her aid. A great hulking fellow, half drunk,
> was savagely kicking his wife as she lay on the floor, struck down by his
> hand. She was horribly bruised. He rushed at the man and pulled him
> away, when, to his surprise, the woman started to her feet with yells and
> curses on his interference. 'Kick me, Teddy', she said, 'as hard as you
> like. You're my husband. You've a right to. Never mind him.'[49]

Yet Jack London, an American socialist, who came to the
city of London to engage in sociological excavation, offered a
superb analysis of the problem. As he saw the situation,
working women were economically dependent on their
husbands who were, in turn, dependent on their 'masters'. In
these circumstances where working men could not articulate
their tensions by beating their masters, they ended up by
beating their wives. He explained that few working men were
sent to jail for beating their wives for the simple reason that
evidence could not be obtained before such cases went to
court; and he added that working women were forced to plead
with the magistrate to let their brutal husbands off for 'the
kiddies' sake'. Moreover, and in contrast to a police magistrate
in Woolwich, London, who, in 1914, told a working man that
he was legally entitled to 'thrash his wife with a stick so long
as it was no thicker than his thumb', sections of the socialist
movement expelled members who indulged in wife-beating.[59]

III

Small as it was, and divided as it often was on the issue of women's emancipation, the socialist movement played a major role in raising the status of women. As well as repudiating and discouraging wife-beating, many socialists 'repudiate[d] the private ownership of the head of the family as completely as [they] repudiate[d] any other sort of ownership'. Long before the socialists, however, free thinkers, Liberals and neo-Malthusians had, and were, disseminating propaganda about the efficacy of family limitation. What differentiated the socialists from these other groups was their repudiation of men's ownership of their wives, and their direct influence within working-class communities.[51]

Socialists contributed to the struggle for women's emancipation in a very significant way by disseminating information on 'birth control'. The phrase 'birth control' is, of course, a tautology. As A.J.P. Taylor put it: 'It only means that conception was restricted and does not explain how.' The phrase birth control was not used in those years, anyway, and the forces of the establishment – the medical authorities, doctors, nurses, politicians, etc. – raged against 'race suicide' without drawing a distinction between the use of contraceptives, illegal operations or drugs designed to produce abortions. From the standpoint of official society race suicide was a crime.[52]

By 1910 the establishment was now less horrified by prostitution than it had been formerly; and it displayed more toleration of prostitution than it did for attempts at family limitation. Incest and prostitution in such cities as London were occurring on a large scale; and juvenile prostitution, too, was widespread. The role of poverty in creating prostitution was now recognised and discussed quite openly – what led the working-class girl to prostitution was appalling poverty. As Mary Higgs, a social investigator, put it: 'When all else is sold she sells herself to live.' In London there were allegedly 80,000 young women 'living, more or less, upon the wages of prostitution', in 1900; in Bradford many factory girls supplemented their poor wages by engaging in part-time prostitution; and in the small Scottish town of Falkirk prostitution was attributed to the existence of '1,500 women workers whose average wage is only seven shillings per week'.[53]

A degree of distressing ignorance about sexual matters existed in all working-class communities; but it is important to emphasise that this ignorance was, according to the women's movement, socially induced by the propaganda and teaching of Church and state. This appalling ignorance was vividly described by Margret Mondfield in her autobiography, *A Life's Work*, where she wrote: 'Many street girls smoked and thought it would act as a preventive to conception. Others used more dangerous methods to procure abortion. Sometimes girls were told they must go out with as many men as possible to avoid conception.'

In reconstructing a picture of working class life during the years before the outbreak of the First World War the historian must subject his source material to critical scrutiny. In her autobiography, *My Fight for Birth Control*, Margaret Sanger clearly misread the British evidence when she wrote: 'At this time [1914] the working classes had not yet been aroused to the possibility of obtaining such information nor to a conscious desire for its benefits, so far as I could ascertain.' The social picture of working-class attitudes to reproduction was, in fact, much more complex than that.[54]

Caroline Nelson, an American socialist pioneer of birth control, who worked in London for several months in 1913, was appalled by the conditions and social attitudes that she encountered. 'In London's poor districts, where the miserable, poor workers have families of from five to a dozen, I told a charity nurse what I thought about it, and I began to give her a piece of my mind for not informing the workers of the preventive means. She said, "My dear I cannot get the women to listen to me. They think that it is a sin against God".' Yet, the most deprived among working-class women frequently had illegal abortions at the same time as they looked upon contraceptives 'as a sin against the Holy Ghost'.[55]

Working men, whether they were artisans or labourers, usually refused to 'permit any mention of sexual matters in their homes' and left 'their children to get their information on the streets'. Artisans as well as labourers were 'prejudiced' against instructing their children in 'their future sexual and parental functions'. Contrary to the argument of the American historian, Peter Stearns, that the artisans were 'more quickly aware of new birth control methods than their fellows in other industries', the important division was often generational. In a book entitled *Seems So! A Working-Class View of Politics*, Stephen Reynolds and B. and T. Woolley described the changes that were taking place in working-class morality: 'And even now [in 1911] working-class morality is on the change. Statesmen are much perturbed by what is termed race suicide. . . . The older fashioned working man will not consider voluntary limitations of the family. To his mind it is unnatural and wicked. But the younger generation is keenly interested in the possibilities and personal advantages, and its advantages to the children who are born.'[56]

Certainly the younger generation of working men were more open-minded about the question of family limitation; and the 'vehement scoldings of prominent people' against race suicide did nothing to arrest the falling birth rate. Socialists as well as neo-Malthusians took information about how to prevent conception to many working-class communities, and for some socialists the fight *for* race suicide was a conscious part of the cultural struggle between 'them' and 'us'. Those individuals who fought for the new ideas were just as courageous as the women strikers who formed the picket lines; and the socialists and free-thinkers who disseminated information on birth control were frequently prosecuted and sent to jail. However, other factors were helping to make the socialists' task an easier one.[57]

In the factory districts of England, but particularly in Yorkshire, where child labour was in marked decline, abortion by means of illegal operations was an accepted part of the culture of working-class women, and in towns like Newcastle women took the abortifacient diachylon 'regularly before each expected monthly period'. The decline of child labour meant that children had much less commercial value, and economic as well as cultural factors helped to trigger the escalation of the practice of abortion.[58]

In her study of the English town of Middlesbrough, *At the Works*, Lady Bell referred to the 'deplorably increasing number of women' who took measures to procure abortions;

moreover, many women were using abortifacients without their husbands' knowledge – even artisans' wives sometimes lived in dread of their men finding out. In York, for example, contraceptives were not adopted by artisans' wives at all, but when pregnancy did occur they resorted to abortifacients.[59]

The decisive factors in determining whether working women resorted to abortion or prevention were poverty, ignorance or lack of information. In 1914 one witness told the National Council of Public Morals that the poorer people could not afford the better methods of prevention such as syringes, oil or quinine. The chairman of the Council wondered if controlling the sale of preventive devices would not increase the number of abortions by means of illegal operations, and he attributed the comparatively higher number of abortions in America to sanctions against herbalists and quacks.

In the eyes of the establishment and the medical authorities, however, the major problem was the falling birth rate.[60] As spontaneous and illegal abortions were not registered as births and deaths, it was not possible to know the full extent of the problem. In England in 1913 the number of children who were born dead was estimated at 70,000 per annum. Indeed something like one out of every four children died before birth from abortion. A woman who belonged to the labouring poor described the social milieu in which illegal operations occurred: 'Self-restraint? Not much! If my husband started on self-restraint, I would jolly well know there was another woman in the case. Nay – with blind contempt – 'tain't that . . . There's any amount of illegal operations. I could mention a thousand.'[61]

If the medical authorities and the establishment were worried by the increasing number of illegal operations, they were also influenced by considerations of social class. Even Karl Pearson, a Liberal defender of women's legal and property rights, wrote in a very elitist way about the problem of the falling birth-rate: 'I do not speak lightly; there is very definite evidence to show that the terrible fall in our birth-rate since 1877 has been a differential fall. It is a fall which concerns chiefly the fitter members of all classes. The fitter of all classes, from the artisan to the executive, have fewer and fewer children, but the unfit maintain their numbers; nor is the reason hard to seek, income and wages are no longer proportional to physical or mental fitness.' Nevertheless many women including 'good church women' were discussing what were the most effective means of prevention rather than the 'legitimacy' of birth control.[62]

Even so, the intellectual debate (as distinct from actual working-class praxis) was dominated by considerations of Social Darwinism and social class. In cases of difficult childbirth doctors refused to administer 'chloroform to the poor', though they did not deny it to their prosperous women patients. But if the establishment was obsessed by considerations of social class, there were important variations in the cultural attitudes and responses of different occupational groups within the working class.[63]

In Rotherham there was no evidence of agricultural labourers or miners making any effort to limit the size of their families; but in some other rural districts in the North of England there had been a fall in the birth-rate among agricultural labourers. More than any other occupational group the miners, who exerted great power over their wives, were relatively untouched by the propaganda for family limitation. Nevertheless miners' wives in Eastington were discussing family limitation with their doctors; and in Chester-le-Spring miners' wives were making active attempts to procure abortions. Nor was this surprising, for the knowledge of how to achieve birth control was spread by word of mouth in mines and factories.[64]

For many socialists the struggle to extend knowledge of birth control was a basic aspect of the cultural struggle that they were waging against the possessing classes. They were not, moreover, particularly concerned about the means they used to reduce the birth-rate; 'race suicide' was the general term that was used to describe the social process of rejecting the dominant views of the establishment. In esoteric discussions a distinction was drawn between ordinary abortions (illegal operations) and abortifacients; yet these discussions did not impinge on the socialists who were waging their own cultural class struggle against the social values of 'them'.[65]

The police and the clergy campaigned against race suicide, and they thereby aroused the hostility of the most militant and class-conscious men and women of the working class. In Huddersfield town council a socialist representative summed up the new attitudes of the militant minority: 'Aye! The time's gone by when we'll breed soldiers to be shot at for a shilling a day or workers to 'addle brass for manufacturers and starve ther' sen.' As the most traditionally-minded of all the occupational working-class groups, the miners were not very receptive to race suicide propaganda. Even so, there were socialist miners in Ardsley who encouraged their wives to take abortifacients. In other ways, too, a minority of working men encouraged the mass, multi-dimensional revolt of working-class women.[66]

IV

A dual consciousness (that is, social conservatism yet a propensity to question) was common to many working-class women; and the small, middle-class women's movement played an important role in both stimulating and yet stifling the mass revolt of working-class women. With a set of middle-class aims and objectives – the 'demand to have the doors leading to professional, political and highly skilled labour thrown open to them' – the women's movement was remote from the harsh realities of working-class life.[67]

If the social conditions endured by the wives of the labourers were unbearable, the conditions of the women in the sweated trades were even worse. The working-class wife was 'the man's economic inferior', and the working man possessed 'absolute power' over her. Even where married women were allowed to work in industry, they were still subjected to domestic tyranny. This situation was described by the authors of *Women's Work and Wages*: 'When the man and wife both work during the day, the woman accepts it as right that she should do all the housework at night while the man amuses himself in any way he thinks fit.'[68]

Not surprisingly, there were many working women who sank into apathy and fatalism. A combination of social isolation and onerous domestic duties did not always inspire working women to fight for a better world, and many of them were even deprived of a fair share of their husband's already inadequate wages. Robert H. Sherard described working-class responses in the North of England: "'Thank God they have gone back" is the elegy that the working-class women sings over her children who have died.'[69] In these circumstances, it was difficult to organise a woman's labour movement.

But if the woman's movement that arose in the early twentieth century was small in numbers, and if its members were middle-class in their origins and social outlook, it was not supported by most middle-class women. The factors that inhibited the majority from supporting the movement for female emancipation were their anti-socialism, their bourgeois individualism and their lack of identification with the women of the 'lower orders'. This was why the woman's movement turned to organised labour for inspiration and moral support.[70]

Indeed, the Woman's Social and Political Union (WSPU) was formed after the Salford branch of the Independent Labour Party refused to admit women members. Already aware of the indifference of most middle-class women, Christabel Pankhurst tried to attract the support of working-class women – this was why her co-worker, Annie Kenney, was told to introduce herself to the WSPU's working-class audiences as 'a factory-girl and trade unionist'.[71]

In *Class and Ideology in the Nineteenth Century*, R.S. Neale did a useful job in debunking the view that the WSPU attracted considerable working-class support; yet he did not realise that the working-class women in the textile industry who sent petitions to the House of Commons demanding the franchise for women were alienated by the indifference of their well-to-do sisters.[72]

A minority of working women did agitate for votes for women; but they were usually discouraged by the labour movement's lack of support. In 1906 only four of the fourteen Labour Members of Parliament supported the agitation for votes for women, and the annual conference of the Labour Party rejected a motion asking the Party to raise the issue in the House of Commons. Apathy and hostility to the campaign for women's emancipation influenced these decisions; but the trades councils also feared that such agitations might result in middle-class women gaining the vote on the basis of a property qualification. Besides, as working women were contributing very small sums of money to the women's movement anyway, a mass women's movement was retarded by the labour movement's sectarianism and lack of vision.[73]

Moreover, while a tiny number of working-class women were involved in the agitation for women's suffrage, the majority of women in industry and agriculture were usually engaged in more basic bread-and-butter struggles. It is therefore not surprising to discover that Sylvia Pankhurst's reputedly more 'proletarian' East London Federation of Suffragettes built up its membership in working-class areas 'chiefly through afternoon tea parties'. Consequently, they were much more aware of their alienation from working people than the WSPU; and they were forced to inform the more middle-class-oriented women's organisations that they could not participate in the 'No Vote, No Rent strike', because it was 'only in the working-class houses that the woman pays the rent'.[74]

In any case working-class women were alienated from the women's suffrage agitation as a result of 'the very different treatment accorded to working-class women and those of another social standing'. In contrast to the treatment meted out to working-class activists, the suffragettes with 'well-known names and a good social position were treated with leniency and in some cases were allowed to do almost anything without arrest or punishment'. It was only the intensification of industrial women's vast spontaneous revolt for higher wages and better conditions that created the climate of opinion in which the labour movement felt forced to campaign for women's suffrage.[75]

Social conservatism was deeply ingrained in working-class consciousness; and, being the outcome – the cultural underpinning – of existence in a patriarchal, capitalist society, it impinged on every aspect of the lives of working-class women. Moreover, if strikes of labouring men encroached on traditional property rights, strikes of working women were inherently revolutionary in the sense that they challenged fundamental notions of women's role in society.[76] And by throwing off the whole weight of past traditions and attitudes, women's strikes undermined working men's social conservatism and helped to change the character of working-class life.

To appreciate just how fundamental the working-class women's challenge to patriarchal attitudes was, we need to consider the plight of women who were engaged in industry. In 1914 the legal maximum number of hours a woman could work a day had remained unaltered for over forty years, at 10½ hours. However, it was not uncommon for girls in dressmaking and the sweated trades to work fourteen hours a day; hostile magistrates imposed derisory fines on employers who encouraged women and girls to work illegal overtime.[77]

The servitude and inferiority of working-class women was seen most sharply in the poverty wages that they received. Their low wages were rooted in 'the ages-old tradition of women's inferiority', and all the trades which secured high wages were 'the monopoly of the male sex'. Married women were often paid less than single women and their wages were so derisory that 'even the small sums that their children earn[ed] for them [were] indispensable additions to the resources of the family'. Poor wages were, however, only one facet of women's inferiority, and to depict the extent to which they reflected their total social situation we can do no better than quote from A.M. Anderson's book, *Women in the Factory*:

> In few places could the framework of bondage be more complete than in a certain 'townland', where the owner of the principal shop and public-house was also the owner of the flax fields and flax scutch mill, and the employer of many inhabitants. The women working for wages in the mill seldom received coin: one girl, whose father and sister were dependent on the same employer, received none during a whole winter. Dealing at the shop was practically a condition of employment.[78]

Trade unions were, and were intended to be, the exclusive preserve of working men; and there were often fundamental 'preliminary difficulties in the way of admitting women to the membership of clubs and unions where the accommodation [had] been provided with a view to the comfort of the men only'. It was commonplace for male trade unionists to voice their dislike of the 'go-to-meetings' woman, and feminine weakness, as Barbara Drake put it, 'bowed to masculine dictums'. Male trade unionists were sometimes opposed to women's trade unions altogether, and a letter from a trade union of men in the Midlands asking the Women's Trade Union League to provide them with a woman organiser concluded thus: 'Please send the organiser immediately, for our Amalgamated Society has decided that if the women of this town cannot be organised, they must be exterminated.'[79]

The prejudice of male trade unionists was, however, inseparable from the social values engendered by a patriarchal society. One trade union leader opposed the admission of women into his trade union because the status of his organisation would have suffered 'if it were known that it contained a large percentage of non-political, non-voting members'. The fact that women did not possess the right to vote in Parliamentary elections helped to perpetuate their low status in working-class organisations as well as in society at large. This was emphasised by the following exchange of opinion between two trade union leaders in the North of England: '"My opinion should have some weight", said the Weavers' secretary at a Lancashire trades council meeting, "for I represent by far the biggest union in the town'. "What's the good of your union", said the Engineers' secretary, "why it's all women; mine mayn't be large, but, at all events, they're voters".'[80]

It could be exceptionally difficult to persuade working women to join trade unions at all, and the leaders of women's unions used insurance inducements to boost their membership. In some cases sickness, death or unemployment benefits or marriage dowries were offered to members, while women members of the mixed unions paid a reduced scale of contributions. Paradoxically, however, with the exception of the women in the textile trades in Lancashire, most women trade unionists were 'drawn from the poorest classes'; and, when the dramatic breakthrough and expansion of female trade unionism occurred between 1906 and 1914, it was at least partly facilitated by the bureaucratic mentality of the male trade union leaders.

This expansion of female trade unionism was initially

stimulated by a new mood of militancy, which, in turn, forced the leaders of the existing trade unions to change their attitudes towards working women. As Barbara Drake put it: 'Men members were enjoined to persuade, or compel, their women-folk to join the union; and some local associations went so far as to lay down that "no person shall be eligible for any official position, whose wife and children, if working, are not members of the union".'[81]

Mary Macarthur became secretary of the Women's Trade Union League in 1903, and the National Federation of Women Workers was formed three years later, in 1906. It was, in fact, a trade union affiliated to the Women's Trade Union League rather than a federation, and it 'had, at first, great difficulty in getting itself taken seriously by employers, who laughed at the idea of a trade union among women'.[82] The Federation's small membership was soon expanded from 2000 in 1906 to 14,000 in 1908 and touched the figure of over 70,000 before the outbreak of the First World War.[83]

In their social outlook as well as in their origins, the leaders of the National Federation of Women Workers and the Women's Trade Union League were essentially middle-class, and they were committed to the basic structure of the capitalist system. By 1914 they had organised a significant number of working women, and they took advantage of the spontaneous strikes of working women to enrol them in trade unions. It is important to emphasise that during this period of unprecedented revolt among working women strikes usually preceded the formation of trade unions; and the middle-class women who led the trade unions taught working women the importance of obedience, self-sacrifice and self-control.[84]

By 1912 the Women's Trade Union League had attracted 160,000 members, and there were 356,963 women workers organised on the eve of the First World War. This enormous expansion of women's trade unionism was partly the outcome of the spontaneous, elemental revolt of women in industry – a revolt which was stifled by these self-same trade unions. Indeed, the important role that women's trade unions could play in disciplining working women was explained, in 1908, by the authors of *Women in Industry from Seven Points of View*:

New recruits to the army of organised labour must learn that a union is not an autocratic machine into which they can drop their pennies and from which they can immediately draw out good conditions and higher wages without any further trouble. They must realise that trade unionism is not magic; [and] that it entails loyalty, self-sacrifice and self-control.[85]

This is not to deny that the women's trade unions often accentuated the latent discontent and potential militancy of industrial women. If employers still looked upon women's strikes as a laughing matter in the early 1900s, they were only able to do so as a result of working women's timidity and sense of inferiority. In a sketch of Mary Macarthur in the *Woman Worker* in 1908, J.J. Mallon described exactly how many working women, who were themselves potential strikers, viewed their employers: 'The "master" is to them a figure of myth and legend: a goblin who eats of those that anger him.' However, these fears were soon forgotten and transcended in the ensuing class struggle.[86]

There is no evidence that the 'labour revolt' of 1909–14 was initiated by women workers; but working women did initiate an unprecedented challenge to the social values imposed on them by the possessing classes. Much of the social reform of the time was designed to discipline working people by introducing compulsory medical inspection of children, compulsory school attendance, temperance instruction, unemployment benefit and the exclusion of women and children from public houses. As working people – and particularly women – became increasingly critical of 'those who wanted to teach them how bad they [were]' class antagonisms found new outlets 'in all sorts of unsuspected ways.[87]

Working-class women resented the interference of outsiders – police, nurses, health visitors, school attendance officers, temperance reformers, etc. – in their lives; and attempts by the authorities to deal with such problems as lice-ridden heads resulted in serious riots. Moreover, the minority of well-behaved workers who opted for such middle-class values as temperance were ridiculed and ostracised in most communities. But if social reforms often penalised the poor 'by forcing upon them useless imitations of middle-class virtues', they also sharpened class antagonisms. And in the resultant revolt cultural and social grievances were just as prominent and deeply felt as economic ones.[88]

Before 1906 the organisation of female labour had been an 'almost "Sisyphean" task', and the chain-makers at Cradley Heath, where the working conditions were deplorable, were 'indifferent to the progress or failure of unionism amongst the girls'. The picture began to change in 1906, when the biggest women's strike in Dundee for ten years persuaded the members of the Socialist Labour Party to campaign against the Rev. Henry Williamson, who had organised women workers, and general male domination of the women's trade unions. A few years later a Scottish correspondent of the *Women's Trade Union Review* described the changing attitudes throughout industry: 'Girls are joining the Federation who used to sneer at the members.'[89]

In the series of women's strikes that began in 1909, the National Federation of Women Workers attracted a great deal of middle-class support; and the strike of women chain-makers at Cradley Heath in 1910 won the support of the press as well as the sympathy of George Cadbury, Lady Beauchamp and the Bishop of Worcester. Moreover, it was the Federation of Women Workers rather than the Women's Trade Union League which played the most important role in the women's strikes. Indeed the Trade Union League was committed to social peace in industry and its political role was summed up by Mary Hamilton:

> The Trade Union League itself was an object lesson in social co-operation. Its members belonged to all parties, and to none. They came from all classes, though the middle class decidedly predominated. Differing on many points, they came together for practical work. With them in mind, tirades against the bourgeoisie became unreal: an idle interruption of the real task.[90]

However, the most important consequence of the women's strike at Cradley Heath was the direct intervention of the British Trades Union Congress – the first time they had ever intervened on the side of striking women workers. As well as collecting money and receiving a deputation on the floor of Congress, the President, J. O'Grady, appealed to the delegates for support: 'I sincerely hope the trade union movement will rise to the occasion, and help these poor white slaves of

England to get their humble demand.' This was the background against which working women in industry and agriculture rose in spontaneous revolt against atrocious working conditions and poor wages. As Margaret Bondfield put it: 'Strikes at Millwall food preserving factory, among the London country charwomen, the Kilbirnie net workers, and notably Cradley Heath chain-makers, all helped to establish trade unionism more firmly among women, largely because of the greater centralisation which the Federation made possible.'[91]

During the years between 1906 and 1914 the consciousness of industrial women was transformed, and even fisher-girls and the women engaged in agriculture struck work to improve their conditions. In 1906 the Scottish fisher-girls, who 'travelled the herrin'' by following the fishing fleet, were assumed to be resigned to 'their circumstances'. As the Rev. Daniel M'Iver put it: 'One might think that the fisher-girls are a solely distressed lot – but no. They are very happy, for they learn to take their sufferings philosophically.' By 1910, however, they were engaged in a 'revolt against late hours', and in 1911 a group of young women at Grimsby struck work against hours that were 'usually sixteen in twenty-four'. Since they had broken their contract and 'could neither claim wages nor return fares to their homes', it was inevitable that their strike should end in defeat. In the future, though, no one would assume that they were resigned to their fate.[92]

In 1912 trade union expansion amongst 'the poorer classes of women workers' was without precedent; and in 1913 striking agricultural women workers were led by Mrs Anns, who was regarded as a legendary scold. As one writer put it: 'She led the women, and in the case of a strike at picking time, she did all the talking; and it did not take much to set her grumbling.' In a world where working women looked upon employers as goblins, men engaged in trade unionism and labour journalism also depicted militant women workers as scolds and even simpletons. But if traditional patriarchal prejudices and stereotypes were not eradicated by working-class women's spontaneous revolt against the status quo, they were severly shaken and undermined.[93]

Moreover, women workers' dramatic intervention in the

making of history came during the national transport strike of 1911. In Bermondsey the strike caught the women's imagination, and every factory employing women was soon emptied: 15,000 women came out spontaneously; millenial hopes inspired the women's unprecedented revolt. As Mary Hamilton put it: 'Afterwards legends flew about as to the cause: a story was told of a fat woman who had appeared in many factories, called the girls out or threatened employers. No-one had seen her; everybody believed in her.' Once they were aroused, women workers demanded more say in the running of their own trade union affairs, too.[94]

In these new circumstances of a mass revolt of industrial women, it became increasingly obvious that the ordinary rank-and-file women had not been trained to run their own affairs. In 1912 it was proposed to set up a Labour College for working women, and on the eve of the First World War working girls in London were taking the initiative by setting up trade unions in the factories themselves. Hostile observers were usually at a loss to explain the reasons for the women's revolt; but a few of them attributed the new spirit of discontent and rebellion to the long, hot summers of those years. In any case the millenial hopes and strivings for a better world were soon interrupted by the outbreak of a bloody and disruptive world war.[95]

4

English Working-Class Attitudes to State Intervention and the 'Labour Unrest', 1883–1914

Such extremes of poverty as one may find in London, Paris, Berlin, or New York today are new in the history of the world, and equally new are other extremes of huge wealth lying side by side, cheek by jowl, with fearful poverty. This violent and unnatural contrast will produce violent and unnatural remedies.

R.E. Hughes

I am not a revolutionist; yet I think revolution may come.

G. Lowes Dickinson

In most histories of the English working class, the emphasis has usually been on the 'unrepresentative minority' of organised workers in the trade unions and in the socialist groups and sects. In recent years those historians who have attempted to chronicle and analyse the role of the 'unrepresentative minority' in the *formal* labour movement have begun to raise questions about the relationships between the organised minority and the unorganised majority. With the growing awareness of the importance of the lives of the unorganised majority of working-class men and women, historians have only recently begun to research workers' culture, social values and social attitudes.

There was certainly a distinction between the so-called 'aristocracy of labour' and the vast majority of unorganised men and women between 1883 and 1914. In drawing a distinction between the small 'aristocracy of labour' and the non-aristocratic workers in England, John Foster argues that: 'Correspondingly, the essence of the non-aristocrats' culture was a rejection of everything associated with their work-time task-masters: discipline, subservience, abstinence.'[1] Although

Foster's distinction is too sharp and schematic, the unorganised workers were often militant, disaffected and hostile
to capitalist values.

Moreover, most English working people were hostile to
state interference in their social lives. From the 1880s onwards
there was an increasing tension between the dominant social
values of the English ruling class and those of most working-
class men and women. This conflict was seen in the almost
'underground' cultural class struggle and the open social
struggle over wages and working conditions in workshops,
mills and factories.

In the presence of strangers – for example, nurses, health
visitors, doctors, and teachers – working people were often
deliberately inarticulate; and there was a wide gulf between
'them' and 'us', '"us" being manual workers in contact with
natural forces or working for a wage with no security of
tenure, and "them" being persons with an adequate income
and security against future privation.'[2] Even the 'most
superior men and women' in working-class communities hated
the representatives of officialdom, and there was a great
dislike of factory inspectors, foremen, nurses and lawyers.
Temperance and middle-class social values were rejected by
the majority of English working people.[3]

I

From its foundation in 1883 until the outbreak of the First
World War the Social Democratic Federation (SDF) always
articulated very elitist attitudes towards English working-class
men and women. A major reason for its hostility to the
working class was the workers' apathy and servility. As A.P.
Hazell put it: 'The workers, generally, display the same
cussedness in regard to every agitation that could be used by
them to advance their interests. It does not matter whether it
is against slums, against rack-renting by house farmers, or
against the prostitution of young females of their own class,
they let the opportunity go by. They don't even seem to care
to do a little bleating.' In attacking 'the cussedness of the
[English] working class', Hazell was upset because they were

largely hostile to the agitation for any sort of state inter-vention.[4]

In the 1880s and 1890s the SDF frequently criticised working people for their ignorance, stupidity and apathy. In 1887 J. Hunter Watts denounced 'creatures who are content to lead the lives of factory drudges, of mill horses, of wage slaves of any kind'. Without offering any hope or way out of the dilemma that he perceived, Dan Irving wrote, in 1893: 'Cowardice, too, plays a not unimportant part in obstructing our onward march. The haunting fear of poverty, nay, the terror or starvation, holds the worker bound. Slavishly does he obey the behest of his masters.' Indeed, the anti-socialist language employed by the nominally Marxist SDF was not very different from the language used by middle-class observers of working-class life.[5]

Towards the end of the nineteenth century the idea of *collectivism* was new to the English labour movement. Despite the advent of the 'new unionism' in the 1880s, the labour movement was still committed to the ideology of thrift, temperance and self-help. In explaining the ideology of the mid-Victorian labour movement, Royden Harrison said: 'When Applegarth commended thrift, he had in mind its exercise through the mutual insurance provisions of his union. When Odger talked of self-reliance, he had in mind the political presence of the working class which was not to be diminished by deference to Conservatives or financial depen-dence upon wealthy Liberals.' But what Harrison described as 'the collective self-help' of the trade unions was sometimes implicitly hostile to the collective doctrine of socialism,[6] and so were most working-class men and women.

In 1885, for example, a rank-and-file worker in Manchester wrote to the national secretary of the Socialist League in London to complain about widespread working-class hostility to socialist ideas as workers understood them. In reporting on working-class opposition to social reform and socialism, Fred Pickles, the secretary of the Bradford branch of the Socialist League, said: 'It is very uphill work, however, and the sneering incredulousness, apathy and lack of enthusiasm we meet with is worse than the downright opposition, of which also we get plenty.'[7] Despite the very real growth of socialist sympathies in many working-class communities such as those depicted in E.P. Thompson's seminal article 'Homage to Tom Maguire', English working-class opposition to social reform and socialism remained formidable before the Liberals began to impose legislative reforms in 1906. In a vivid description of workers' attitudes in Salford, Robert Roberts wrote: 'Before 1914 the great majority in the lower working class were ignorant of socialist doctrine in any form, whether Christian or Marxist. Generally, those who did come into contact with such ideas showed either indifference or, more often, hostility.'[8]

In the major English cities the unorganised workers and their families were always at odds with the police. In rural as well as in urban communities the police were hated by many working people, and in Oxfordshire in the 1890s, 'the village constable was still regarded by many as a potential enemy, sent to spy on them by the authorities'. The police did indeed spy on trade unionists and socialists; but the police throughout England antagonised the unorganised workers for other reasons. As Joseph Toole, who was brought up in Salford, explained:

> If we played games, we played them in the streets, or on a 'croft', always in danger of the police, who seemed to have little else to do but chase poor lads playing innocent games, summon them to attend the local police-court, and get their already too poor parents fined two shillings and sixpence.[9]

By then 'the growth of conscious class hatred' was generally recognised by the English ruling classes. As the social causes of poverty, prostitution and 'overlaying' (the suffocation of babies and infants) were increasingly pinpointed, a section of the middle class began to agitate for social reform. In 1885 the socialists' argument that prostitution was a direct result of poverty was innovatory; but by 1890 even the leader of the Salvation Army admitted that prostitution was rooted in social conditions, and he linked the prostitution of ex-servant girls to 'quarrels with their mistresses and their sudden discharge'.[10]

As a small army of social investigators 'rediscovered' the poverty of the English working class, Charles Booth and

General Booth championed the cause of state intervention and 'state socialism'. Yet the socialists own increasing emphasis on the need for state intervention to cope with working-class social problems actually widened the existing gulf between many unorganised working-class men and women and the SDF and the Independent Labour Party (ILP).[11]

Throughout the years between 1883 and 1914 the 'dialectical' struggle between the socialists' socialism, ruling-class interference in workers' social lives and the values and attitudes of the unorganised workers raged with varying degrees of intensity. With the upsurge of the strikes of the unskilled workers in the 1880s and early 1890s, militant democratic socialism dominated English working-class politics. As J.M. Budish and George Soule noted: 'The "new unions" were characterised by the absence of benefit funds or any of the vested interests which tend to make labour conservative. They were not exclusive, and were thought of chiefly as instruments of economic warfare. At the same time they welcomed state interference in the form of laws regulating everything except the hours of labour.' In depicting the 'new unions' before the First World War, Louis Cazamian said: 'Instinct with the feeling of class hostility, the younger unions turned to socialism; they accepted its doctrines in a large measure or entirely.'[12]

Furthermore, workers' hostility to socialism was sometimes rooted in older working-class traditions, and the socialists' agitation for state interference in the sphere of education often sharpened the existing antagonisms of the unorganised workers. When strikes of the unskilled workers failed, the size of the socialists' constituency was narrowed and scaled down. Some London dockers were, for example, 'the descendants of scuffle-hunters, whose traditions still survive [in 1896], perhaps in an unconquerable hatred of government.' Furthermore, there was still widespread working-class hostility to state education; J.R. Clynes described the attitudes of the spinners in the North of England: 'In advocating wider universal education, too, I received much bitter opposition. Elderly spinners claimed bitterly that "learning only made the youngsters discontented, and taught them to cry for the moon".'[13]

Socialists and trade union leaders often regarded workers' opposition to the compulsory education of their children in state schools as evidence of their lack of sympathy with socialist ideas. In practice such opposition was usually a negative rejection of middle-class authority and social values. But although the reasons for working people's opposition to compulsory education was motivated by many factors, an undoubtedly strong motive was the importance of children's earnings.[14]

The educational system was the focal-point of the cultural class struggle between 'them' and 'us' in the late Victorian period. In Elsing, Norfolk, workers' hostility to education resulted in their children's infrequent attendance at school, and in Airedale, Yorkshire, an Inspector of Education attributed the poor attendance at the state schools to a long tradition of hostility to 'authority'. In the poorer districts of London there were 'hundreds of children running about the schools all day long', and a distinct dimension of workers' opposition to state education was 'the antagonism between the schools and working-class homes'.[15]

Furthermore, the state schools were instrumental in taming 'wild young spirits' – Joseph Toole summed up education in the schools in Salford as 'merely instruction classes with a view to one's later removal to a factory'. An important aspect of the cultural class struggle in the state and Church schools was evident in the day-to-day 'lectures' one Oxfordshire headmaster delivered to working-class children:

> The children must not lie or steal or be discontented or envious. God has placed them just where they were in the social order and given them their own especial work to do; to envy others or to try to change their own lot in life was a sin of which he hoped they would never be guilty.[16]

In those communities where socialists displayed sensitivity towards working-class men and women, socialism began to make some progress. But elsewhere there was considerable hostility to socialists and socialist ideas. As Frank Hodges said: 'It [the socialism of the ILP] was not a popular cause in Gloucester at the beginning of the present century.' In the coalfields in the North of England, Jack Lawson observed that: 'Those who talked of Labour representation and socialism were treated with indifference.' In Salford 'all kinds of abusive epithets were hurled at you. You were told you believed in free love and had no belief in the Almighty – that is, if you were not accused outright of being an atheist.'[17]

In a study describing social conditions in Oxford before the spate of Liberal social reforms in 1906, C. Violet Butler explained that working-class culture and social attitudes were a formidable barrier against socialism. As she put it: 'It is probably owing in part to these last two forms [the Post Office Savings Bank and the Co-operative Society] that collectivist ideals have so little hold on the town.' Socialism was also associated with 'compulsion', and working-class opposition to vaccination in the 1880s and 1890s was motivated by a general dislike of compulsion. In discussing this controversy in his autobiography, *About Myself*, Ben Turner wrote: 'All I know is that compulsion is wrong, and that was the chief issue – the liberty of the subject.' In an article in *The Nursing Record*, P.W. Young wrote: 'Others there are who object to vaccination, simply because it is compulsory. An Englishman ought to be a freeman, they will tell you, and treat his own children in any way he pleases.'[18]

II

As the 'explosion' of labour unrest before 1914 was accompanied by a revolt against the Liberal Government's social welfare legislation, it seems strange that some historians should deny the existence of an 'anti-capitalist cultural resilience' in British working-class communities.[19] Far from 'the dominant working-class view of state "welfare"' being one of 'sceptical acceptance', the imposition of social welfare provisions on working people unleashed working-class opposition to middle-class social values and attitudes. In any case the labour unrest at least partly arose, in spite of Henry Pelling's assertion to the contrary, from working people's hostility to state interference in their social life.[20]

Though the social behaviour of the vast majority of British working men and women was known to be influenced by a traditionalism in which inherited superstition played an important role, the representatives of the bourgeois world were often so ignorant of the overall pattern of working-class life that they were initially taken aback by the fierceness and the aggression articulated in the mass, spontaneous strikes between 1910 and 1914. The resistance to the imposition of social welfare legislation on working-class communities from 1906 onwards ought to have prepared official society for the subsequent insurgency of British labour in 1910–14, for there was a growing recognition of the workers' resentment over the dictation and 'benevolent effort working from above' and of the double-standards in moral judgement. In 1906, for example, one prominent trade unionist observed that working men and women were responding to the representatives of the middle-class social world by saying 'mend in yourself what you see wrong in me' and 'who made you a judge?'.[21]

Far from playing a disruptive, divisive class-struggle role before 1910 when there was a vast elemental upsurge of working-class militancy, trade unions actually assisted official society in imposing middle-class social values on their members. Alfred Marshall, the English economist, praised the artisans' trade unions for exercising 'an elevating influence by punishing any member who conduct[ed] himself badly, or who [was] frequently out of employment from excessive drinking'; and Richard Bell, a leader of the railway workers, sought to justify trade unionism by emphasising its importance in restraining 'immediate impulses for the sake of [an] eventual advantage'. Indeed, the leaders of the agricultural workers also attempted to assist the upholders of the status quo by imposing the middle-class social values of temperance, thrift and self-help; and, though they also perpetuated a double-standard, the artisans' trade unions repeatedly imposed fines on members who used bad language. But if the main impetus for social change often came from the 'new unions', it would be inaccurate to suggest that there was a clear-cut ideological difference between the 'new' and the 'old' trade unions.[22]

Trade unions as a whole played a dual, contradictory role in the day-to-day affairs of working men and women; for while they transmitted middle-class social values and attitudes from above, they also articulated the socialist aspirations of the minority of persistent militants in working-class communities. As the 'new unions' of the unskilled and the semi-skilled workers projected a strong socialist dimension from the 1880s onwards by rejecting what they characterised as 'the glorified goose and coffin club' conception of trade unionism, they unwittingly provoked an overall social and political response from the bourgeoisie which led the Liberals to seek state control over the whole spectrum of working-class life.[23] Furthermore, the social welfare legislation which was used to impose middle-class social values on working men and women unleashed an upsurge of spontaneous, elemental protest from a large number of unorganised workers who no longer just resented but were now prepared to struggle against ever-increasing state control of their lives. The unprecedented wave of mass strikes which erupted between 1910 and 1914 cannot be understood unless the workers' earlier opposition to the Liberals' social welfare provisions is kept in mind.

In 1912 Charles Watney and James A. Little attributed the 'industrial warfare' they saw raging around them to the fact that only one per cent of the British working classes seemed to 'understand the values of capitalism'; and the labour unrest contributed to a new recognition of the vastness of 'the gulf between "them" and "us"'. This unrest certainly led an increasing number of middle-class social investigators to engage in the sociological investigation of working-class life and the *class* attitudes behind the unsurgency of striking workers; but even before then workers were always suspicious of the representatives of the middle-class world whether they were policemen, factory inspectors, doctors, nurses, health visitors or temperance missionaries. The exclusiveness of 'working-class society' and the respectability which inhibited many workers from joining trade unions, 'going on the parish' or ignoring the ritual of wearing black clothes at funerals were a fundamental part of the workers' culture which had evolved from mid-Victorian times in response to the harsh, impersonal world of *laissez-faire* industrial capitalism.[24] Those contemporary observers, including most socialists, who ignored this workers' culture were unable to explain the well-springs of the labour unrest.

For Harry Quelch, a leading theorist in the SDF, the

'direct, immediate cause' of the labour unrest was 'a simple economic one' of wages lagging behind the increased cost of living. A trade union leader, who was also a member of the SDF, saw the labour unrest as a spontaneous 'upsurge of elemental forces' in which 'the dispossessed and disinherited class in various parts of the country were all simultaneously moved to assert their claims upon society'. But though economic factors unquestionably played an important role in the labour unrest before the break of the First World War, the upsurge of elemental forces was unleashed and sustained by what John Carstairs Matheson of the Socialist Labour Party depicted as 'the untutored discontent' of working men and women who were really unfamiliar with socialist ideas. As this untutored discontent was explicitly acknowledged, but not so frequently analysed, by a host of contemporary investigators and observers, it is somewhat surprising that most historians should insist on treating workers' attitudes to state intervention and the labour unrest as divisible strands in a phenomena of working-class protest.[25]

As the vast majority of unorganised men and women already articulated their opposition to compulsory school attendance in a situation where child earnings were often important for family survival, it was clear that they would not welcome the additional social reforms of the New Liberalism. Compulsory education was resented by a large section of working-class parents; many mothers complained that 'they could not make both ends meet' when they were forced to send their children to school; and since working-class children were not disciplined in 'the pastor and master sense of the word', the intervention of the school attendance officer was usually seen as 'harsh and inconsiderate'. But the fundamental hostility to compulsory attendance was as much cultural as economic in motivation as state education resulted in class judgements by the other class.

Just as working men and women resented and resisted the 'compulsory' state education that was often imposed on them by the members of 'another class', so did working people resent and oppose the temperance propaganda of the middle classes. Temperance was ridiculed in many working-class communities; and agricultural workers refused to go to their village reading-rooms where the squire and parson 'talk[ed] their temperance stuff'. Even in the strictly managed factories the teetotallers, whether men or women, were often compelled to 'face unlimited ridicule'; and the worker who refused to conform to 'the drinking usages' of his shop was soon 'made to feel in innumerable ways that his presence [was] not wanted'.[26] Yet if working-class England was no longer altogether an unknown country to middle-class social investigators, the endemic and unrelenting conflict between working-class and bourgeois social values was clearly evident before the spate of social welfare legislation in 1906–14.

This conflict was exemplified by traditional working-class attitudes towards the police, though hostility to the bourgeois state *per se* was not personalised until the crystallisation of new workers' attitudes after 1906. In 1911, for example, Stephen Reynolds and Bob and Tom Woolley captured this new mood of workers' hostility towards the state when they wrote:

> The laws they passes for the poor up to Parliament only chucks 'ee into the hands of policemen, an 'spectors, an' lawyers, and' such-like - out o' the frying-pan into the fire – an' they rises the taxes on the little you have got for to thic lot going. Us don't want their kindness of that sort. Us'd rather muddle on our own old way.

But just as social investigators discovered that most factory girls 'looked upon the [Factory] Inspectors as personal enemies', so were the police universally suspected and hated by the working classes.[27]

In a book entitled *The Hunger Line* dealing with the protest movements of the unemployed, Bart Kennedy argued that the police played a directly political role in reinforcing the status quo. Policemen 'disguised' in the crowd were, in his personal experience, always 'ready' to 'act as agents of provocation if those that governed thought it would be a good thing to provoke disorder, so that they might crush it horribly and provoke fear'. Thus he did not hesitate to sum up the consequences of covert police behaviour in a country which claimed to be 'the land of the free' when he asserted:

And there was crystallised into words a Satanic paradox which ran thus. *Free speech and free movement is used in England for the enslaving of* the people. All things in England were used against the people. And so in the end this hunger-line had come slowly forth from the holes and dens of London to show itself. This line that was the sign of the coming doom of this world-town of wealth incalculable.

The police were just as much disliked in the countryside as in the towns and cities. Agricultural workers observed that 'middle-class boys' did 'not get into trouble with the law', and in the consequent conflict between the contending classes there was 'probably no lonelier man in the [country] parish than the constable'.

The most intense antagonism towards the police sprang from their role in enforcing the laws against working men who swam naked in canals and rivers, and who gambled. As the police were seen as the servants of one class in attempting to 'impose a certain social discipline on another', they were feared and hated for the reasons that W.J. Brown explained in his autobiography:

Poor folk instinctively distrust and dislike policemen. They did so even more in those days even than now. To the poor, the policeman is not a kindly fellow who holds up the traffic so that children may cross in safety. He is the instrument which, in the experience of the common people, never operates equally as between rich and poor. The advent of the policeman to a home in a poor street foretells misfortune. In may be distraint for non-payment of rent, may be news that a woman's husband has been found drunk and disorderly and locked up; it may be that 'one of the boys' has got himself into hot water.

But if this constant working-class antagonism towards the police arose from state interference in workers' social life, it could quickly flare up into violence in strikes and labour disputes.[28]

In the countryside the state was regarded as 'an instrument' of 'benevolent tyranny'; in the towns and cities even 'the most superior' of working people displayed a 'great horror' of inspectors, foremen and officials; and most working men and women found it difficult to hide their 'quite insurmountable aversion towards embarking upon anything' which involved their coming into 'contact with officials or filling up forms'.

A great deal of this antagonism towards the state *per se* arose from traditionalism and their experience which the representatives of middle-class charity organisations in the mid and late Victorian period; yet the new factor in their more intense hostility to state interference was a heightened awareness of the nature of the status quo and growing 'totalitarian' controls. This was alluded to by Stephen Reynolds and Tom and Bob Woolley when they tried to explain the causes of the labour unrest:

> Labour unrest, the spontaneity of some recent strikes, are not the only signs that the economic questions of capital and labour and wages are becoming matters of feeling, and, therefore, sooner or later, of action. Trade unions are supposed to represent the most advanced working men; but while the trade unions have been spending their energies in political action, working people generally have advanced a step further. Silently, so far as the reading public is concerned, they have been learning to question the whole of the present system of wages and earnings and social position. They do question it now, with a growing resentment.[29]

III

Yet much of the new intensity of workers' hostility to the growing state interference in their social life sprang from their traditional attitudes and suspicion of the representatives of the alien social world of the middle classes. Most trade union officials and rank-and-file activists were usually much closer to the middle than the working classes, at least in some of their social attitudes; and the opposition of the majority of unorganised working people towards, for example, trade union agitation for pit-head baths cannot be understood in isolation from inherited superstitions and workers' traditionalism. There was still widespread distrust of doctors and hospitals. Trade unions had trouble persuading miners and other workers to go to hospitals for treatment; general medical practitioners were accused of 'running after the rich and cutting about the poor'; and miners often refused to wash certain parts of their bodies because of an age-old belief that 'washing weaken[ed] the muscles'. It was this traditionalism that made it difficult for trade union officials to persuade miners to pay fees to the colliery doctors; and the various attempts to spread medical enlightment were not helped by *Lancet*'s discovery that public baths were contributing to the problems of lice infestation.[30]

Workers' traditionalism was just as important as the active propaganda of the capitalist political parties – the Liberals and the Tories – in making it very difficult for socialist ideas to penetrate the social consciousness of working men and women. All observers and participators in the English social scene, irrespective of their political bias, were at one in their *shared* perception of widespread working-class opposition to the agitations for socialism or even social reform. Socialism was not 'a popular cause' in the English and Welsh (as distinct from Scottish) mining communities; in the English and Scottish towns and cities socialism was identified with 'free love' and a rejection of 'belief in the Almighty'; and socialist doctrine was treated with hostility.[31]

In fact traditionalism and workers' beliefs in the need for independence from middle-class institutions and charity were the major motives in their hostility to social reform and socialism. In a world where working people clung to 'their hereditary' beliefs in the efficacy of a bottle of medicine and where working-class mothers usually paid more attention to one another than to doctors, the representatives of Edwardian Liberalism were not exactly unfamiliar with workers' suspicions of the middle classes. But though workers' opposition to state interference in their lives really began to crystallise in the mid-Victorian years, it was only intensified and prodded into widespread active militancy by the new social welfare provisions.

When this new welfare legislation culminated in the Children's Act, the compulsory medical inspection of school-children, and national insurance, it was inevitable that class antagonisms would be sharpened. Just as Stephen Reynolds recognised the intensity of working-class opposition to further social welfare legislation, so did R.H. Tawney assert that working people were clearly opposed to 'an increase in state intervention in the form of inspectors whose sole purpose seemed to be to interfere in other people's lives'. Yet some Liberals were fully aware of the class antagonisms that they were sharpening by imposing the social reforms of the 'New Liberalism'. This was summed up by J.M. Kennedy:

> Even when a careful social reformer goes among the working classes and endeavours to ascertain their views he will not find his task an easy one. The suspicion, natural enough, with which the workman has come to regard all attempts to pry into his economic and domestic affairs, his dislike of the methods of the school inspector, his more recently developed contempt for the Insurance Act officials, and the 'proper pride' of his wife . . . lead inevitably to different attitudes for different circumstances.[32]

As the Edwardian Liberals were therefore aware of the antagonisms that their social welfare provisions would create between the working classes and the state, it is important to examine some of the real (as distinct from the articulated) reasons for the controversial departure from their traditional *laissez-faire* outlook. While exponents of the new policy tried to justify it by arguing that the compulsory medical inspection of schoolchildren was dictated by the 'ignorance' of working-class parents, the real reasons were not always so humanitarian. Certainly, the problem of what the Victorians had called 'physical deterioration' was a constant element in the inspiration behind the new social welfare legislation; but, when the Boer War forced Parliament to face the reality of thousands of army recruits being rejected every year because of 'defective teeth alone', the Liberals were soon galvanised into action. The very abruptness with which the New Liberals imposed a whole spate of legislation led many working men and women to see the state and 'the compulsory military service movement' as 'a huge plot'.[33]

While many working people now openly articulated a suspicion of the motives of the New Liberals in imposing compulsory medical inspection on their children, traditionalism was often the dominant motive in working-class opposition to 'strangers examining their children'. For just as suspicion of nurses, health visitors and district visitors and a general working-class stigma against asking for free medical treatment were manifestations of traditional attitudes, so the workers' resistance continued to express itself obliquely when children were 'kept off school during the visit of the school nurse'. The practice of cutting away parts of the children's hair which were infested with lice meant that the poverty and distinctiveness of working-class children could no longer be so easily hidden; and many working people thought the real purpose of medical inspection was simply to 'experiment upon' their children.[34]

As British workers' culture was at least partly developed to achieve some sort of 'equality' of appearance with the middle class, it is not too difficult to understand what motivated the widespread riots against the compulsory medical inspection of working-class children. When working-class children could be identified by the coloured chemicals that were painted on the infected parts of their head, the equilibrium of class relationships was upset. Resentment was therefore so great that 'riots and assaults were fairly frequent'. One such riot in a mining community was reported in the journal, *Lancet*.

At the St. Helens police court a woman named Maria Johnson was recently fined 10s. and costs for assaulting Agnes Jolliffe, a nurse employed by the school authorities, who had been charged with the duty of removing the child of the defendant for the purpose of having her cleansed from vermin. Notice of the child's condition had been duly served upon the parents, but nothing had been done by them. When the nurse appeared at the school to remove the child she was surrounded by a crowd of between two hundred and three hundred colliers' wives, who rescued the child, and the nurse was stated to have been struck on the forehead by the mother.

In fact working people who were taken to court in various parts of the country for resisting the medical inspection of their children were prepared to defend themselves in the courts by arguing that Britain was 'supposed to be a free country'.[35]

Similarly, though the Children's Act 1911 was motivated by a desire to improve health and control working-class social life, it also aimed at the laudatory objectives of keeping children out of public houses and eradicating the serious social problem of 'overlaying' (or the suffocation of children in their parents' beds). As very young children had long been the victims of drunken parents and were sometimes thought to have been 'murdered' for the insurance money, the Children's Act made it illegal to take children into public houses and enabled magistrates to impose stiffer penalties on parents who were found guilty of overlaying when under the influence of drink. Working people resented the indiscriminate range of this Act and the class assumptions behind it, but even more importantly they resented this new interference in their lives. Some of the working women's objections were explained by Anna Martin: 'The Bill will put a stop to our chief bit of pleasure. Our husbands often take us out on the trams or out into the country in the summer evenings, and we go and sit with them in a respectable public-house for half an hour . . . but it will be different if the men have to go in by themselves and we have to stand outside with the children.' Stephen Reynolds and Bob and Tom Woolley reported working-class responses to the 'overlaying' section of the Children's Act: '"They'll hae some difficulty to prove thic", said Mrs. Perring. "And when a baby's overlaid by accident they'll be sure to try and bring it in drunkenness, an' wi' liars enough they'll prove it, whether or no".' Consequently more and more working people agreed with writers like C.H. Norman and Hilaire Belloc who characterised the legislation as evidence of the advent of 'the Servile State'.[36]

This quite sudden and dramatic imposition of social welfare legislation on working people had two important results. In the first place, it created a new atmosphere in which working men and women were less reluctant to articulate their views; and secondly, it intensified existing suspicions of and opposition to middle-class interference in their day-to-day lives. For if opposition to compulsory national insurance was motivated by a variety of factors, including a traditional repugnance to compulsion, the poverty of farm labourers who grudged the compulsory contribution of 4d a week and a deep suspicion of the motives of the New Liberalism, a common response was reported by Christopher Holdenby: 'I say it be more plague nor profit, and them as invented it be no friend o' the workin' man.'[37]

But though traditionalism was probably the dominant factor behind the widespread working-class opposition to state interference, it also influenced the 'explosion' of workers' aggression which found another outlet in the labour unrest. This was summed up by one contemporary observer when he wrote, 'Change prepares itself for birth in the *Vie Intime* of people, not politics. I doubt if the governing classes and those who talk are in any degree aware of the ferments now at work among the governed, who at present have only the illusion of governing themselves.' Yet the new articulation of the traditional 'mentalities' behind the labour unrest was intertwined with the social tensions created by greater urbanisation and the growth of an anti-capitalist (though not distinctly socialist) consciousness.[38]

Moreover, this new anti-capitalist consciousness was fed by such diverse streams of thought and 'primitive' stirrings as 'millenarianism', populism, cultural revolt, social banditry, cinematography and, though much less frequently, utopian socialist aspirations. Millenarianism was a particularly powerful factor in the spontaneous strikes of the women workers. Mary Hamilton described the millenial hopes of the 15,000 women workers who struck work spontaneously in London during the national transport strike in 1911. And, during the years between 1910 and 1914, when labour unrest was articulated in strikes, riots and demonstrations, cinematography was regarded as one of 'the most remarkable phenomena of modern times'. Though it was considered to be 'the simplest of all forms of expression – pictures which tell a story', the possessing classes were inclined to attribute the strike wave to the advent of the silent cinema. Besides, it was not only blamed for undermining 'habits of industry and thrift', but it was also seen as one of the major reasons for the labour unrest. As Charles Watney and James A. Little put it:

> They read of costly menus, and they know their own outlay on bread and dripping – if that – for their children. They see the pictures in the papers, which love, both from interest and inclination, to chronicle the doings of the famous. They even witness it all in the cinematography shows which are springing up – in legions. People do not always rightly appreciate the influence of these two factors in moulding popular thought.[39]

Certainly the decade before the outbreak of the First World War was characterised by the acceleration of intense class antagonism. As the social and political authority of the possessing classes was being increasingly challenged, it was clear that 'social pride' was no longer preventing so many working men and women from joining trade unions. For if the 'lower middle class' were now becoming involved in the labour unrest, the most establishment-minded bourgeois elements were determined that 'the few' would continue to 'command' while the majority obeyed. Clearly, this demise of widespread 'social pride' and 'respectability' which had hitherto kept working men and women out of the trade unions played an important role in class conflict; and the workers' opposition to the new social welfare provisions loosened many of the social and cultural restraints which had just previously led Karl Kautsky to depict the English working class as 'dumb' and 'docile'.[40]

In a harsh, poverty-stricken world, docility was enforced by the tyrannical behaviour of a host of employers. Certainly the poverty was real and tangible enough. In one city in Yorkshire over 3000 children were undernourished; and 'deaths from starvation [were] only too common amongst dock workers'. Moreover, potential working-class individuality was crushed by primitive means of discipline such as those described by Robert Roberts: 'On some building sites a foreman might find fifty labourers pleading for a mere half-dozen jobs. It was not unknown for him to place six spades against a wall at one hundred yards' distance. A wild, humiliating race followed; work went to those who succeeded in grabbing a spade.' And in countless communities a small minority of trade unionists were often victimised and blacklisted by employers who nevertheless appreciated the role of trade union leaders in disciplining the 'explosions' of the untutored discontent of working men and women.[41]

As trade union officials were now seen as 'third parties intervening between employers and employed' or as the chief agency for creating the 'disciplined masses', rank-and-file workers frequently concentrated their hostility on trade union leaders as well as employers and the police. For if every trade union agent in the mining communities was a Czar, and if the agents had to 'take part in leading the local strikes' they disapproved of, there was nevertheless a new awareness of the dual, contradictory role played by trade unions in the functioning of British society. Thus in their book *The Road to Freedom*, Josiah and Ethel Wedgwood offered a vivid description of how some contemporaries saw the role of trade unions in containing the militancy and insurgency of working people:

> In fact, the trade unions are now generally recognised as most valuable bodies and a credit to the working man of the country, not because they voice grievances and keep up wages, but because they make it possible to handle large bodies of men securely, without calling in the military or even the police. In reality, they act as breakers-in for the Lib-Con-Lib governments. And if their power is menaced (as the 1911 Insurance Act, which turns them into Government agents), it is only to transfer the workmen into still stronger keeping – that of the state – which, by feeding, lodging, nursing, doctoring, educating and drilling them, soul and body, from the cradle to the grave.[42]

IV

The greater role of the trade unions in disciplining the labour force was simultaneously accompanied by an unprecedented wave of strikes in which class antagonisms were sharpened. As Stephen Reynolds put it: 'Class antagonism is a very powerful force, growing rather than diminishing, acting in all sorts of unsuspecting ways, and in a moment it flashes out: "Ignorant fellow! – Bloody gen'leman!"' Moreover, if widespread socialist sentiments were not evident in the labour unrest, negative anti-capitalist sentiments were. For though economic factors were present in the struggle for higher wages, the dominant *motif* of the labour unrest was *the* expression of a fundamental challenge to the hegemony of the possessing classes.[43]

However, the evident participation of left-wing organisations in the labour unrest led the authorities to overestimate the influence of socialist and anarchist elements. Thus Basil Thomson, the head of the Special Branch, subsequently wrote:

> We date most of our social troubles from August 1914, as if politically England was a Utopia before the War, I was reminded by a friend the other day that during the summer of 1913, in a conversation about labour unrest, I had said that unless there was a European war to divert the current, we were heading for something like revolution. That was before

the railway strike of 1913. I suppose that the dock strike, the growth of bodies like the anarchists and the Industrial Workers of the World, and the unrest that had upset even disciplined bodies like the police and prison warders in all civilised countries, had induced this unwanted pessimism.

But though these organisations were not without some transitory ideological influence during actual strikes, the workers' challenge to authority was essentially spontaneous and untutored.[44]

The spontaneity and the untutored nature of this mass discontent made it very difficult for even the most perceptive socialist to discern 'any definite objective' in the labour unrest other than a protest against 'the general condition in which working men have to live'. But far from the labour unrest simply expressing discontent with low wages, poverty and long hours of labour, it also coalesced with workers' resentment over state interference in their social lives. With the unleashing of these 'long pent-up forces of discontent', some observers argued that 'the influence of economic causes was a comparatively restricted one'. The intensity with which workers now conducted strikes was seen during the transport strike in 1911 when over 100,000 men paraded through the streets of London with banners indicating their alienation from capitalist society.[45]

In the labour unrest of 1910–14 working men and women restricted themselves to expressing a basic discontent with the authoritarian conditions in which they lived. As this vague and sometimes even unspecified discontent was transcended, there was clear evidence of a transformation of the consciousness of an increasing number of working men and women. One index to the new challenge to the authority and control of the employers was summarised by Henry Clay in a two-part table showing the number and duration of strikes between the beginning of the twentieth century and the eve of the First World War. But if a number of complex factors, including the fact that many Labour Members of Parliament had lost touch with the rank-and-file of their own unions, contributed to the increasing incidence of strikes in the years before 1914, the trade union leaders acted as bulwarks of the established social order.[46]

Average Annual Number of Stoppages		Annual Duration in million days
1902–1909	465	3.6
1910–1913	947	18.0

The contemporary role of the trade union leaders in the labour unrest was seen in their response to the mass, elemental upsurge of disaffected working men and women. As they increasingly lost control of their own rank-and-file members, they expressed their fears and anxieties over the spontaneous revolt of the unorganised and the organised workers alike. As one trade union leader put it: 'The present situation has its dangers, as there is a growing feeling that all that is necessary is to go on strike and the workers can have anything they care to ask for, and if only the trade union officers would get out of the way the workers would do things.' But the fundamental nature of the strikers' demands pushed some of the moderate trade union leaders into militant postures. This was summed up by Mary Hamilton: 'In this year [1911] feeling was so intense that at the Trades Union Congress a sedate textile leader cried, amid enthusiasm, "Let those strike who have never struck before, and those who have always struck, strike all the more" – a remark received with wild applause.'[47]

But this fierce class-consciousness would not have broken out at the annual conference of the TUC in 1911 if working people had not already mounted an unprecedented challenge to the authority of the possessing classes. Moreover, there was profound, if somewhat reticent, unrest in the fields as well as in the factories; farmers in Essex were astonished when farm workers left their homes rather than give up their trade union. In very difficult circumstances, where farmworkers taught their children to feign inarticulacy before the parsons and the farmers, the agricultural workers' trade unions were sometimes kept in being by railwaymen and other workers acting as their branch secretaries.[48]

As the farmworkers became much more open in their opposition to the parsons and their employers, class tensions were heightened as never before. This new development in the labour unrest in the countryside was described by Ernest Selley: 'Some farmers were obliged to sell their sheep and cows owing to the shortage of labour. It was said that rather than give way, the farmers were prepared to lose the harvest.' A London daily described their attitude in the following lines:

> Be danged to their impudent cheek –
> They want sixteen shillings a week!
> But rather than pay
> I'll waste all my hay
> And thus my revenge on 'em wreak!

As employers organised blacklegs and rival employers' trade unions to curb the revolt of the labouring poor and the artisans, wages, hours of labour and working conditions were no longer the main bone of contention between the contending classes. As Edward Tupper put it: 'I honestly believe that for some of these employers the rate of pay was no longer the real issue; they were smouldering with hate and outraged pride. They simply could not face the recognition of an organisation amongst the serfs they had enslaved under the system for so long.'[49]

Indeed, what made the labour unrest of 1910–14 an unprecedented social and political development was precisely this new working-class assault on 'the system'. For just as working men and women were opposed to the state welfare legislation which interfered with their personal lives, so they now struck against the employers' interference in their social and working lives. In most industries there were certainly strikes for higher wages and shorter hours; but the strikes which challenged the hegemony of the possessing classes were much greater in magnitude and much more far-reaching. There were, as W.W. Craik put it, 'strikes because of the victimisation of one man, strikes because of the intolerable conduct of some petty official, strikes without trade union sanction and strikes in the teeth of the leaders' expressed opposition'.[50] The transport strike of 1911 was fought for the abolition of 'the infamous ticket' of the Shipping Federation which imposed a slave status upon the men in the mercantile marine; and one of the most 'famous of all reinstatement cases was the "Knox strike" of 1911 when six thousand men came out, in the words of the Government report, for the reinstatement of an engine-driver who had been reduced in rank owing to alleged drunkenness off duty for which he had been fined in the Police Court'. As this was only one of several similar successful strikes, it was clear that new relationships were being made by workers who had already opposed state welfare legislation.[51]

Far from 'the revolutionary impact of post-1909' being reduced by the largely apolitical nature of the labour unrest, the far-reaching nature of the demands raised by the unorganised as well as the organised workers gave the Government every reason to be extremely nervous. In one strike 3000 dock workers 'struck for three days demanding the suspension, pending enquiry, of a dock policeman who had arrested a workman on a charge of using obscene language'; in South Wales 'a thousand miners struck work for three days alleging that they had been prevented from attending the funeral of a comrade who had been killed at work'; and a strike of pottery workers secured the 'reinstatement of a manager who, the men said, had been discharged for refusing to bully his workmen'.[52] As working-class opposition to state welfare legislation merged into the labour unrest,[53] the disturbed equilibrium of traditional class relationships imposed new stresses and tensions.[54] By attempting to control what had only been a potentially revolutionary working class before 1906 by means of an encroaching 'Servile State', the New Liberals transformed themselves into their own gravediggers and thus changed the face of British political life.[55]

PART TWO

5

The First World War and the Recasting of Bourgeois England, 1914–1939

> In England at the end of the First World War a section of the working
> class made a great attempt to establish workers' control of production.
> They failed, and the whole thing seems to be buried beneath later events.
>
> C.L.R. James

The question of whether the First World War was an agent
of stabilisation or destabilisation revolves around the assertion
that the English working class 'came out of the whole
experience only to a minute extent infected by socialist ideas'.
In a 'revisionist' interpretation of the impact of the First
World War on working-class men and women, Ross
McKibbin and other historians of the Right and the Left have
sought to play down the significance of wartime opposition to
the state. As McKibbin puts it: 'The industrial disputes of the
war, for example, were no worse than those which occurred
immediately before it, and arose out of traditional
grievances.'[1] By ignoring the wartime context of censorship,
the anti-war repression imposed by jingoistic mobs, legal
sanctions, social criticism, government propaganda and police
interference and spying in the labour movement, McKibbin
seems to present a convincing account of English working-
class history.

The context was the crucial thing. Alongside state repression and police infiltration in the labour movement, the press
were forbidden from reporting many anti-war activities.
Because of the wartime restrictions on the freedom of the
press, it is particularly important for historians to consult the
autobiographical accounts of anti-war activists. In a vivid and

heartrending account of the war resisters who were, in her phrase, 'on the run' between 1914 and 1918, Sylvia Pankhurst also deals with the less 'political' and sullen resistance of ordinary working people:

> Anti-war feeling was by no means confined to sophisticated intellectuals. One found it perhaps most firmly rooted amongst the simple, unlettered people of rural areas. . . . Yet the talk in the cottages was not of victory, but of grief and bereavement, scarcity and high prices. . . . People said that the farmers dare not sell their wheat and hay except to the War Office, and that bacon seized by the Government was going mouldy in the docks. Those who had relatives in the Channel seaports told heartrending tales of the grievous return of vast numbers of the wounded.[2]

I

At the beginning of the war the national trade union leaders agreed to refrain from strikes. But they did so against a background of intense social tensions and bitter class hatred. Social tensions and class hatred are always a part of the dynamic dialectic of social change within class-divided industrial societies, and bourgeois England was no exception. In his autobiography, *Westering*, Rowland Kenney described the simmering class hatred which still existed on the eve of the First World War:

> In the years immediately preceding the Great War the British industrial world was in chaos. There were endless squabbles and quarrels, often ending in strikes and lock-outs, with black suspicion on the men's side and hatred of the men on the side of the owners.[3]

Far from the 'black suspicion' and class hatred being eradicated by the war, they were deepened by the visible injustices, state repression, brutality and stark inequalities.[4]

Although the First World War evoked initial enthusiasm amongst many working men and women, the first signs of popular disenchantment were seen within less than a year. By 1915 there was, according to William Orton, 'serious trouble among the London dockers, Edinburgh navvies, Dundee jute workers and other trades'. Indeed, 'it marked the end, in fact, of the truce in industry, and started in certain sections of the "popular" press an undiscriminating campaign against Labour'.[5]

There was moreover much more opposition to the war in Scotland and South Wales than in England. Despite the 'revisionism' of such historians as Christopher Harvey and Iain McLean, Scotland and Wales were much further to the Left than England between 1914 and 1921. As Arthur Gleason put it at the time: 'The Clyde area in Scotland and the valleys of South Wales are two regions where the winds of doctrine blow increasingly'.[6] At the same time Whitling Williams, an American sociologist, observed that 'Of this, at least, I am sure – Glasgow is certainly the most revolutionary and also the most rum-ridden and degraded city I ever yet have seen.'[7] In a hard-headed analysis of British history during and after the war, Victor Kiernan has argued: 'Scotland, or at least Clydeside in its great days, stood apart; it was preserved by the Scots intellectual (including theological) tradition, more widely shared than any systematic thinking in England. But the Red Clyde of 1915–21 found itself isolated (the other militant area was South Wales), and thereafter Scottish Labour was to relapse, along with Scottish education, towards the English average.'[8]

While the process of radicalisation and the challenge to the capitalists' cultural 'dominance' went much further in Scotland and South Wales than in England, the growth of the English workers' confidence in their collective ability to restructure society cannot really be ignored. To gain some measure of the transformation of the class-consciousness of English working men and women during the First World War, it is useful to glance back at the state of affairs between 1883 and 1914. In his study of *The White Slaves of England*, R.H. Sherard described how militants were intimidated in the late nineteenth century: '"None of Healey's men need apply" was an edict recently given forth in Widnes and St. Helens. Patrick Healey is the secretary of the Chemical Workers' Union in these two towns, the adherents to which, as stated, were boycotted on this occasion, as on many others.'[9] But if Healey's men and other trade unionists amongst the unskilled and semi-skilled workers were still being victimised up to the outbreak of the war, the most 'primitive' bullying techniques were reserved for women workers. As Geoffrey Drage put it:

> Two East End firms were mentioned in this connection, in one of which 'the employer told his women distinctly that if they joined the union he would sack every one of them, if he had to shut up his shop'. In the other case a newly-formed union was destroyed by the action of the employer, who 'dismissed forty of his oldest and best hands merely because they belonged to it. The other girls remained in the union till they were watched to the union office and the girls' club by a man employed as a searcher to the factory and also to follow the girls to their club. The girls were at last afraid of being seen, and gradually dropped out of the union.[10]

Although there was much less overt anti-militarism and anti-capitalist sentiments expressed in England than in Scotland between 1914 and 1918, a cumulative process of radicalisation was nevertheless at work in English society. To grasp the scale of the 'explosion' of workers' resentments between 1918 and 1921, a number of new factors – the elements of discontinuity – need to be taken into account. In the first place, workers' confidence grew because labour was quite obviously scarce. Secondly, there was a quite dramatic growth of organised labour. Thirdly, there was a marked improvement in wages and living conditions. Fourthly, there was the growth of militant trade unionism around the shop stewards' movement. Finally, there was the impact of the revolution in Russia in October 1917.

A few years before the 'unloosening of discipline due to war-weariness and demobilisation', unrest and resentment were already accumulating. The First World War was 'followed by one of the greatest social upheavals of modern times'.[11] Keith Hutchison, in a book published in 1925 on *Labour and Politics*, described the links between the silent, sullen resentments of the war period and the post-war 'explosion' of social tensions and class hatreds: 'Their [the unions] funds had accumulated; their membership increased; and they now demanded the better conditions they had been promised. Consequently there was an outbreak of strikes, in which, on the whole, up till the end of 1920, the men obtained the advantage. Labour began to think that the strike weapon might be put to other uses; that it might force urgently needed legislative and administrative changes which the Parliamentary Labour Party was powerless to effect.'[12] Between 1892 and the eve of the First World War trade union membership jumped from 1,500,000 to just over 4,000,000. By 1924 the figure was 5,200,000.[13]

The elements of discontinuity in English labour history were already evident by 1916. As William Orton argued: 'The years 1916–18 were marked by such a series of apparently spontaneous and heterogeneous movements as almost invariably heralds a period of revolutionary change in organised society.'[14] Material developments during the war were certainly relevant to the militancy of English labour after the war. As J.J. Mallon and C.T. Lascelles argued: 'In the classes of unskilled labourers, from which most of those in "primary" poverty have been drawn, the general desire for better things has been stimulated by actual experience during the war. Under war conditions the earnings of labourers' families rose to a level of which they had never dreamed, and many of them learned what life might be with regular earnings and a higher standard of living.'[15] During the war itself one change fed upon another. The disappearance of the employers' 'primitive' techniques of intimidating unskilled and semi-skilled workers gave working men and women a new confidence in themselves. And a new confidence and the new social space in which they strengthened labour organisations broadened their horizons and stimulated their aspirations for a better life.

Throughout their book on *British Labor and the War* published in 1919, Paul Kellogg and Arthur Gleason focused on what they called 'the move to the Left'. Although the roots of this development were planted in the very beginning of the First World War, they did not begin to flower until the strikes of 1916. While the strikes in England during the war were less radical than those in Scotland, they displayed the signs of the pent-up frustrations of countless working men and women. As Kellogg and Gleason sum up: 'The swing towards the Left in British labor, which we have followed in its organised front in foreign and domestic politics, showed itself still earlier in the economic field in the new movements for workers' control.'[16] This comparatively new agitation for workers' control was, of course, accompanied by the growth of the shop stewards' movement and unofficial trade unionism.

In denying that the English working class was radicalised by the experience of the First World War, Ross McKibbin focuses on the elements of continuity in the development of the labour movement. He sums up his argument thus: 'It is difficult to argue that the British economy before 1914 was significantly less suited to working-class politics than after 1918. Those aspects of vocational and cultural consciousness that labour exploited after 1918 pre-dated the war.'[17] Moreover, in *King Labour*, David Kynaston argues that the working class on the eve of the war 'failed in a cultural and ideological as much as in a political sense to move on to the offensive'.[18] Yet despite the no-strike deal made between the national trade union leaders and the Government, the pent-up resentments of working men and women were to 'explode' at the end of the war. The cultural consciousness of the pre-war years was anti-capitalist; and the cumulative grievances of the war years actually resulted in a discontinuity in the development of working-class politics and culture at the end of the war.

Between 1918 and 1921 the evidence of a new working-class aggressiveness was visible everywhere. Contrary to what McKibbin argues, the growth of the organised labour movement was not simply the outcome of a steady and unceasing process of evolution. In one sense David Smith touches on what happened between 1914 and 1918 when he argues that: 'The hope expressed in *The Ragged Trousered Philanthropists* was given some encouragement four years after the book's publication when, in February 1918, the Labour Party, now over three million strong, adopted as part of its new constitution a clause which for the first time explicitly committed the Party to a socialist basis.'[19] A major reason for this move to the Left was the radicalisation of millions of English working men and women. The Labour Party reflected rather than led the new mood of radical disaffection from the capitalist state.

In academics' and activists' accounts of the English working class after the first World War, the titles of their books were eloquent testimony to the elements of discontinuity in working-class politics and culture. The sharp distinction between the English working class and the labour movement which was crystal-clear before the war began to blur after the war. In such books as *What the Workers Want*, *Labour in Transition*, *The New Labour Outlook* and *Fed Up and Full Up*, Arthur Gleason, William Orton, Robert Williams and Whitling Williams reported on the new cultural attitudes of the unorganised working class as well as the new mood of militancy amongst those who belonged to the organised labour movement.

In 1920 Arthur Gleason reported that the elements of discontinuity in English labour history were now obvious to any objective observer. As he put it: 'The social revolution, now under way in Britain, has been hastened by the fact that the capitalists and employers have lost control of Labour.' And added: 'For the first time in history partly conscious of their power, the workers are now determined to create a new social order in which they share the benefits, the responsibility, and the control.'[20] Although he denied that either socialist or Syndicalist ideas had mass influence, C.F.G. Masterman, the Liberal Member of Parliament and writer, acknowledged the workers' opposition to 'the present rulers of Britain'.[21] Though often unsympathetic to socialist aspirations, the witnesses that I have just quoted were in no doubt about the emergence of a new mood of working-class disaffection as a consequence of the changes wrought by the war.

In a scholarly monograph on *The Children of the Unskilled*, E. Llewelyn Lewis observed that the English 'working class now exhibits itself in the movement towards industrial unionism and a demand for a national policy for unemployment'.[22] Unorganised men and women were now just as concerned about the problem of unemployment as the activists in the labour movement. The new mood expressed itself in novel cultural as well as in novel political attitudes and expectations. As early as 1917 Ben Turner, a trade union official, noted that: 'There is not the fear there used to be. There is a sober independence that is better for all concerned.'[23] Although the new mood of militancy in the factories, coal mines, shipyards and workshops was somewhat weakened by the emergence of serious unemployment in 1921, Will Thorne, could still, in 1924, sound an optimistic note based on a lifetime's experience in the labour movement: 'How far that confidence has been justified may be seen in the vast growth of the Labour and trade union movement from a comparatively modest position to its present powerful proportions.'[24] But though the growth of the labour movement was an expression of new working-class hopes and dreams, it did not altogether embrace the much more widespread mood of working-class disaffection from the established social order.

In stressing the elements of discontinuity in English working-class politics and culture between 1914 and 1924, it is important not to lose sight of the basic continuity of the 'labour unrest' from 1883 onwards. Moreover, there was a distinct line of continuity in the fierce class conflict which raged throughout England during the years between 1910 and 1924. At the end of the war F. Dudley Docker, the President of the Federation of British Industries, looked to the future with a sense of foreboding: 'There is no doubt that the outbreak of the present European War occurred at a very critical period in the history of Britain. There was an immediate danger of civil war in Ireland, and throughout England, Scotland and Wales class antagonism had reached an acute stage.'[25] In his pamphlet on *How to Avoid Revolution*, Arnold Freeman wrote: 'Yet the warnings uttered by those prophetically-inclined colliers, railwaymen and engineers ought not to be merely dismissed and forgotten. They voice an immense resentment of the wage-earners against the governing classes and against things in general which has shown itself too palpably in various directions (e.g. in the police strike of 1918 and the strikes of 1919) for its existence to be in question.'[26] Although he acknowledges 'the potential fraying' of 'the liberal institutional framework' of 'a self-confident Establishment' in staving off the challenge from the Left, Charles Maier focuses on what he depicts as 'the silent revolution' in England during and after the war.

Though the real 'explosion' of working-class resentment did not come until towards the end of the war, social tensions between 1914 and 1918 were held in check by the substantial concessions made by the ruling class. As Charles Maier puts it: 'Challenging the upper classes after the war was not only the immediate thrust of the Left, but what they might well have termed the silent revolution, the transformation of economic and social status threatened by the growth of state intervention or inflation. Total war meant social transformation, the centralisation of power, equalisation of income, the concession of new rights to the working classes.'[27] Even so, soldiers who had been recruited from the working class in 1914 and 1915 did not behave with exemplary docility throughout the war. Early in 1918 discontent in the army was widespread. As Robert Williams put it: 'Soldiers home on leave had made a violent demonstration at Folkestone, and had refused to return to their units abroad, and if the War Office had not been prompt in granting the men's full request for demobilisation, this would have given rise to the gravest and most far-reaching complications throughout the whole of the Western Front.'[28]

The national conference of the Labour Party in January 1918 met at Nottingham. It was of decisive importance in signalling the 'discontinuity' in the history of the English labour movement. Although the basic emphasis of the left was on exploiting the industrial power of the working class, sections of the Left were willing to see the workers' anger channelled into the liberal institutional framework of Parliamentary democracy. The two inherently warring developments went hand-in-hand without a sufficiently searching debate on the issues involved outside of the small left-wing sects.

The Nottingham conference was important for three reasons. In the first place, it allowed some of the new working-class hopes and sometimes almost messianic dreams engendered by the October Revolution in Russia to find an outlet. Secondly, the pressure exerted by a radicalised rank-and-file forced Labour representatives to leave the Coalition Government and declare war on the unfair policies of the employers. Thirdly, it allowed the labour movement to reaffirm its commitment to internationalist principles. As Paul Kellogg and Arthur Gleason put it: 'In contrast, there was a very evident resurgence of feeling of working-class brotherhood at Nottingham, and the fraternal delegates from Allied countries were made to feel by the applause which followed their speeches that the things in common were bigger than the things in difference.'[29]

By 1918 the evidence of widespread disaffection was everywhere. Disgruntled and embittered soldiers demanded immediate demobilisation; and in London the police came out on strike. In 1919 there was a city-wide strike of policemen in Liverpool. As Herman Mannheim put it: 'A special place amongst post-war strike movements is due to the Liverpool police strike in August 1919.' It was particularly important because it led to considerable looting and culminated in the military and police being brought into Liverpool from other cities and military centres.[30] Although 'labour unrest' was constant from 1910 onwards, the English ruling class unwittingly aggravated the situation during and after the war by contributing to Labour's new sense of importance and self-importance within the nation. As Robert Williams observed: 'In order to allay the unrest and increasing misgivings in the minds of the workers, every Jack-in-office declared that Labour must never be allowed to sink back to the pre-war status.'[31]

In contrast to the period between 1906 and 1914, when mass strikes and Syndicalist sympathies contributed to 'the decline of the Labour Party's prestige', the advent of the First World War compelled the Liberals to develop 'a sustained courtship' which ended in their own ultimate eclipse instead of the marriage they desired.[32] Despite the Labour Party's reorganisation and the new socialist structure and objectives, many working men and women continued to support and express their sympathy for 'direct action' and extra-Parliamentary agitation. In looking at the somewhat different responses of the conferences of the Trades Union Congress and the Labour Party in 1919, Robert Williams concluded: 'There can be no gainsaying the fact that Labour in its industrial sphere is far more ready to take revolutionary action than would appear from the number of votes cast at election times, although it must be stated that increased militancy on the industrial field, by reason of the constant challenging of the status of the employing class, does create a class solidarity which in turn finds expression in the ballot-box.'[33]

II

Although the Labour Party's emergence at the end of the war as a major political force committed to socialist goals was inseparable from the subterranean changes in workers' culture and consciousness, the process of social change was already evident during the years between 1883 and 1914. By insisting that the English working class was radicalised by the process of total war, I do not want to convey the impression that workers' culture – that is, their distinctive way of life and social values – was transformed beyond recognition. Despite the crucially important transformation of *aspects* of their culture without which the process of fundamental radicalisation could not have occurred, some traditional attitudes and social behaviour survived into the 1930s. Before focusing on the important changes in working-class culture during and after the First World War, I shall sketch in those aspects of the traditional attitudes and behaviour which survived the process of radicalisation.

To understand the wartime and post-war radicalisation of the English working class, it is necessary to identify and compare the elements of continuity and discontinuity in the workers' culture and way of life. What emerges from an examination of the major characteristics of workers' culture after 1914 was the survival of some pre-war attitudes and forms of social behaviour. This was more obvious in some occupational groups than others, though the surviving historical evidence does not justify very sharp distinctions in every case. It is also possible that the sociological evidence gathered by middle-class investigators obscured important generational differences. However, it is probably a major paradox that some of the most radicalised occupational groups politically sometimes remained the most conservative socially. The coal miners were an obvious example.

In an account of English working-class life from the inside, Margaret Eyles, a working-class activist, argued that doctors, nurses and welfare workers did not understand working-class life. And, in her Foreward to Eyles' book, Norah March complained that those who engaged in 'promoting social reforms' were unaware of 'the real nature of the problems with which they would deal'.[34] This was a variation on an old theme. When she published a study of working-class life in the North of England in 1911, Lady Bell observed: 'Many among them have a quite insurmountable aversion towards embarking upon anything which would necessitate coming in contact with officials, filling up forms, etc.'[35] Although such attitudes were probably mitigated by the experience of total war, they survived in many communities into the 1930s. As Hubert Smith explained: '"Never sign you name" is a working-class maxim which has grown out of the bitter use of a signature to a paper written in confusing legal language.'[36]

The lay-preachers were critical of the coal miners who played pitch-and-toss on Sundays; and the coal miners continued to resent 'police interference' with their gambling and social life. But although the coal miners were less touched by the experience of the First World War than other occupational groups, workers' hatred of the police was quite general. It was rooted, too, in the same pre-war resentment at police interference with their way of life – that is, those aspects of it which conflicted with bourgeois cultural values. In a careful study of Easingden, a coal-mining community, John Sinclair documented the miners' cultural class struggle with official capitalist society when he reported on the miners' hostility to middle-class outsiders:

> There was so much that required to be done. Not, of course in respect of housing, baths at the pit-head, or to argue the merits of an increase in wages. These were secular questions, outside the province of the onlookers. Your soul and body were not such private concerns. The welfare workers sought to save your soul from hell, and your body from fornication.[37]

The labour process was of fundamental importance in shaping the social outlook, attitudes and social and political values of the men and women in the coal-mining communities. Yet despite their persistent social conservatism, elements of discontinuity in their culture and way of life were obvious after the war. Although socialist ideas sometimes began to impinge on the miners' consciousness to a greater extent than before the war, this was not true everywhere. In a community like Easingden, where there was a fierce and distinctive anti-capitalist consciousness, elitist socialists from the outside made little impact. What John Sinclair said of Easingden was probably true in other coal-mining communities: 'The big words beat the listeners every time; but instinctively they knew that the speakers were as aloof from themselves as the welfare workers, and they sniggered accordingly.'[38] And yet in contrast to other less radical coal-mining communities, the coal miners in Easingden wanted the coalowners to provide baths at the pit-heads.

The elements of continuity in English working-class culture were also seen in the traditional attitudes towards gambling, temperance and the police. Although almost every factory had its own starting price bookmaker before the war, workers' gambling developed and spread still more after the war. Though disapproved of by right-wing and left-wing social reformers, gambling on football, cards and horse-racing grew by leaps-and-bounds. Instead of opting for the self-improvement offered by the Workers' Education Association, many workers, whether men or women, clung to 'an old and stubborn evil' which the law could not 'suppress entirely'.[39]

The mass drunkenness of the pre-war years declined in the years after 1918. Activists in the labour movement including many Marxists maintained an unrealistic hostility towards workers who consumed alcohol; and the gap between the socialists' middle-class values and the workers' behaviour (that is, forms of behaviour often induced by particular labour processes) was only narrowed.[40] Hubert Smith attributed the decline of working-class drinking to 'legislative restriction' rather than the moral persuasion of middle-class reformers. But the 'teetotal working man' was still unable to escape 'a good deal of unpopularity and ridicule among his mates'; and welfare supervisors in factories and works were 'coldly received and harshly criticised by most trade unionists'.[41]

Militant socialists' and anti-militarists' hatred of the police was intensified during the First World War as a result of their experience as victims of state repression.[42] But although workers' dislike of the police declined after the war, it continued to be a marked feature of working-class culture, and was kept alive by persistent police interference in workers' gambling and other social activities. Indeed, in some communities suspicion of the relationship between the police and the courts deepened after the war. As Wyndham Childs put it: 'A popular feeling seems to have grown that if an accused person is acquitted by a magistrate the police evidence must necessarily be perjured.'[43]

While patent medicines of dubious value remained popular, wartime experience of medical examination and state welfare provision lessened many of the pre-war prejudices against GPs a great deal; overall, the war had a beneficial effect on the health of the working-class. Although working-class women's opposition to the compulsory medical inspection of their children decreased, it still existed amongst the 'poorer women' including dockers' wives.[44] On the other hand, *the process* of changing working-class attitudes was already beginning to manifest itself before the war. Despite the 'repugnance for the parish doctor' as inimical to working-class 'respectability', a minority of organised workers in the trade unions were as early as 1905 'availing themselves of the services' of hospitals and infirmaries.[45]

Before the First World War the father in most working-class families did not play 'a very active part in domestic matters'. It was the mother's role to 'interview the teacher, the inspector, or the magistrate'; the father was 'only called in to administer punishment in its more severe forms'.[46] Although some fathers in working-class homes were beginning to take a greater interest in their children by 1919, this was probably not the rule. In many homes the mother did 'all the housework' and brought up the children 'with too little money and no help'.[47] In her autobiography, *Remembering My Good Friends*, Mary Hamilton described what she encountered in Blackburn in 1924 when she stood there as the Labour candidate in the general election:

> 'Lancashire women are beasts of burden' said one of them to me, when I had become an accepted fact, even a citizen. It was quite normal, there, for the wife not to know the amount of her husband's wages, and for any reduction in those wages to affect the sum he handed over to her for housekeeping, not that which he retained for himself.[48]

Old and new working-class attitudes, social values and anti-capitalist sentiments existed side-by-side in the early 1920s. Nevertheless the presence of a discernible counter-ideology amongst the working class could be seen almost everywhere. Alongside the visible subordination of many working men and women, there was a working-class resistance, too. Indeed, at the formal level of workers' consciousness, subordination and resistance sometimes existed in the same heads at the same time. Although bourgeois reformers like H.A. Mess, Arnold Freeman and H.A. Secretan wanted to utilise the state schools, the Workers' Educational Association and the cinema to integrate working people into a humanised social order of liberal capitalism, the war contributed to socialists' increasing awareness of the role of the school within capitalist society as an instrument of subordination.

Indeed, bourgeois reformers, who were often humane men and women themselves, increasingly acknowledged that 'the schools existed to supply employers with competent and willing workers'.[49] Moreover, at the same time as they sought to use right-wing Labour leaders to popularise Liberal-Labour ideas in working-class communities through the medium of the Workers' Educational Association, there was a distinct decline of scholarships to enable working-class children to 'make it' to universities.[50] Also, socialists were much more critical of the bourgeois elite's domination of the educational system. In a much sharper critique of the educational system than socialists articulated before 1914, Margaret Pollock wrote in 1924:

> Many people, whether they admit it or not, dislike an extension of educational opportunities for the following reasons: They are glad of cheap, juvenile labour, because it increases the profits of industry, and, consequently, the interest on their investments; they are glad of social inequality, because it gives them a feeling of superiority which they otherwise find it difficult to merit; they are afraid that the education of the working class will increase their discontent with existing conditions; and they are glad to maintain the professions as a monopoly for their own class instead of opening them to wider competition.[51]

Although such organisations as the Socialist Labour Party had complained as early as 1902 about the 'drill sergeant methods' and the 'repressive and terroristic system of discipline' in state schools, they did not encourage antagonism between school teachers and working-class pupils.[52] In the early 1920s the British Communist Party (CP) attempted to foster antagonisms in the classrooms in the communities where it had some influence through their organisations the Pioneers and the Young Comrades League. Instead of attempting to democratise institutional arrangements within the schools, the Pioneers and the Young Comrades League waged a class war on teachers in state schools who belonged to the Independent Labour Party (ILP).

While the CP took over the traditional left-wing socialist critique of authoritarianism and corporal punishment, the communists were so obsessed with the Leninist commitment to foster the maximum disruption in state schools that they departed from the libertarian education traditions of the indigenous Left. Rather than cooperate with the ILP's attempt to democratise the educational system as a step towards socialism, the CP tried to foster disruption in the classrooms between the unprivileged and the 'privileged'. In appealing to workers' children to inform the Young Comrades League about the 'ill-treatment of children by teachers or instances of favouritism shown to children of parents who are supposed to be "well to do"' the young 'communists' were seeking to create insoluble tensions within the labour movement as well as in the schools.[53]

Nevertheless there was also an unbroken continuity of the indoctrination of working-class children. As Jack Common explained: 'In the council schools you are taught a respect for white collars, punctuality (the best prizes usually go for this), a certain amount of docility, patriotism, religion, and the rest of the half-baked precepts which school teachers are unwittingly pushed into spreading.' Yet despite the indoctrination of working-class children, many of them remained rebellious and intractable. In accounting for the rebelliousness of working-class children in modern industrial societies Stanley Aronowitz focuses on the egalitarian aspects of 'most child's play'. Similarly, Jack Common sought for the explanation of working-class children's immunisation from the infection of bourgeois social values and attitudes taught in the state schools in the reality of the streets. As he summed up: 'It is outside in the street, where there lives a tradition which does not naturally breed the qualities necessary for the factory. . . . A white collar is not only the teachers' insignia, it is the bosses'. And their sons'.'[54]

If the qualities which were necessary for the resistance in the factories and workshops were created in the streets, the oppositional culture of the dockers and the agricultural labourers survived into the post-war world without any evidence of dramatic political radicalisation. While 'deaths from actual hunger' were quite common before 1914, deaths from starvation were most common 'amongst dock labourers'.[55] Despite the marked improvement in the docker's standard of living after the war, they remained a particularly deprived occupational group within the working class. This was summed up by Arthur Creech Jones: 'Docks and poor social conditions seem to go together. Bad housing, indifferent health and poor conditions of life are the rule for the working population in these areas, even after allowing for the advance in recent years in general social amenities.'[56] In a vivid description of the conditions of dock workers in 1924, Margaret Pollock observed that: 'Every day at the Docks the sight may be seen of despairing, disappointed men, who offer themselves again and again, only to be refused. This alone is sufficient answer. "Gaze at the faces of the rejected", said J.J. Mallon, "see them crawl off broken and stricken".'[57] And yet the organised minority of trade unionists amongst them were, as always, on the Left.

Both before and after the First World War the agricultural labourers were difficult to organise into trade unions, though their resentment against the farmers' tyranny and exploitation were frequently articulated through non-institutionalised forms of protest.[58] Just as there was a continuity of agricultural workers' 'respectability' and feigned 'inarticulacy', so the traditional suspicion of working people in the towns survived, too.[59] The feigned 'inarticulacy' of the pre-war years as a very marked feature of the ongoing cultural class struggle was still strong in the 1920s. As W.J. Shingfield reported in Margaret Pollock's collection of essays by working-class activists: 'This has taken such a hold on the farm workers that they have studied a mode of procedure which they still teach their children – such phrases as the following: "Keep a still tongue in a wise head". "If asked any questions about home matters by the farmer, parson, or strangers, always say 'Don't know'".[60] Shingfield argued that this was why workers in the towns and cities applied to 'the farm workers such terms as "John Hodge", "Hayseed" and "Clodhopper"'. In the event 'deference' towards their 'superiors' in the countryside was also feigned.[61] Yet despite the continuity of these aspects of their culture from at least 1883, the agricultural labourers in many communities began to vote for Labour and socialist candidates in Parliamentary elections.

In 1913 Christopher Holdenby reported a farm worker's assessment of the dominant attitudes: 'They talks of their womenfolk just as they would of a glass o' beer, or rather they reckons them a bit lower, for if they had a day off they can't get along without the beer, but they never thinks of taking their wives with 'em.'[62] Patriarchal attitudes survived after the war, though the status of working-class women was raised almost everywhere. While many working-class women began to speak of themselves as 'the likes of us', they were less oppressed than they were before the war. The growth of sport and annual holidays amongst working people in the 1890s and later signalled the advent of new and more progressive attitudes towards women.[63] Although the First World War accelerated the process of social change in working-class communities – a process already underway in the late nineteenth century – the discontinuity in workers' culture was more obvious in some occupational groups than others.

The most radicalised groups were the engineers, the railwaymen and the miners. Yet the miners' social advances were not quite so marked as that of other occupational groups. Although the miners were radicalised and moved to the Left politically, they retained many of the pre-war features of their own distinctive culture and way of life. But in acknowledging the miners' social conservatism, the tendency of some historians to ignore the process of social change in the mining communities before the war should be recognised. Certainly, the elements of continuity and discontinuity in the miners' culture were evident in their attitudes to the agitation for pit-head baths.

In 1911 the Coal Mines Act stipulated that the coalowners would have to provide pit-head baths provided that two-thirds of the miners at a particular pit 'voted in favour of them and if the total cost did not exceed three pence per head'. Most miners before the war were hostile to the socialists' agitation for pit-head baths, because of the survival of an old superstition that washing weakened the back or the muscles in the arms.[64] Although this particular superstition took slightly different forms in different parts of England, it was nevertheless very real.

In post-war Easingden the miners washed 'all except the small of the back', which was 'left untouched, in the traditional belief that water weakened that vital part'.[65] Yet before the war many miners refused to wash themselves 'beyond the hands, forearms, face, and neck' because of the widespread belief among them that 'washing weakens the muscles'.[66] By 1924 there were only a minority of pits where a two-thirds majority had voted for pit-head baths under the 1911 legislation.[67] But although this represented a considerable achievement on the pre-war years, the process of changing social attitudes was visible before 1914. In reporting on these changing attitudes in 1909, H.W. Swanwick captured the new mood amongst the militant minority: 'After the [suffrage] meeting, a group of miners came up to me to ask me, formally, if I would address a meeting of miners on the need for pit-head baths. I laughed and said "Surely you don't want a lady from London to come and tell you what you want". But they declared that the men had been fed with anti-bath propaganda and did not rightly understand the proposals. So I said I would come, on condition that I was allowed to make suffrage propaganda at the same time, and they agreed.'[68] This was an advance on the miners' attitudes in the 1880s and 1890s when they would not tolerate the middle-class women who agitated for the female suffrage.

During the years between 1918 and 1924 a cultural class struggle was waged by the coalowners and the miners around the issue of pit-head baths. In 1919 Joseph Shaw, the chairman of the Powell Duffryn Steam Coal Company, told the Royal Commission on the coal industry that: 'You often find the cocks and hens in the bathroom. We would provide baths tomorrow if the people would use them.' The context in which this ideological struggle took place was one in which an increasing number of working people were agitating for better housing conditions including the provision of baths. While the governing class was prepared to make many concessions to the working class down to 1921, they nevertheless ridiculed the agitation for baths in workers' homes.

Writing in 1919 Lawrence Weaver argued that 'No-one believes that the working classes prefer to keep coal in the bath.'[69] Yet the denigration of the miners' agitation for pit-head baths continued unceasingly throughout the interwar period. In contrast to the pre-war period the labour movement argued the case for pit-head baths and the provision of baths in working-class homes. Middle-class prejudices were no longer allowed to pass unchallenged. In acknowledging the lack of enthusiasm amongst some working people for pit-head baths, Margaret Eyles argued that 'this [was] largely due to the obstacles put in the way of tired people ready to go into bed, dirty or clean'.[70] A major role in the struggle for baths in working-class homes was played by the Women's Labour League.[71] In contrast to the pre-war period general anti-capitalist sentiments merged with a Labourism and socialism which were more sensitive to workers' attitudes and culture than ever before. Without this development, the Labour Party would not have been able to mobilise a mass working-class vote in the general elections after the war.

III

Despite the very tangible features of continuity in English working-class culture during and after the First World War, the aspects of discontinuity were much more important. The discontinuity is the key to understanding the rise of the Labour Party as a major political force within English society. Although the process of social change was evident between 1883 and 1914, and although some decades-old features of working-class culture survived into the early 1920s, the class-consciousness of working men and women underwent an identifiable change during and after the war. In countless

articles and essays in the middle-class quarterly press, the
'labour crisis' and the mass disaffection of working people
were discussed and agonised over. In one such article
published in the *Contemporary Review* in 1922, Theodore C.
Taylor, a large employer, observed that 'In many cases, so far
has the creation of a false class opinion gone, that the
conscientious worker is reckoned a blackleg.'

Moreover, the unorganised as well as the organised workers
were so disaffected from English society that Theodore C.
Taylor was astute enough to realise that the type of repression
used during the war would no longer work. He therefore
suggested that the 'labour crisis' should be met by utilising
new methods. As he put it: 'I am convinced that most
employers of labour have yet to learn the true secret of how
to kill "ca' canny". That way is the way of sacrifice. It is the
will to give and the fact of giving to one's workers more than
one is compelled to give. It is the spirit and the practice of the
principles of profit-sharing and labour co-partnership.'[72] This
was the most crucial development after the war, though the
employers reversed the policy recommended by Taylor after
1921. As Charles Maier put it:

> Given the state of the estimates, it is hard to say which nation's
> bourgeoisie fared most harshly, but a significant change is evident. Great
> Britain experienced the sharpest decline in the share of national income
> earned by capital assets, as a result of the war, but then Britain had
> previously bestowed a far higher proportion of its income on capital
> assets than had been the case elsewhere. Even after a major change in
> the distribution of income, Britain still remained a country of vast
> inequalities.[73]

A redistribution of wealth was, therefore, the fundamental
price paid for recasting the social order in what Charles Maier
depicts as 'bourgeois England'. At the same time as the
established social order was being recast as a result of the new
economic and political demands being presented by a radicalised working class, some Labour politicians were already
complaining in 1922 about the 'drift back to pre-war days' and
'the standards of a generation ago'.[74] In discussing the setback
after 1922, W.T. Cloyer, a Marxist lecturer in the National
Council of Labour Colleges, acknowledged that there had

been 'a temporary change of attitude for the better' after the war. By 1922 bourgeois England was so effectively recast that unemployment was once again blamed on the unemployed themselves.[75]

A major factor in the growing post-war militancy of the English working class was the radicalisation of working-class women. The 'average' factory woman was now 'less helpless'; and as *a class* *factory women* were 'more confident, more independent and more interested in impersonal issues'. What was even more striking than anything else was that *'the class [was] evolving its own leaders'.*[76] Moreover, the oppositional working-class culture – a culture which manifested itself in the revolt against social welfare legislation and in the 'labour unrest' between 1910 and 1914 – was politicised by the experience of four years of total war.

In the first place, the general hostility to socialist ideas declined very markedly from the end of the First World War onwards. Secondly, there was no visible growth of *socialist* sentiments amongst working people during the war. But the wartime resentments against inequality, militarism and injustice 'exploded' into a widespread sympathy for socialist ideas between 1918 and 1924. The old hostility to socialism had gone. In a book published in 1921, G.A. Gardiner observed: 'The ILP is mainly a propagandist organisation and if one is to judge by the great meetings it holds and the measure of support its speakers there obtain, one is bound to accept the conclusion, not only that its influence is out of proportion to the names on its register, but also that after the cloud under which the Party and all its leaders fell during the war, it is surely gaining the ear of the people.'[77] Even if G.A. Gardiner exaggerated the *degree* of general working-class support for socialist goals, the 'primitive' and uninformed hostility to socialist ideas described previously had passed away.

Although only a minority of the English working class embraced socialism after 1918, the new post-war socialism merged with the already existing oppositional working-class culture. As the two came together, the workers' oppositional culture was politicised and raised to a higher level than had existed for decades beforehand. In contrast to the earlier period when a separate but oppositional workers' culture existed more or less independently of the socialist minority's critique of the established order, the conscious socialist critique merged with the widespread 'unconscious socialism' of working men and women.

While G.A. Gardiner's observations of the new and extensive working-class interest in and sympathy for socialist ideas were verified by other witnesses of the English scene, an equally important development was the transcendence of the workers more traditional Labourist philosophy and world outlook. For example, inspectors employed by and sympathetic to the Government reported that 'the stigma which formerly attached to the receipt of poor relief was disappearing, and that there was much less reluctance on the part of working people to accept relief from the Guardians than there had been formerly.' The new evidence of a qualitative change in working-class culture had important political consequences. It certainly reflected itself in the growth of workers' support for the socialists' agitation to squeeze concessions out of the established social order. The new attitudes were also seen in the greater sympathy for the socialists' campaign against unemployment and demands for 'work or full maintenance'.

In *Full Up and Fed Up: The Worker's Mind in Crowded Britain*, Whitling Williams, the American sociologist, cited evidence of a new anti-capitalist consciousness amongst English workers: 'Yes, the worker is much to blame. . . . But with all that, I think we must have a new system of society simply for this one reason: Management and Capital just can't be trusted. With the lure of profits, you understand, it finds it too easy to be dishonest – just personally dishonest and with society in general.'[78] At the end of the war, too, welfare work and welfare supervision in the factories and workshops were 'the subject of severe criticism from the Labour movement and radicals in general'. Just as many working people had always criticised and ostracised temperance advocates in the factories and mines in the pre-war years, so they now intensified such criticisms and identified temperance advocates as propagandists for the established social order. But in contrast to the pre-war period left-wing socialists (with the exception of the communists) were now much more sensitive to the workers' culture and self-activity.

The qualitative change in workers' culture after the war was seen in the way that the workers' 'untutored' hostility towards 'welfare supervision' in the factories and workshops merged with the socialists' critique of English capitalism. Thus Mary Macarthur, the secretary of the National Federation of Women Workers, reported that 'welfare' was 'the most unpopular word in the terminology of the factory worker'.[79] Indeed, as Irene Osgood and Margaret Hobbs reported: 'There are few kind words for "welfare supervision". The ideal of the "welfare supervisor" was docile, obedient and machine-like women workers.' The crucial difference between the pre-war, the wartime and the post-war response of working men and women to exploitation at the point of production was the workers' emergent support for the socialists' plan to substitute 'workshop committees' in place of welfare supervisors.[80] Strengthened and transformed by the growing numerical force of organised labour, this more insistent cultural revolt was reflected in the political radicalisation of working men and women.

Although both the ILP and the Ministry of Health admitted to a common dilemma in offering 'a strict definition' of the term 'the working classes', they defined the working class as 'any persons belonging to the classes who work for their living', or 'who are domestically employed, or are supported by the earnings of wage-earning children'.[81] However, after the war the same traditional lack of mobility prevailed amongst unskilled workers such as the dockers.[82] In some working-class communities social mobility did not exist for the unskilled, though the pattern varied from one part of the country to another.[83] The mobility of capital was the essential factor in opening up some skilled jobs to the children of the unskilled. Even so, it seems that 'influential friends were the chief means whereby sons of labourers were respectively apprenticed as a painter, a signalman, wire-drawer, upholsterer, a clerk or a chemist'.[84]

The traditional social distinctions within the English working class survived after the war. But they were no longer so divisive as they had been formerly. While the pawnshops were still very busy in the early 1920s, the workers' pre-war conceptions of what constituted 'respectability' did not die out altogether. The goose and burial clubs which existed in most communities before the war were still extensive afterwards.[85] While traditional notions of 'respectability' in relation to such things as asking for state assistance during periods of unemployment were seriously weakened by the war, aspects of traditional 'respectability' survived in workers' attitudes towards the pawnshop.[86] Without the continuity of some aspects of working-class culture human survival itself would have been much more difficult than it was; and without the discontinuity the mass strikes, militancy and disaffection would not have 'exploded' in so many communities.

As bourgeois cultural 'dominance' was broken towards the end of the war, the workers' militancy reached new levels. The strike wave reached a peak between 1919 and 1921. The Government responded to the 1919 railway strike with 'all the paraphernalia of press propaganda and military preparations'. Just as the shop stewards' movement rose to prominence and authority amongst rank-and-file workers, so did the trade union leaders at the national level (including many nominal 'Marxists') attempt to impose their authority on a rebellious membership.[87] Although the emergence of the CP as 'the Party of a new type' retarded the development of the indigenous socialist movement, the October Revolution in Russia played an enormous role in radicalising working men and women. By 1921 'bitterness and a widening gap between the classes' led to nine million days being lost in 'industrial warfare'.[88]

The features of workers' social conservatism could be seen everywhere in the early 1920s. But within the context of the history of the English working class between 1883 and 1924, the elements of discontinuity were more prominent than anything else. This was seen, for example, in working men's attitudes to sex. Before the First World War working men would 'not permit any mention of sexual matters in their homes' and allowed their children to 'get their information on the street'.[89] In private letters sent to Margaret Eyles in the early 1920s, some working-class women confessed that they could now 'tackle the problem of telling their children the facts of life'.[90] The discontinuity in workers' culture was that working women were now discussing such questions with

Leonora Margaret Eyles and other women in the Women's Labour League. An important consequence of these discussions was that a growing minority of working women threw off the ignorance and inhibitions of the pre-war years.

Moreover, Leonora Eyles reported that 'There is in the Labour ranks a spirit of "no compromise" fighting the slower war of attrition that many Labour people have been hoping to wage.' At the same time as the Women's Labour League was criticising 'imperialism and jingoism' in the state schools, Eyles and other socialist women were now for the first time urging 'working-class women to get on to the Education Committees as much as possible'.[91] Although C.F.G. Masterman tried to reassure the readers of the *Contemporary Review* that the Labour Party would not introduce socialism if it 'came to power', he was really ignoring a new reality.[92] The Labour Party was, in fact, waging a cultural class struggle against the established social order.

It was a *different* English working class which emerged from the experience of total war in 1918. In accounting for the process of social change within working-class life, it is clear that consciousness was at the centre of the dynamic of history. The process of cultural change was an interaction between past and present, and the cultural sediment of the past was of key significance in shaping the history of the working class in the post-war years. Besides, in the dynamic dialectic of social change, the right-wing middle-class elements often unwittingly raised the political temperature. They did so by protesting in letters to the newspapers that 'the lower classes did not want to work'. By 1921 they were asserting that working people 'would rather "live in luxury" on the dole than take a job'.[93] In doing so, however, they were contributing to the heightening of social tensions and class antagonisms.

The attacks on the unemployed were answered in books and pamphlets produced by the labour movement. In demanding work or full maintenance and carrying banners in the May Day processions encouraging the unemployed not to pay their rents ('unemployed – don't pay your rent'), the labour movement was much more aggressive after the war. On the question of education, for example, Labour men and women, who were not always Marxists, went over to the offensive.

Like Margaret Pollock, Leonora Eyles encouraged working women to educate themselves and their children. As she summed up: 'Many Tories have said to me that higher education is a mistake because it only makes for the discontent of workers' children – which is, of course, what we hope for. *Discontented people are usually dynamic people.* We need more of them.'[94] Because the gap between the labour movement and unorganised men and women was narrowed after the war, it is meaningless to use such analytical categories as 'Labourism' to describe English working-class history between 1883 and 1924.

IV

In defining Labourism before and after the First World War, John Saville argued that it was 'an ideology which looked to Parliamentary methods for the redress of grievances and the long-term solution to working-class problems'. Moreover, Labour's commitment to Parliamentarianism was 'integrally linked' with 'at least part of middle-class thinking on self-help and personal redemption as the basis upon which social advance could be achieved'.[95] Inspired by such Leninist books as Theodore Rothstein's *From Chartism to Labourism*, the communists' concept of 'Labourism' has never been very useful as an analytical category for explaining the history of the English working class. It is even less able to explain developments in the labour movement. Far from the English labour movement capitulating to middle-class thinking on self-help, it developed its own *morality* in the mid-Victorian period. The collective self-help of organised labour was in fundamental conflict with middle-class thinking.

The Lib-Labism which played a crucial role in the formation of the labour movement in the mid-Victorian period was already hostile to middle-class concepts of self-help before the advent of socialism in the 1800s. As Royden Harrison puts it: 'Collective self-help with its virtues of brotherly care for one another, solidarity and discipline, was prior to the individual, self-help morality of Samuel Smiles.'[96] By the 1880s the mid-Victorian 'Labourist' ideology was challenged by the socialist doctrine of the 'new unions'. As the 'new unionism' reappeared within the 'labour unrest' of 1910–14, 'Labourism' was being repeatedly challenged by the counter-ideologies of militant socialism and Syndicalism.

Although Labour leaders always attempted to incorporate the organised workers into a partnership with capital, they did not get their own way. At critical moments before and after the First World War they sometimes lost control over their rank-and-file. In a letter that he sent to all trade union secretaries in 1902, John Hodge wrote on behalf of the Labour Representation Committee as follows: 'If Labour representation was to be a reality they must drop every "ism", except Labourism.'[97] But 'Labourism' before the introduction of individual Party membership in 1918 sometimes meant socialism in at least some working-class communities. From 1918 to 1924 'Labourism' in may working-class communities was a euphemism for the conscious cultural class struggle being waged by rank-and-file as well as intellectual workers whose story has been chronicled in the preceding pages.

The inadequacy of the concept of 'Labourism' to describe the history of the English working class between 1918 and 1924 ought to be illustrated in the growth of the shop stewards' movement and the mass vote for the Labour Party. In the general election of 1918 the Labour vote was 2,245,000. By 1923 it had almost doubled to 4,348,000. With the simultaneous growth of Parliamentary and extra-Parliamentary agitation from 1918 onwards, the conflict between the right-wing and the left-wing elements in the Labour Party were intensified. But as had happened in the past, the Parliamentary representatives of Labour did not reflect the growing working-class radicalisation in the country at large.

In 1917 the news of the Bolshevik Revolution gave 'a fresh impetus to the expanding popular movement'.[98] Yet despite the enormous enthusiasm engendered by the Russian Revolution, English Marxists did not initially associate it with socialism. As the *Socialist*, the organ of the Socialist Labour Party, put it in an editorial entitled 'Hail! Revolutionary, Socialist Russia': 'We do not know how much our Russian comrades can do without a thoroughly organised industrial movement. But if they manage to extricate Russia from this bloody war, much indeed will have been accomplished.'[99] Meanwhile as the Labour Party introduced individual membership in 1918 and attracted more and more working-class support, the Leninist communist groups in England broke completely with the traditions of indigenous socialism.

At the same time as the Leninists played an increasingly divisive role in the English labour movement, the bourgeois elite sharpened its cultural and ideological war against the workers in general and the Labour Party in particular. As it became more obvious that the mass support for the Labour Party would continue to grow, the press and bourgeois politicians began to argue that 'Labour was unfit to govern'. As Mary Hamilton explained in 1924 in a book entitled *Fit to Govern*: 'Less than four years ago, Mr. Winston Churchill asked, in contemptuous tones, "Is Labour fit to govern?" and gave himself the answer, "No". On January 21, 1924, the House of Commons, in its historic division, gave the answer "Yes".'[100] But the discernible counter-ideology of the English working class was not articulated in the House of Commons except through the negative argument that Labour *was fit to govern*.

In 1924 the first *minority* Labour Government behaved like 'nothing more than a moderate working-class wing of British Liberalism'. In this specific sense there was very marked evidence of the continuity of the corporative mentality of the *dominant* political leadership of the English labour movement. Furthermore, the Ramsay MacDonald who had cooperated with the Liberals in 1906 now wanted to prove that Labour could govern Britain without being a divisive political force. Indeed, he declared that even if he were to be the Prime Minister for fifty years, 'the pledge I have given you from my heart would still be unfulfilled . . . not because I fainted or failed, but because the corn was still green'.[101] But in the localities away from the House of Commons socialist men and women were developing and sharpening their own counter-ideology against bourgeois cultural 'dominance' and the 'Labourism' of the Labour leadership in London. However, they were hindered rather than helped by the disruptive, divisive role played by the communists in many working-class communities.

Despite the traditional Labourist philosophy of the leaders of the labour movement in London, mass disaffection existed side-by-side with a qualitatively new sense of solidarity. Denied expression in Parliament between 1918 and 1924, mass working-class discontent finally found an outlet in the general strike of 1926. As Jack Common put it: 'The general strike in this country marked the peak, in this country, of this crude harvesting of an immense solidarity to a petty demand. The general strike failed because it asked for too little.' However, if the general strike asked for too little in 1926, the origin of the failure was located in the socialist' failure in 1924 to articulate socialist demands in Parliament. A major reason for this tragic failure was the denigration of the indigenous socialist tradition by those who had been influenced by Leninist doctrines. As Frank Budgen put it: 'Communist parties sprouting up everywhere. Secret meetings. Do what the Russians tell you. Dictatorship of the proletariat. . . . A couple of thousand armed men grab and hold on to the levers of government and, hey presto! The revolution's there.' The consequence was that De Leonite socialism was rejected in favour of an inappropriate Leninism. As one of De Leon's supporters told Budgen: 'No. That's all old hat. No time to think any more. Action. Direct action.'[102]

One of the most tragic consequences of the advent of Leninism within the English labour movement was the rewriting of working-class history. Between 1883 and 1917 the counter-culture of the workers was, in Richard Price's phrase, 'decidedly un-Leninist'. By rewriting the history of the years before the advent of Leninism in England, the communists assisted the bourgeois elite to mystify the past. This pseudo-Marxist mystification was evident in the use to which the British CP put Robert Tressell's novel, *The Ragged Trousered Philanthropists*. It was also visible in the post-1917 denigration of the whole of the previous English socialist tradition.[103] A source of totalitarian tendencies in the twentieth-century labour movement, it demands analysis and confrontation.

By 1924, when the first 'minority' Labour Government took office, the recasting of bourgeois England was essentially complete. Although there were profound changes in workers' social life and attitudes during the decade between 1914 and 1924, the Labour Party's coming to office did not make any great impact on working-class social life between then and the outbreak of the Second World War in 1939.

Far from threatening the capitalist system, the first 'minority' Labour Government was committed to the status quo before 1924. Although genuine discussions took place during and immediately after the First World War on how socialism could be introduced incrementally within the framework of Parliamentary government, J. Ramsay MacDonald had ceased to be a socialist in any meaningful sense of the word by 1923. In fact, the very last discussions among the leaders of the Parliamentary Labour Party on 'socialism as an alternative to capitalism' had taken place in 1923.[104]

During and immediately after the First World War, the tremendous influx of middle-class recruits into the Labour Party, and the Parliamentary Labour Party, was a guarantee of the future stability of capitalist England. The role of the former middle-class radicals who increasingly entered the Labour Party was of crucial importance in the fashioning of Labour policy for the defence of the British Empire. But what E.D. Morel wrote in a private letter to Count Max Montgelas in 1920 summed up the role of such middle-class figures in the whole process of recasting bourgeois England. As Morel put it: 'The only influence since the war broke out which is "intellectualising" – in the international sense – this vast mass of ignorance [the Labour Party] is the influence wielded by our small group. . . . We are educating it daily and have been.'[105]

Although the Labour leaders' commitment to the status quo was not overt before 1924, it was evident beforehand. As John Scanlon, a Labour MP, who was writing from inside experience, put it: 'They seldom saw workmen, except from platforms. They lived middle-class lives and took their impressions from middle-class people. Even before the fall of 1931, Cabinet Ministers have told me how Mr. MacDonald would return from dinner in Mayfair and sorrowfully tell how some of Labour's actions were not pleasing in the eyes of the best people.' Moreover, during the strike involving 110,000 dock workers in 1924 – a strike against the casualisation of labour – Richard W. Layman reported that 'Arthur Creech-Jones, who was then national secretary of the Transport and General Workers' Union, recalls a letter from Wedgwood to the Transport Workers, warning that the military would be used to keep food supplies moving if the strike continued.' Fortunately for the Labour leaders, the employers capitulated to the transport workers demands after the first 'socialist' Minister of Labour had set up a Court of Inquiry.[106]

Although the leaders of the Parliamentary Labour Party were, in 1928, influenced by the European socialists' emphasis on the need for 'credit control', MacDonald's 'lack of clear ideas about finance' in 1931 was responsible for his ultimate betrayal of the labour movement. But because the ruling class had already moved bourgeois England away from its lurch towards 'collectivism' during the First World War, it had nothing to fear from the first 'minority' Labour government. Indeed, as Richard W. Layman reported in his book, *The First Labour Government*, the Labour leaders lacked confidence in their own ability. On 24 September 1924 Beatrice Webb noted that J. Ramsay MacDonald had told his Cabinet he was 'sick of it' – that is, the socialist dissidence in the labour movement – and had wondered if they were really 'fit to govern'.[107]

The second 'minority' Labour Government took office in 1929. It had even fewer progressive claims to its credit than the first 'minority' Labour Government. It was very orthodox in its approach to financial and Empire problems; and it did not really impinge on English workers' social lives. However, if the first 'minority' Labour Government pushed through John Wheatley's progressive housing legislation, increased the allowances of unemployed men, and reduced the waiting period known as 'the gap', the second 'minority' Labour Government was distinctly hostile to working people.

After J. Ramsay MacDonald's betrayal of the labour movement in 1931 in the face of a world economic collapse and the formation of a National Government, the Labour Party suffered an unprecedented crisis. It eventually recovered and bourgeois England was not yet again recast until the election of the first 'majority' Labour Government in 1945.

As the economic crisis in contemporary England deepens,

the hidden history of the working class will be rediscovered. The rediscovery of the hidden history of the working class and the indigenous socialist tradition will, in turn, impinge on political struggles and the struggle for democratisation. While the outcome cannot be predicted, the interaction of these diverse political and intellectual forces will be of decisive importance. This interaction and the debates it will create about the future shape of English society – that is, the dynamic dialectic created by the working-class presence – will hopefully form a barrier against the threat of totalitarianism in the years ahead.

6

Racism, the Working Class and English Socialism, 1914–39

The amount of cant about Empire history which most of us have absorbed from our orthodox education is pretty considerable. Most of us in our heart of hearts would like to believe that we belong to a master-race; and we are loath to admit that men of our race (even when they were of another class) were ever anything but saints and heroes.

J.F. Horrabin

The outbreak of the First World War was a turning point in the development of English working-class racism. What the war did was to transform the workers' covert racism into an aggressive overt racism. As James Walvin has argued: 'World War I produced an enormous increase in Britain's black population. Workers were in a sellers' market as the armed forces drained industry of its manpower'.[1] The 'exposition' of aggressive and undisguised racism was seen in many English towns and cities during the very serious 'race riots' in 1919. The year 1919 was also marked by the beginning of overt anti-black racism in England as a whole.

I

Although English working-class pacifism was vitiated by the jingoism engendered between 1914 and 1918, it soon revived at the end of the war. Yet the war did not eradicate working-class pacifism; and in the rural areas, according to Sylvia Pankhurst, many working-class women were comparatively untouched by the ruling class's war propaganda.[2] In depicting the complexity of working-class attitudes to the war, Hugh Cunningham has argued that 'In working-class soldiers' letters of the First World War patriotism can be seen to derive from a sense of duty and obligation; it had no adventurous flamboyance about it, more of a feeling that mates should stick together and see things through. Concealed in this may lie an important willingness to accept what the State demanded of you, and this may distinguish working-class patriotism with its suspicion of the state.'[3] But just as working people expected more from the state after the war, so they – or at least a significant number of trade unionists and unorganised workers – agitated for various forms of state discrimination against black people. And overt racism simply 'exploded' in 1919.

The reasons were material, psychological and political. If the major material factor in the growth of aggressive working-class racism from the outbreak of the war onwards was the more visible presence of black people in English towns and cities, new psychological and political factors were at work, too. In some of the 'race riots', and particularly in Liverpool, a great deal of the violence against black Britons was the work of ex-colonial soldiers who had retained rifles. Although no one was killed in Liverpool, blacks were shot at. Furthermore, as a result of serious unemployment in post-war England, some of the 'trade unions now insisted on the employment of [white] Englishmen in preference to Negroes.'[4]

A new and aggressive type of working-class racism was created during and after the First World War by such new factors as sexual jealousy, the insecurity induced by unemployment and a heightened sense of white superiority. Despite the fact that '"scientific racism" had passed its peak of popularity in the universities and in scientific circles, racist ideas were increasingly popularised by the middle classes. By the 1920s some of the middle-class advocates of women's liberation could not separate the campaign for 'birth control' from an obsessive worry over the threat of over-population in Asia and Africa. As Elsie M. Lang put the argument: 'But if the white races follow this wise counsel and practise birth control have they any guarantee that the coloured races will follow suit; and if not, now that education is spreading so widely in Asia, will not fresh dangers arise of a far more terrible character?'[5]

By 1918 England was an overtly racist society; and in the early 1920s the 'colour bar' was introduced in many hotels and restaurants as well as in some sports. While many socialists and trade unionists disapproved of the development of post-war racism, the labour movement as a whole took some time before it acknowledged the problem. James Marley, a nominally socialist Member of Parliament, protested against the 'colour bar' in hotels, pubs and restaurants, yet he insisted that working-class racism was 'harmless'.[6]

The First World War was a watershed in the emergence of overt working-class racism in the labour movement as well as in society as a whole. But the new complexity of old and new working-class attitudes – for example, a continuing suspicion of the law-makers with a heightened intolerance towards black people – was captured in the dialogue overheard by Whitling Williams, an American sociologist, in the London docks in 1920:

> 'See them Lascars', said a red-faced, unshaven fellow in a badly soiled coat, greasy handkerchief for necktie, spotted, corduroy pants, and the heaviest of boots, all in great contrast with the East Indian's bare feet, gray, denim trousers and jumper, black beard and dish-rag of a turban. 'The law's been lettin' them things and the Chinks get the places on the boats that should belong to us. 'Taint right.'[7]

Middle-class Africans who came to England after the First World War were often horrified by the unexpected hostility they encountered. As Peter Esedebe, the African historian, has argued:

> Most, if not all, persons of African descent came to Britain with an idealised concept of the 'mother country' and its reputation for 'fair play' and 'justice'. Their sense of membership in a 'British Empire' often received a rude shock, and the boast *Civis Britannicus sum* was shown to be empty and hollow when they had to face social ostracism at the hands of white Englishmen who were often their 'social inferiors' educationally and professionally in terms of normally understood class differentiations in Britain.

Furthermore, there was, as Esedebe insists, a tangible

relationship between the growth of Pan-Africanism and English racism: 'The significance for the Pan-African movement of racial discrimination consisted in the fact that it provided the exiles with a rallying point. It is worth noting that all the five Pan-African conferences held in the first third of the present century unequivocally condemned racial prejudice.'[8]

The origins of widespread working-class racism in England can be traced back to the growth of black communities in London, Liverpool, Hull, Cardiff, Bristol, Newport and Newcastle. In the fascinating autobiographical volume, *Old Man Trouble*, Ernest Marke, a black Briton, who subsequently took up residence in Britain, attributed the notorious 'race riots' in 1919 to unemployment and the competition for jobs. As he explained: 'Those [demobbed servicemen] who did not get their jobs back immediately, began taking it out on the Negroes.' In Liverpool an African friend told Marke, 'There are a lot of John Bull gangs who go out beating up coloured people. I don't exactly know why, but it's getting serious.' When he returned to Liverpool in 1924 from a trip to Africa, he discovered that 'even some members of the Liverpool police force had become so prejudiced against coloured men that their behaviour towards them had become nothing less than hooliganism.'[9] By the early 1920s a pernicious, overt racism was a dominant feature of English life.

Just as English society became very race conscious, so a strong substratum of racist thinking existed in the working-class movement. Seen through the lens of the dominant English 'socialism', the Africans were members of an 'inferior', child-like race. Being 'backward' and 'primitive', the Africans could be exploited until the advent of English socialism in the always distant future. In the absence of a major anti-imperialist tradition, racism inevitably influenced the consciousness and thinking of English socialists and communists. Even when some English socialists did not themselves regard black Africans as being 'inferior' or 'primitive', they seldom challenged racism in a serious, systematic way.

The British Empire was, as R. Palme Dutt, an Anglo-Indian communist, put it, 'the unspoken premise of all labour and trade union politics';[10] and socialist propaganda was 'almost exclusively national in character ("Britain for the British")', not Africa for the black Africans.[11] England was a very racist society – a society in which the English workers took their racial 'superiority' for granted.

Yet English socialists and communists usually emphasised the material benefits that the workers gained from the Empire, and not the heritage of imperialist and racist propaganda.[12] In the early 1920s, for example, R. Palme Dutt insisted on the importance of the material basis of the Empire for the survival of British capitalism. At the same time, he argued that 'The propaganda of the Empire as a cult for popular consumption has been assiduously cultivated in this country, but has never taken root.'[13] By contrast, in her book *Women's Problems of Today*, published in 1926, Leonora Eyles lamented the role of the state schools in fostering racism and war fever. As she summed up: 'It is difficult, when the schools are run with a background of imperialism and jingoism, to get the idea of war out of the public consciousness.'[14]

In practice the British Empire played a crucial role in the economy before the First World War, yet overt racism and jingoism did not get a real grip on workers' consciousness until 1919. A major factor in the creation of mass working-class racism after the war was the propaganda surrounding Empire Day. In *The Autobiography of a Liverpool Irish Slummy*, P.O. O'Mara described the role of the state schools in inculcating imperialistic propaganda:

> The Empire and the sacredness of its preservation ran through every textbook like a leitmotif. Our navy and the necessity of keeping Britannia ruling the waves is the rather indelible mark left on my memory – though the reasons for this was never satisfactory explained. Pride in our vast and far-flung colonies and the need for their protection and preservation were emphasised, as was the confidence that in any crisis the colonies and the motherland stand as one.[15]

Although the English labour movement was less covertly racist before the First World War, socialists such as Robert Blatchford fostered racist propaganda before and after 1918. In assessing the role of Blatchford's socialist newspaper, the *Clarion*, Logie Barrow argues that: 'On black people, the

Seamen campaigned for the Coloured Alien Seamen's Order. This Order became law in 1925.

The Coloured Alien Seamen's Order was designed to prevent coloured seamen from settling in Britain. Although individual socialists throughout England protested against the racist legislation in 1925, it was supported by the most paternalistic Labour and Liberal politicians. In fact the most 'enlightened', paternalistic Liberals and Labourites argued that the 1925 Act was completely inadequate. In Muriel Fletcher's report on the 'Colour Problem', the Liverpool Association for the Welfare of Half-Caste Children – a committee composed of academics, clergymen, headmasters and social workers – argued that:

> Useful as this Order has proved in checking any further influx of coloured seamen to this country, in Liverpool it has had little effect as it applies only to aliens, while the majority of West African firemen on the ships of Liverpool firms are in possession of British passports.[24]

By 1930 the fear of unemployment was undoubtedly an important factor in deepening the racism of the white seamen in the National Union of Seamen. In a vivid portrait of the situation in the Homes and Missions for seamen in Liverpool, Muriel Fletcher wrote:

> The general view of the Superintendents appeared that the white man and the coloured do not get on together and two reasons were put forward for this:
> (1) The white men feel that the coloured ones are responsible for unemployment among white seamen.
> (2) A strong resentment exists on account of the intermixture taking place between coloured men and white women.
> Although there has never been any outbursts in these buildings, the white men show their resentment and discuss it with the Superintendents. The coloured men feel that the atmosphere is hostile and do not come again.[25]

Although some working men and women no doubt 'offended coloured people by questions which were', as Peter Esedebe argues, 'really posed because they were sceptical of racist myths', the general sense of white superiority antagonised and alienated the black population.[26] Besides, though some English workers were sometimes suspicious of racist

Clarion purveyed a large number of lengthy contributions from South African correspondents, the most anti-African being the most frequent.' Nevertheless, Barrow warns us that 'the temptation to regard him [Blatchford] as a proto-Mosley must be resisted as overhindsightful.'[16]

In a pamphlet published by the Independent Labour Party (ILP) in 1926, Fenner Brockway drew attention to the racism in the English labour movement: 'There is sometimes a tendency in the trade union movement to raise colour barriers. The ILP welcomes coloured people on a basis of absolute equality into the ranks of labour.'[17] Indeed, Margaret Cole told James M. Winter that racism was 'unexceptional in the labour movement'.[18] And in documenting racism in England, James Marley said: 'Most of my hostile letters are anonymous, showing that certain types of mind find an outlet by hiding within the pack and raising hosannas to race-superiority; thus receiving the amount of emotional satisfaction they would get were they able to subdue the coloured man alone.'

In *Negro Victory: The Life Story of Dr. Harold Moody*, David Vaughan quotes the letters African students sent to Dr Moody before the League of Coloured Peoples was founded in London:

> Here is the story of a medical student in London in his own words. 'I am in my final year. My father has had a disaster at home and cannot send me any money. I would do anything to help myself and to save enough to pay the rest of my fees until my father recovers from his losses but I cannot get anything anywhere. Can you help me to find a job?' Another said: 'I am a British subject. I studied in America and am a graduate of a reputable American University. On my first arrival in London, I could not obtain accommodation anywhere and at two o'clock in the morning I was smuggled into a large hotel by the night porter who took pity on me.'[19]

While racism and imperialistic jingoism permeated the whole of Britain from the First World War until 1939, it was much worse in and around London than in Scotland or the North of England. The late Dr Archie Lamont argued that Scotland was much less of a racist society than England during the interwar period. As he told me in a private letter: 'There was never any anti-black feeling in Scottish towns, but in the Highlands (Wester Ross) I know from the late John M.

Mackenzie, that the population in one village escorted a black
African to the next village when he looked like settling. That
would be around 1924 or earlier.'[20] Furthermore, Dr Harold
Moody's biographer, David Vaughan, quotes from a letter than
an African doctor of medicine sent to Moody in the early 1920s:

> I came here with my family to undertake post-graduate study in London.
> Although I tried for a whole day I could not discover any place where I
> could obtain lodgings of any sort. I therefore had to take a nighttrain to
> Scotland where I had received my medical education, and where I knew I
> would be treated with more courtesy.[21]

Despite the liberal traditions of the Scottish universities in
providing black men with a medical education from the
nineteenth century, Scotland was just as racist as England. But
the Scottish labour movement seems to have been more hostile
to imperialism and racism than its English counterpart, though
both movements contained racists and anti-racists in their ranks.
For example, in reporting that 'certain restaurants and dance
proprietors in Edinburgh' had placed 'a bar upon Indians and
other coloured people', the *New Leader* seemed to be surprised
by the extent and intensity of the protest demonstrations
organised by the Scottish branches of the ILP.[22]

Although many English trade unions were racist, the worst
offender was the National Union of Seamen. The leaders of the
latter were out-and-out racists. While the practice of employing
African and Lascar seamen on British ships began about 1870,
the seamen's trade union was not an overtly racist organisation
until the First World War. When she published a *Report on an
Investigation into the Coloured Problem in Liverpool and other
Ports*, Muriel E. Fletcher wrote:

> The practice of employing coloured seamen on the ships plying between
> Liverpool and the West Coast of Africa is not a new one. An official of the
> firm which employs the largest number of these men states that in the case
> of his firm the practice originated sixty years ago [in 1870] and during the
> last twenty-five years West Africans have entirely replace white men as
> firemen and trimmers on the ships in the African trade. These dates are
> borne out by the fact that there are several half-caste women, who were
> born, and are resident in Liverpool, between the age of 40 and 50 years of
> age.[23]

In the wake of the 'race riots' in 1919, the National Union of propaganda, Kobina Seky, a philosophy student in London, wrote about his own experience of racism:

> It does not take him [an African] long to find out that he is regarded as a savage even by the starving unemployed who ask him for alms. Amusing questions are often put to him as to whether he wore clothes before he came to England; whether it was safe for white men to go to his country since the climate was unsuitable to civilised people; whether wild animals wandered at large in the streets of his native home town.[27]

By the opening decade of the 1930s racism was commonplace in England. In reporting on a conference on the 'colour problem' in London in 1931, the newspaper, *The Afro-American*, noted: 'A warning to the English people that colour prejudice is undermining the British Empire is issued by the Joint Council to Promote Understanding between White and Coloured People in Great Britain.'[28] At the same time, the *Negro Worker*, an organ of the communist Third International, emphasised that racism operated 'not only in America but in "democratic" England also'.[29]

Moreover, African and Indian students, and aristocratic Africans and Asians who visited England were often victims of 'the colour bar'. When the nephew of the reigning Prince of Akeokuta in Nigeria was refused hotel accommodation in London, the editor of the *Negro Worker* wrote: 'This case should be an eye-opener to Negro workers in Africa and the West Indies who are made to believe that the British capitalist class is different to the American.'[30] At approximately the same time another African said: 'One of the essential causes of recurrent ill-feeling among Africans is the persistent ill-treatment Africans have to experience repeatedly at the hands of inn-keepers and hotel managers.' In one of the early issues of *The Keys*, the journal of the League of Coloured Peoples in England, Dr Harold Moody wrote: 'The colour-bar as it operates in Great Britain, especially in Cardiff, Liverpool, Hull and London, is getting worse daily.'[31]

II

Although racism, imperialism and jingoistic white 'superiority' were inextricably linked in ruling-class propaganda about the Empire and the Royal Family, devotion to the Royal Family was very uneven in working-class England. In the *New Leader*, the organ of the ILP, a socialist journalist observed: 'The feeling of loyalty to Royalty is, of course, strongest in London. It is not really so strong in the industrial centres of the North or South Wales or Scotland.' But Harry McShane, the veteran Scottish socialist, confirmed the presence of racists and anti-racists in Glasgow in the inter-war years.[32]

Moreover, Tom Murray, who was a Communist Party organiser in the 1930s, has described the constant physical attacks on Nigerian students who lived in Leith. Although the Nigerians were communists engaged in sending agitational literature back to Africa, they were not accepted by the white workers in and around Edinburgh. Yet both Harry McShane and Tom Murray insisted that the Leith and Glasgow branches of the National Union of Seamen were much less antagonistic to black seamen than their counterparts in Liverpool, Hull, Cardiff and London.[33]

So although sections of the Scottish working class were probably just as racist and imperialistic as their counterparts in England, it is possible that the Scottish labour movement was rather more anti-imperialist and anti-racist than it was elsewhere in Britain. There would seem to be some evidence for this view in Ras Makonnen's book, *Pan-Africanism from Within*. An advocate of Pan-Africanism, who lived in England in the 1930s, he later recalled that:

> There were two main trends in English adult education, and one of these looked very relevant for adaptation in Africa. There was the Workers' Educational Association (WEA) first of all; this seemed to us more of a bourgeois, middle-class affair. . . . Then there was the National Council of Labour Colleges (NCLC) – the really hardcore Keir Hardie-type of class education. This was much more what we were looking for, and both Jomo Kenyatta and I had seen something of their operations in Scotland. The approach was strictly Marxian, and a lot of miners and other Scottish workers were brought in so that you would get a more enlightened trade union leadership.[34]

The NCLC did protest against racism in the labour movement. They also protested against the exploitation of black seamen employed on English ships. In an article in the *Plebs* magazine, the organ of the NCLC, 'Internationalist' protested against the poor wages paid to black seamen and concluded:

> None of us among the whites can feel much enthusiasm about our own past record, as a movement, in relation to members of other races. We have been too preoccupied with immediate struggles at home to take overmuch interest in the wrongs and sufferings of subject races. The inter-racial and international ramifications of modern capitalism are compelling us at least to take a new line.[35]

But the internationalists in the NCLC were in a minority within the English labour movement. In London, Cardiff and Liverpool such champions of black emancipation as Chris Jones, Arnold Ward and Harry O'Connell worked in the branches of the communist Negro Workers' Welfare Association. In 1933 they marched on May Day under a banner marked: 'Races, United against Imperialism' and 'Our children are compelled to honour the Union Jack, the symbol of colonial slavery and oppression'. In reporting the Negro Workers' Welfare Association's participation in the London May Day, the *Negro Worker* carried an article denouncing English imperialism: 'What is Empire Day? On "Empire Day" the League against Imperialism exposes the horrors of colonial exploitation, robbery, shootings, imprisonments and its colossal death role.'[36]

Furthermore, in circumstances where 'coloured men in Cardiff were given less transitional unemployment pay than white seamen', the *Negro Worker* began to campaign for the rights of black workers. Chris Jones, Arnold Ward and Harry O'Connell all contributed to the *Negro Worker* in the early 1920s, and the signs of strong Pan-African sympathies were already evident in their writings. In any case, Chris Jones resigned from the Communist Party in 1933; George Padmore was expelled by the International Control Commission of the Communist International on 23 February 1934; and Arnold Ward dropped out of the Communist Party as the new Popular Front policy led to the abandonment of anti-imperialist agitations. Of the major leaders of the black people in England, only Harry O'Connell remained active in the

Communist Party throughout the 1930s.[37]

With the collapse of the Negro Workers' Welfare Association, the National Union of Seamen intensified their racist criticisms of the black seamen and their families in English towns and cities. By 1935 this led to the formation of the Coloured Colonial Seamen's trade union. The leading figures within it – for example, Chris Jones, Arnold Ward and Harry O'Connell – became more sympathetic to the philosophy of Pan-Africanism; and, although they were critical of the moderate policies of the League of Coloured Peoples and the ILP, they increasingly cooperated with Dr Harold Moody, Fenner Brockway and James Maxton. As the leader of the League of Coloured Peoples in the 1930s, Harold Moody played a major role in exposing the rampant racism in English society.

For reasons explained by W.G. Brown in an article in *The Keys*, the organ of the League of Coloured Peoples, the Shipping Assistance Act of 1935 played a pernicious role in sharpening existing racist antagonisms. As Brown put it:

> Thus a new monument to economic ignorance and racial animosity rises in England. Fresh, vigorous and dynamic, abundantly nourished by the poisons of the depressions, this tower threatens all intelligent attitudes, and submerges the vital problems still unsettled among shipping labourers. . . . The *Trade Unions*, the Police and the Shipowners appear to co-operate smoothly in barring colonial Seamen from signing on ships at Cardiff. The legislative history of this policy has been traced chronologically, and the emphasis placed upon the stipulation to carry only British seamen which accompanied the two million pound grant to the shipping industry. These plans and methods were never unknown to the colonial seamen.[38]

Yet despite the very concrete material basis for the racism of the National Union of Seamen, the white seamen's sense of racial 'superiority' was beginning to assume something of an independent dynamic.

In the important pioneering study of *Negros in Britain*, Kenneth Little tends to gloss over the pernicious racism within many English trade unions. Ignoring the very strong racist attitudes in the English trade unions, he asserts that:

> The National Union of Seamen, however, contended that far from

wishing to dispose of the British-born coloured men, or at any rate the West Indians and the West Africans, they were actually fighting their battles against the exclusion of domiciled British crews. It is just possible, therefore, that once again the word 'British', which to the ordinary citizen of this country does not convey any meaning beyond a white citizen of the Empire, was mainly responsible for the misunderstanding. In short, as the *Seaman* (the official organ of the National Union of Seamen) subsequently admitted, too much was made of the employment of aliens, as such, by union officials and other white members of labour organisations.

But as the *Daily Worker* had already reported in 1934, the 'National Union of Seamen have been agitating against coloured seamen for some time'. Furthermore, the immigration officers were victimising British-born West African seamen and preparing the way for a 'repatriation drive'.[39]

Although Indian students in London, Cardiff and Bristol were attempting to organise Indian seamen into trade unions in the early 1930s, they did not enjoy very much success. From the mid-1930s the communists were more interested in creating a Popular Front than in organising working men and women in the black communities in England. Before the advent of the Popular Front, the *Negro Worker* exposed the racism and racist propaganda of the National Union of Seamen. In an editorial in the July 1934 issue of the *Negro Worker*, it was revealed that:

In the May 30 issue of the *Seaman*, the official organ of the National Union of Seamen, appears an editorial entitled 'Relief Money for Ten Years – Keeping Coloured Loafers'. A few quotations from this editorial will show to what extent these labour fakers will go to incite friction between the white and colonial seamen and keep them from united struggle against the shipowners: 'A world-wide reputation has been earned for Liverpool as the happy hunting ground of the colonial loafers. . . . There are over 1,000 West Africans, Indians and Arabs in Liverpool, and some hundreds of them are living in idleness and comfort on relief money. . . . A sinister position has arisen due to the scale of relief money for a man and a woman being 20s per week, as in order to obtain this extra money some coloured men are living with white women. Thus not only are these men content to settle in Liverpool as pensioned idlers, but they also welcome the inducement to get money for a wife. Here thus looms the prospects of a half-caste community to add to the problems, financial and otherwise, of Liverpool's citizens.'

By 1935 James Maxton was writing in the *New Leader* as follows: 'It appears to be the object of certain interests to deprive colonial seamen of British nationality, and the situation of men born in British Protectorates is particularly difficult.'[40]

Throughout the years between 1919 and 1939 economic insecurity, sexual jealousy and a rampant sense of white 'superiority' kept racial tensions and antagonism in English towns and cities of 'half-caste children'. The trade unions did not make any serious attempt to create solidarity between white and black workers. As James Walvin explained: 'Their [the African seamen's] plight was worsened by the refusal of the trade unions to accept them for what they really were: "a section of the same labouring class striving for a livelihood on exactly the same basis as any other union member".' Meanwhile, the Parliamentary Labour Party endorsed the trade unions' complaints against 'coloured labour'; and in openly siding with racism, Labour Members of Parliament were, in Walvin's phrase, 'guided by the amazing belief that the working class was, necessarily, white'. And when black workers were again beaten up in several English ports in 1932 and subjected to 'similar outrages' to those of 1919, the labour movement did not speak out.[41]

The English trade unions were also very backward in relation to the anti-imperialist work being carried out by the ILP in South Africa. In an article published in the *Plebs* magazine, in 1934, entitled '"Democracy" in the British Empire', J.F. Horrabin reported on the work of W.G. Ballinger:

> In every Labour or Co-operative meeting in which I have referred to the African problem, there has always been unanimous agreement that the British trade union movement owed a debt to the African workers – a debt which they might pay by helping the latter to organise. W.G. Ballinger, a Scottish trade unionist, has been doing something to pay that debt. He has not, for the most part, had any backing or even encouragement from the British trade unions.

In circumstances where the Labour Party did very little anti-imperialist education, the task of fighting racism and jingoism was left very largely to the ILP and the NCLC.[42]

In 1935 Harry O'Connell helped to form the Coloured Colonial Seamen's Union. From then on close relations developed between such advocates of Pan-Africanism and the League of Coloured Peoples. In reporting from Cardiff, Cecil Lewis wrote:

> To protect their rights, the coloured seamen formed an organisation called the Coloured Colonial Seamen's Union, and sent one of their number, Mr. Harry O'Connell, to London, to seek assistance.
> While in London, Mr. O'Connell interviewed the Society of Friends, the Overseas League and the League of Coloured Peoples. The League of Coloured Peoples at once became interested, and the matter was placed before the Executive Committee who unhesitatingly voted a sum sufficient to defray the cost of an investigation in Cardiff.

By 1937 both the League of Coloured Peoples and the Coloured Colonial Seamen's Union were insisting that the National Union of Seamen were much more responsible for unemployment amongst black seamen than the shipping companies.[43]

In June 1937, Chris Jones, the President of the Coloured Colonial Seamen's Association, told delegates to a conference of the League of Coloured Peoples that 'the question of the employment of coloured seamen was not so acute at present on account of the boom in shipping, but maintains that this boom will not last, and expressed a fear that as they were the last to sign on, they would also be the first to be fired'. A few months later a contributor to *The Keys* said that the members of the League were 'disturbed by the propaganda which is made in Parliament and elsewhere' for 'the repatriation or segregation' of African and Indian citizens living in England.[44]

Although Arnold Ward was not so prominent in politics after he left the Communist Party, he remained sympathetic to Pan-Africanism. He also continued to publish articles against the racism of English working-class men and women. Despite their political differences, Harry O'Connell and Chris Jones protested against the racism of English workers at the same time as they organised black workers living in English towns and cities.[45] Ras Makonnen has left a vivid description of the role played by Chris Jones:

Another grouping of blacks at this time in England was the Colonial Seamen's Union led by Chris Jones; it was one of the commonest occupations at that time for West Africans, and had arisen quite naturally from the white seamen's fear of West Africa being a white man's grave. . . . It became one of our jobs along with Chris to persuade such people to join the union; otherwise we were attacked by enlightened white trade unionists who were afraid that the blacks would act as scabs. So the Colonial Seamen's Union was not really a union in the strict sense – we did not want a separate black union – it was more of a welfare and propaganda grouping which would get the colonial seamen together and persuade them to join the white union.

But the Coloured Colonial Seamen's Union collapsed with the outbreak of the Second World War.[46]

III

The most difficult and complex problem facing the militant socialistic Pan-Africanists in England was how to foster and reconcile their dual goals of African emancipation from British imperialism with international socialism. In an article in the *Negro Worker* in March 1933, George Padmore expressed a strong scepticism about the motives of the Quakers and other middle-class reformers who were attempting to promote better relations between 'white and coloured peoples in England'. In setting out the reasons for this scepticism, he said: 'The real purpose of this movement is not to expose British imperialism and its ideologists who foster and spread race hatred, but to put a brake upon the growing resentment of the coloured workers and students against the shameful way they are being treated in this so-called democratic country.'[47]

A serious difficulty for the historian attempting to reconstruct a *social picture* of the lives of black Africans in England is the somewhat contradictory evidence presented by George Padmore and Ras Makonnen. In sketching in the history of the League against Imperialism between 1927 and 1935, Padmore wrote:

Yet despite the excellent work of enlightenment which the League performed in left-wing circles, it never succeeded in recruiting a colonial membership. But the objective conditions were even more unfavourable

then than they are today. The majority of the coloured population, apart
from the itinerant seamen living in the dock area of London, Liverpool
and Cardiff, were made up chiefly of students. These African and West
Indian intellectuals came mostly from prosperous and middle class and
religious families.

On the other hand, Ras Makonnen argued that the Africans
in England were not middle-class – at least in their consciousness. As he put it:

> The other important distinction from America was that in Britain blacks
> were at that time so few that there was none of that social stratification
> within the black community that one had seen in Harlem or Boston. . . .
> In Britain on the other hand if there had been some outrage in Accra or
> elsewhere in West Africa, and a constitutional delegation came across to
> England, its members were not removed from the local population. So
> when your Danquah or Sekyi came over to hold some brief before the
> Privy the locals saw this as prestigious for themselves: 'Our big man is
> around, and I put on my black suit and go to Mayfair to see these big
> fellows.'[48]

What was not in doubt, however, was the pernicious and
poisonous racism of English society. Furthermore, the overt
racism of many white workers drove the blacks in England in
upon themselves.

Alienated from the white working class in England, the
early black movements sought alliances with the middle-class
philanthropists. When the first number of *The Keys* appeared
in July 1933, it could not escape confronting the problem of
racism. As David Vaughan explained: 'It was a quarterly
publication and it derived its title from the inspiration of that
distinguished African, Dr Aggrey, who asserted that the
fullest musical harmony could be expressed only by the use
of the black and white keys on the piano. The first issue
explained that the name was symbolical of what the League
was striving for – the opening of doors now closed to the
coloured peoples and the harmonious co-operation of the
races.' Confronting the major problem of survival in a very
hostile society, the Africans, Indians and West Indians and
other black people could not escape the dilemmas created
from them by racism. The dilemma of how to reconcile the
advocacy of race solidarity and inter-racial cooperation in a
racist society was quickly seized upon by the critics of

Pan-Africanism.[49] Class and race created often insoluble dilemmas and the opportunism of many white socialists did not help the black Africans to overcome the problems they faced in England.

In the introduction to *The Keys*, Roderick MacDonald says that the League of Coloured Peoples was 'the first conscious and deliberate attempt to form a multi-racial society, led by blacks, although with a membership that for its first ten years included a large proportion of whites'. Furthermore, when Dr Harold Moody founded the League in 1931, he sought to bridge the gap between such paternalistic and nineteenth-century-oriented bodies as the Anti-Slavery and Aborigines' Protection Society' and 'the small but assertive, largely student and wholly black organisations'. Also when the African Service Bureau was founded in the late 1930s, the Marxian socialists within it cooperated with white socialists in England and Europe.[50] In fact Ras Makonnen was the only Pan-African *leader* in England who questioned the fundamental *principle* and efficacy of cooperating with such white socialists as Fenner Brockway and James Maxton in the ILP.

Although the Communist International had previously advocated race unity and class unity simultaneously, the new policy of *realpolitik* around 1934–35 produced some startling attitudes. As a result of the new Popular Front policy in England, the communists attacked both George Padmore and Dr Harold Moody for advancing 'race unity instead of class unity'. In 1934 the *Negro Worker* had already criticised the League of Coloured Peoples, the Society of Friends, the Missionaries, and the white friends of the Negro for allegedly opposing the struggle for colonial freedom. An article on 'A Conference on the Negro in the World Today' concluded with the assertion that: 'There were those black Britons like Dr. Moody, who advocated a curiously confused and contradictory programme of race solidarity on the one hand and inter-racial co-operation on the other.' By 1937 Reginald Bridgeman was criticising George Padmore for failing to draw 'any distinction between the white ruling class and the exploited and oppressed white masses, and thus adapting himself to the imperialist policy of dividing white and coloured workers'. And yet Padmore was the most sympathetic of the black leaders in England towards 'the whites carrying on the traditions of the Abolitionists'.[51]

Racism was much stronger in the English labour movement after than before the First World War. It was, in fact, made respectable by the influx of middle-class 'experts' on colonialism during and after the war; though the most critical anti-colonial critics and opponents of racism were to be found in the ILP and the NCLC.

While many white socialists were nominally critical of imperialism and racism, they did not develop a critique of the role of racism in vitiating white workers' solidarity with their black counterparts in England and the Empire. Although the Indian historian, P.S. Gupta, depicts Dr Norman Leys as a critic of racist theories, Leys never abandoned the racism he articulated at the end of the First World War. In 1918 he sent a private letter to the British Colonial Secretary in which he said: 'When barbarians are turned by the thousands into a vagrant proletariat . . . every meeting point between men of different tribes and traditions destroys superstitions that gave security to property . . . the cement that made government of any kind possible is being dissolved.'[52]

The sense of white 'superiority' was dominant in the English labour movement, and it vitiated solidarity with the anti-imperialist struggles of the blacks. When Gilbert Murray, a left-wing socialist, contributed an introduction to Norman Leys' book, *Kenya*, in 1924, he insisted that 'white rule in Africa' was 'an absolute necessity'. In the same year, Archibald Robertson, the Marxist historian, wrote a review of Bertrand Russell's book, *The Prospects of Industrial Civilisation*, in which he stated:

> Even Bertrand Russell, pacifist as he is, admits that, supposing socialism be established among the white races and threatened with attack from the more prolific races of Africa, the former would have to defend themselves 'by methods which are disgusting even if they are necessary'.[53]

Norman Leys joined the Labour Party in 1920, and he quickly emerged as an expert on the 'colonial question'. He contributed articles to the *Plebs* magazine and gave lectures at the summer schools organised by the NCLC and the ILP. Because he exerted so much influence on colonial policy in the English labour movement, the article he published in the *Plebs* magazine on Africa in 1930 deserves to be quoted at length:

> There are two things that make it specially difficult to persuade people to the wise and just policy for the Africans. The first is that it is so difficult to explain to people who have never lived in Africa how dreadfully ignorant Africans are and what a disabling thing barbarism is . . .
> One has to have first-hand dealings with uncivilised people to realise how lazy and unreliable they are, how impossible it is for them to be accurate or to distinguish clearly between a fact and an opinion, how they always let you down when you try to help them.[54]

When Eden and Ceder Paul contributed an article to the *Plebs* magazine in 1924, they posed the question, 'Why do so many of the workers thrill to the "Idea of Empire"; why are they so proud – yes, poor devils, proud – because they bear part of the "White Man's Burden", because they belong to the "Empire on which the Sun never sets"?' Then they answered their own question thus: 'Undoubtedly, one of the main sources of this pride is the universal will-to-power, the widespread and natural reaction against the sense of inferiority, against discontent with the actual conditions of existence.' Yet they never once mentioned racism either in England or the Empire.

The English Left's failure to develop adequate solidarity movements with the black Africans in the interwar period was deeply rooted in the soil of working-class racism. As far back as the Second Congress of the Communist Third International, Tom Quelch, 'the son of the revolutionary socialist who spoke up so boldly against English imperialism at Stuttgart', declared that 'the rank-and-file English workers would count it treachery to help the enslaved peoples in their revolts against English rule'. So at the same time as working-class racism became more open and aggressive, English socialists usually expressed reluctance to develop anti-imperialist agitations.[55]

The increasingly aggressive racism in English society was acknowledged within the ILP and the NCLC. When George

Padmore and C.L.R. James became members of the ILP in the mid-1930s, English socialists were forced to confront and acknowledge the reality of racism in the trade unions and labour organisations as well as in the wider society. Also, the English socialists devoted more and more attention to combating Empire Day propaganda and atrocities against black people in the Empire. In a letter sent to a working-class socialist in Glasgow in 1938, George Orwell described his impressions of English and French imperialism:

> [French Morocco] is a tiresome country in some ways, but it is interesting to get a glimpse of French colonial methods and compare them with our own. I think as far as I can make out that the French are every bit as bad as ourselves, but somewhat better on the surface, partly owing to the fact that there is a large indigenous white population here, part of it proletarian or near-proletarian. For that reason it is not quite possible to keep up the sort of white man's burden atmosphere that we do in India, and there is less colour-prejudice.[56]

In a penetrating study of the socialists' problem written from America in 1939, C.L.R. James commented:

> Even in England where race prejudice is very strong, personal relationships between white and coloured revolutionaries are exceptionally good. Little trouble ever arises about Negro or other coloured comrades staying in the homes of white revolutionaries, slighting of Negroes and their friends at socials, etc. There the radical movement in England differentiates itself sharply from *English bourgeois and petty-bourgeois society* which was *the most race-conscious in Western Europe* before the Nazis came to power in Germany in 1933.
>
> Yet the English revolutionary movement is eaten to the marrow with a most dangerous anti-Negro chauvinism. An English revolutionary, in thinking of the colonial revolution, thinks always of India, but very rarely of Africa . . . But this same Englishman, who when he wants to go to a dance, calls up his Negro friend instead of an Indian, finds it hard to think of an African revolt. He speaks always of the English revolutionaries winning power in England and then 'granting' freedom to Africans. He has accepted almost completely the evaluation of Negroes propagated by British imperialism. He sees Africans as incapable of independent action on a large scale, unable to organise a revolutionary struggle, to seize power and hold it. In other words, he sees them essentially as the bourgeois sees them. The African for him is the revolutionary white man's burden.[57]

And yet there was a strong myth that England was not a racist society during the years between the two World Wars. It was left to the American historian, Roderick MacDonald, to refute the myth that England did not possess either a 'coloured population' or a 'coloured problem' before the arrival of the 'Empire Windrush in 1948'. In reporting on the widespread racism in England between 1919 and 1939, he was recovering a major aspect of the hidden history of working-class life in which racism found expression in trade unions and other labour organisations.

7

English Working-Class Women and Organised Labour, 1914–1939

Successful revolutions have a trick of blurring their own successful outlines; in proportion as they are successful, their early stages vanish in the midst of the past. With revolutions in opinion, accompanied as they are by slow stages and largely underground, this is especially the case.

Ray Stranshey

One of the great myths of British social history is that the First World War emancipated women and lifted them out of 'the anonymity of a species'. However, if there was a much greater tendency after the war of 1914–18 to question 'ancient sanctions', many working-class women remained the 'slaves of slaves'. Sociologists as well as the advocates of women's rights claimed that women's status and role in society had been transformed as a result of the enormous demand for female labour.[1]

This enormous demand for female labour during the war was supposedly the reason for women's new status in industry. Millicent G. Fawcett, a leading advocate of women's rights, argued that the war found women 'serfs and set them free'. Moreover, women's emancipation from pre-war slavery was partly attributed to such a subjective factor as a change in men's conceptions of women arising from the war experience. Indeed, one historian of women's rights argued that what more than three-quarters of a century of persistent agitation had failed to accomplish was effected within four years of catastrophic upheaval.[2]

Many historians have often failed to understand the changes and the impact of the First World War – or sometimes the lack of a dramatic impact – on working-class women. By generalising about British women as a whole and by ignoring important differences of social class, they have exaggerated the role of the war in emancipating working-class women and depicted a false picture of their actual history. If the war played an important role in facilitating divorce in circumstances where it would have been impossible beforehand, and if it contributed to 'the relaxation of sexual conventions', it did not create the paradise for working-class women depicted by a number of historians.[3]

As a result of the general lack of knowledge of the history of working-class women before the war, a number of historians have attributed the emergence of the 'New Woman' to the impact of the war itself. Unaware of the *beginning* of family limitation or birth control before the war, Arthur Marwick asserted that 'what the war did was to spread promiscuity upwards and birth control downwards'. Even more exaggerated claims were made for the alleged relationship between the war and the emancipation of women by John Collier and Iain Lang when they argued: 'For the first time expert advice on contraception became readily available to *every* young man and woman, and Dr. Marie Stopes's manual on *Married Love* abolished a major risk of unmarried love.'[4]

By intensifying the 'labour unrest' of the pre-war period and by weakening the ancient sanctions of religion, the First World War made a dramatic impact on working-class consciousness. Moreover, if historians have sometimes exaggerated the war's impact on the lives of working-class women, it is important to realise that some of the changes in working-class life after the war were at least partly a result of processes that had been at work beforehand. In an important book entitled, *The Consequences of the War to Great Britain*, Francis W. Hirst quotes the perceptive comments of one contemporary:

> In many cases it is extremely hard to distinguish between the effects of the war and the natural development of processes which were at work before the war. For example, the standard of living was steadily rising before the war. Education, public health and other social services were extending. Motoring, wireless, aviation, were all developing. More and more women were entering the professions. Naturally it is very hard to

disentangle the normal processes of development from what is due to the war.[5]

There was closer contact between middle-class and working-class women during the war than there had been previously. In Sidmouth middle-class women made and hawked 'undecorative chemises' to the poor; in Glasgow middle-class suffragettes took on the task of visiting and administering to the needs of working-class babies; and in London the East End Federation of Suffragettes were involved in community work in the working-class districts. As the middle-class suffragettes discovered the realities of working-class life – and particularly the problem of drinking among women – they were often horrified; and even in the East End of London the suffragettes led by Sylvia Pankhurst were conscious of their alienation from working-class women.

In the 1920s advocates of women's rights – and later on historians, too – ascribed women's post-war emancipation to their mass employment in industry. As they equated women's freedom with mass employment in industry, it is important to emphasise what happened in the post-war years. For if the Sex Disqualification Removal Act 1919 opened the doors to 'many hitherto male professions including the Bar', it was more than counterbalanced by the Restoration of the Pre-War Practices Act of the same year. If upper- and middle-class women gained access to professions that had been closed to them before the war, many working-class women were driven back into the home.[6]

As women were 'discharged wholesale' after the war, the National Federation of Women Workers as well as the mixed trade unions of men and women supported the principle of restoring the pre-war practices which had kept many working women out of industry altogether. In the actual conditions of the 1920s, it must have been difficult to refute the view of one advocate of women's rights that working women presented themselves to industrialists as 'cheap labour or as the potential mothers of cheap labour'.[7]

Moreover, as the leaders of the suffragette movement saw the emancipation of the women of their own class in the shape of new career openings, and as the women's movement faded into relative oblivion, it seemed that some of Peter Kropotkin's earlier comments on women were more valid than ever before: 'It is always upon the shoulders of another woman that the enfranchised woman passes on the burden of domestic labour. The emancipation of woman means to free her from the brutalising labour of the kitchen and the washhouse.' As English trade union and government officials were determined, in 1918, to force married women back into the home and domestic service, there were few chroniclers who were interested in describing what was happening to working-class women.[8]

As soon as the Armistice was completed, the trade unions began to play a major role in pushing women out of industry. By 1923 'the reversal of the process of substitution which was so striking a feature of the war-time industry' was practically complete. In 1921 there were just over two million women and girls employed in British industry, and the ratio of female to all workers did not exceed 35 per cent. By 1928 there were only 699,000 married women employed in industry; and the women who were employed in industry continued to experience the inferior status that had characterised their lives before the war.[9]

In 1918 the female membership of all trade unions (excluding artists' and teachers' unions) was about 1,086,000. This represented an increase of 750,000 over the pre-war figure. As women were pushed out of industry and as the post-war slump deepened, this figure dropped to 615,349 in 1922. By 1923 there were only 480,000 women members of trade unions. A further factor which did nothing to stabilise the membership of women trade unionists was the incorporation (perhaps cooption is a more apt word) of the Women's Trade Union League into the new General Council of Trades Union Congress (TUC).[10]

I

Moreover, although the consciousness of many working-class women was enhanced by social processes going back to pre-war years, certain reverses were experienced, too. If the Trade Boards set up in the wake of the new Act of 1918 contributed to raising the status of women in industry, there were still male-dominated trade unions whose leading figures refused to admit women on 'grounds of sex alone'. This was the background against which Barbara Drake argued that most male trade unionists found it very difficult to practice democracy in relation to working women. Nor was this elitism confined to the Lib-Labs or the Labourist elements in the labour movement.[11]

In practice the growing influence of Leninist ideas in the labour movement contributed to a new form of elitism towards working-class women. The reality of working-class women's still further withdrawal from activity in the labour movement was captured in a pamphlet published by the British Communist Party in the mid-1920s, where this extraordinary statement occurs: 'The idea of "strikes" is very obnoxious to the women and especially to the girls of the working class.' Quite apart from the obvious exaggeration of this statement, it was alien to the spirit and content of pre-war *left-wing* socialist formulations of the problems facing socialists who wanted to mobilise working women for class struggle.[12]

By 1924 there was a general recognition that very few working-class women were actively involved in the labour movement; and a contributor to *Plebs*, the journal of independent working-class education, argued that 'family limitation' was 'absolutely indispensable' for women's activity in the labour movement. But if the practical realities of working-class life prevented the socialist elements from making much impact on working women – the reality of a 'weariness so profound that no propaganda could get into their heads' - elitism was an even more important barrier.[13]

Working-class women who were active in less elitist socialist organisations before the war did not adapt to the new situation in the Communist Party in the 1920s without a great deal of internal conflict over the issue of women's rights in the labour movement. Outside the Communist Party altogether, elitist attitudes often constituted formidable barriers between socialist organisations and working-class women. As a gifted and articulate working woman put the point: 'It is because we are so dull and heavy that we are not getting more women into our movement. Those outside think we are so "clever", so "highbrow". I thought so myself; I fought shy of the labour movement because I thought it was much too clever for me; I imagined I would never grasp its points.' Even when the socialists cycled into the mining village of Easingden in the summer months, the miners and their wives were alienated by the elitism of the middle-class socialists.[14]

The emergence of a unified, confident and sexually emancipated working class was inhibited by traditionalism, social divisions within the working class and the lack of social mobility. The sons of artisans were guaranteed jobs at their fathers' trades and the sons of labourers were unlikely to move out of their inherited social strata. Moreover, the deepening economic depression made it much harder for even the most sensitive socialists to win much support for their programme of emancipating working-class women from their traditional drudgery.[15]

In a wide range of working-class communities 'influential friends' were crucial for those young people who were searching for jobs; and even the unemployed artisans were better placed to search for jobs outside their own communities than labourers, since they could afford to use the cheap trains. A consciousness of the social differences between labourers, semi-skilled workers and artisans inhibited many young people from moving out of their own strata, and the social divisions within the working class contributed to pessimism, apathy and the lack of any hope for the future. Class solidarity was also vitiated by the jealousy engendered by these social gradations within such relatively well-organised groups as the cotton workers.

Moreover, while there had been a modification of pre-war poverty, this did not always apply to the mining communities. Mining children went to school with 'gaping holes in their boots'; and sometimes 'a woman was found wearing her husband's coat and in one case between them they had one pair of boots'. In the pits there was often 'an attitude of uncompromising revolt', and wife-beating remained quite common.[16]

The poverty of the miners contributed to the strength of traditionalism; and, if the miners' traditional militancy continued to inspire socialists, other features of their traditionalism were less attractive. In contrast to other working-class communities, wife-beating did not diminish quite so much, and birth control propaganda made little impact in the mining communities. The miners were 'hostile to change of any sort', and women were only worth 'keeping because of their craft'. Moreover, the marriage bed was 'a child-rearing bed', and 'childless marriages were a source of disquietude in the Rows'. Far from being emancipated by the war, the plight of the miners' wives was summed up by J.G. Sinclair:

> It was not until they were dead that the women of Easingden reached the Happy Isle. While they were alive it was always work, work; washing, mending, sewing, cooking, running to the store for groceries; and sometimes to the Portland Arms with a mug to be filled with beer, for the men-folks' dinner.[17]

As many women had been driven back into the home after the war, they had been deprived of a possible source of emancipation. Economically dependent on their men, there were clearly limits to the new status of women that had been predicted by the advocates of women's liberation during the war. For in 1926 the proportion of wage-earning women to the total female population had not changed since 1911, and there was still a strong working-class stigma against the married woman who wanted to work.[18]

In some very tangible ways there was, in fact, a retreat from the gains that women attained before the war: in the London hospitals would-be women medical students were refused admission. Sir Thomas Oliver, a distinguished medical expert, argued that the home was 'the highest sphere' of women's activity; and married women teachers were dismissed in various parts of England. This was, indeed, part of a general tendency among the public authorities, and even the mills in Bolton refused to employ married women. In 1927 a Bill to prevent public employers from refusing to employ married women was voted down by 'an almost empty' House of Commons.[19]

For those women who were employed in industry working conditions were certainly better than they had been before the war, however; and, although sexual assaults on factory women were not unknown, they no longer continued to dominate the reports of the Factory Inspectors. Outside the factories sexual assaults on women increased very sharply, and the authorities could only speculate about the possibility that 'the increased activity of women on behalf of their sex [had] resulted in bringing more offences to light'. Certainly women felt less inhibited about reporting sexual assaults than they had been in the past.[20]

Women workers' hours of labour were reduced, though the economic depression was the most important factor responsible for this improvement. Working women were also opposed to 'scientific management'; and, in spite of often violent quarrels between women in the factories, there was a strong sense of community. As some working women told Margaret L. Eyles: 'Of course we have a good time when we can. The workshop is our life!' Fines were still imposed on women for a whole range of petty offences, and some workers preferred fines to dismissal for being late or singing. As late as 1921 the High Court in England upheld an employer's legal right to impose fines on workers for singing.[21]

Insecurity remained a marked feature of working-class life, though women workers were prepared to challenge employers' rights in the courts. The deep sense of insecurity resulted in women workers who were ill concealing their ailments from their employers; and patent medicines were taken by women workers who 'whipped themselves like tired horses'. One consequence of an identifiable working-class culture which crystallised before the war was the isolation within factories and workshops of workers who advocated temperance; and, although more working women were still interested in votes for women, there were still working men who opposed the agitation because men were superior and 'did all the work'.[22]

There was a very profound sense in which the miners' culture was not altered by the war at all. Though there was certainly a conflict between the miners' unions and the coalowners for pit-head baths, some left-wing historians have failed to understand most miners' own profound indifference to the agitation. In Britain as a whole superstition was still widespread in working-class and rural communities, and most miners voted against the provision of pit-head baths. Being largely indifferent to the problems of their womenfolk – or, to put the point another way, caught up in traditional superstitions – the miners were opposed to the socialists' agitation. There was still a strong traditional belief that 'water weakened the vital part of the back'; and a daily 'sluicing of one's back' was a sign of a miner's 'premature decay'.[23]

There was still a profound ignorance of working-class life. Outsiders such as doctors, nurses and welfare workers were viewed by working people as 'them', and state intervention in workers' social life was often resented. An unbridgeable gulf existed between 'them' and 'us', and working-class culture was intended to protect its own from the interference of outsiders.

II

The experience of working-class women was inseparable from the existence of a traditionalist male workers' culture; and, while there were important ways in which the status of working women improved, a surprising number of pre-war social attitudes survived.[24] If government inspectors reported that 'the stigma which formerly attached to the receipt of poor relief' was disappearing, and that there was much less reluctance on the part of working people to accept relief from the Guardians than there had been formerly, resort to the Poor Law was still unpopular. If the new attitudes among some workers strengthened the unemployed agitation, many other workers still regarded 'a visit from the relieving officer a degradation indeed'.[25]

Although workers' 'respectability' no longer inhibited trade union membership to the same extent as formerly, trade union activists were still victimised. Working women could still be discriminated against for complaining about the violations of the Factory Acts, and the fear of dismissal was a marked feature of workers' mentality. The fear of the pauper's grave, though in decline, survived and burial clubs continued in most communities. While the pawnbrokers were 'as busy as the bakers', an estimated 40 per cent of working people 'would starve rather than go to the pawnshop'. Workhouses were hated as passionately as ever before; and there was sometimes a strong reluctance 'to go on the parish'.[26]

Old and new working-class social attitudes existed side-by-side; and it was quite clear that the war had made more impact on middle- than on working-class women. If domestic service was still seen by many women as a form of slavery, sexual attitudes were somewhat more relaxed or less repressive than ever before. Working women were less hostile to the compulsory schooling of their children, and the change in the appearance of the British woman was described by one historian as 'almost revolutionary'. By 1925 the amount of material needed for a woman's outfit had been reduced quite dramatically by pre-war standards, and many women were said to be in a revolt against 'involuntary motherhood'.[27]

As a result of the refusal of some romantic left-wing historians to examine the social history of working-class women critically instead of glorifying their proletarian status, a false picture of the real experience of working women has dominated British social history. A large number of working men (it is impossible to quantify the number) still regarded their womenfolk as inferior beings; and this was why the emancipation of women wrought by the war was at best only partial for the women of the working classes.

Traditionalist attitudes were as strong as ever in some working-class communities. As Leonora Eyles put it: 'I have heard it said by working men that they have no pleasure in life but "beer and the missus", and this, I think, is typical of most working men except true socialists. Most wives seem to be domestic drudges, wage-earners, child-bearers and ministers to their husbands' physical appetites. They are not loved for themselves, but for their usefulness.' Working-class women were often expected to be sexually subservient, and there were still working men whose 'primitive ideas' of marital rights expressed the traditionalist notions of women's role in society.

A profound failure to repudiate the Leninist tendency to glorify the proletarian status *per se* is at the root of romantic left-wing historians' inability to understand the real experience of working women in those years. Ignorance, superstition and outright brutality were prominent features of workers' social life, and many working men refused to use contraceptives as a result of a widespread belief that they caused consumption. Moreover, if a growing number of working women resented their role as child-bearers, many working men thought that child-bearing was the woman's pre-ordained role in society. However, in the face of all the evidence to the contrary, Sheila Rowbotham insists that: 'It was not their unkindness or insensitivity but sheer ignorance which prevented them from understanding women's attitudes to sex. It was the same with contraception.'[28]

The ignorance was not only tangible, it was also induced by capitalist society at large. If such historians as Charlotte Haldane, Hamilton Fyfe and Gerald Heard exaggerated the extent to which birth control permeated downwards in the 1920s, this is not to deny that a growing minority of working people were in sympathy with the birth control movement. Left-wing socialists did much to push birth control propaganda; and a minority of working women were less reluctant to articulate their views in public than had been the case before the war. A meeting of such women in Glasgow was described by Margaret Sanger:

> That evening I spoke in a hall under socialist auspices, Guy Aldred acting as chairman. One old-timer said he had been a party member for eleven years, attending Sunday night lectures regularly, but never before had he been able to induce his wife to come; tonight he could not keep her at home. 'Look!' he cried in amazement. 'The women have crowded the men out of this hall. I never saw so many wives of comrades before.'[29]

The statistics revealed that birth control was much more common amongst the upper and middle classes than the working class, however; and the reasons were not difficult to perceive. For in addition to the obstacles thrown up by a traditionalist workers' culture, contraceptive devices such as the gold spring were too expensive for working people; though there was clear evidence that more and more working-class people resented their function as 'child-producing automata'. Furthermore, society as a whole was still hostile to birth control.[30]

In 1923 Guy Aldred was jailed for selling Margaret Sanger's book on *Family Limitation*; and in 1924 John Wheatley and the minority Labour Government refused to allow doctors employed in maternity and welfare centres to give birth control information to mothers who desired it. Moreover, birth control provision remained in the hands of about twenty voluntary associations until 1930; and even Dr Marie Stopes, who was well known as a pioneer of birth control, sent letters to the *Nation* defending the imprisonment of such past and present advocates of birth control as Charles Bradlaugh, Annie Besant, Margaret Sanger and Guy Aldred.[31]

Marie Stopes was much more critical of abortion than Guy Aldred – a pioneer socialist who understood the social causes of abortion – and she persistently advocated the use of contraceptives. When she opened a birth control clinic in the East End of London in the 1920s, she received thousands of requests for abortions from working-class women who simply did not know that abortion was illegal. The social gap between the 'haves' and the 'have-nots' was clearly as big as ever.[32]

In the 1920s abortion increased dramatically and the working-class women used both drugs and mechanical means to procure abortions. Between 1910 and 1930 the increase in the crime of abortion was as high as 183 per cent; and these increases in the offence occurred in spite of the fact that it was 'very difficult to get a jury to convict for criminal abortion'. Besides, if the law on abortion was being modified, abortion was still seen as a greater crime than rape or wife-beating.[33]

An important factor in workers' social life in the 1920s was the absence of the influential middle-class women's movement which had publicised such social problems as working-class wife-beating before the war. There can be no doubt that the relative dearth of information and statistics on wife-beating in the 1920s is related to the relative absence or apathy of such a movement. Moreover, there was from the end of the war a very marked tendency for journalists and writers to exaggerate the freedom being enjoyed by the new woman. When Arnold Bennett, for example, argued that a husband could no longer 'beat his wife with impunity', he was confusing changes in the law with real changes in social customs in working-class communities.[34]

From an impressionistic perspective, it certainly seems to be the case that wife-beating declined by comparison with pre-war experience. Moreover, there seems to have been rather less of the savage brutality that working women had suffered; and the general reduction of crimes of violence was far from unusual. But the impressions of contemporary observers or historians of workers' social life can sometimes be measured against much harder and more sociological evidence. For while one writer attributed wife-beating in working-class communities to drink, the report of the Royal Commission on Licensing demonstrated a much greater complexity.[35]

In the coal-mining communities in the Rhondda and Pontypridd there was a direct correlation between wife-beating and drunkenness; but in other parts of England the statistics for drunkenness and wife-beating were not always correlated. The increase in the number of working-class women who applied for and gained separation orders in the 1920s, was attributed to working women's refusal to tolerate the beatings that were common before the war. Indeed, it was even claimed that a minority of working women were driving their husbands to 'desert them by their own various misbehaviours' to obtain separation and maintenance. British culture was still patriarchal, capitalistic and unsympathetic to the women of the labouring poor.[36]

In working-class communities in Middlesbrough and Glasgow 'considerable brutality was shown by some of the husbands towards the wives'; and in those communities wife-beating was accepted with a resignation that puzzled outsiders. If the clergy took a more sympathetic interest in the problem than previously, they tended to attribute wife-beating to the drink problem. In a vivid, though illiterate, letter from a working woman in Glasgow, who was refused a separation order in the sheriff court, it was clear that wife-beating remained an important part of a traditionalist workers' patriarchal culture. Moreover, influential sections of the society presided over by the possessing classes were either indifferent to the problem in working-class communities or actually approved of it. One police magistrate confessed that he did not know how to cope with husbands who appeared before him for 'persistent cruelty' to their wives; and an English lawyer, who was in sympathy with the agitation for further reform of the divorce law, defended wife-beating in the following words:

A workman who finds that his wife has spent all the money he had given her on drink and has neither provided nor cooked him his dinner when he comes home tired, may perhaps be let off with a light sentence if he beats her, but apart from beating, he has no redress.[37]

In a situation where divorce was still practically impossible for working-class women, the emancipation of working-class women in terms of their ability to secure separation orders in the courts was exaggerated. If there were five times more divorces for upper- and middle-class women after the war, the statistics for separation show how little things had changed for the women of the labouring poor whether they were the wives of labourers or artisans. For if the statistics for separation increased from 4566 in 1925 to 7366 in 1928, this was little more than half the figure in the abnormally high year of 1914 when the annual figure reached 14,000.[38]

Moreover, though a wide range of progressive legislation coloured the bitter-sweet 1920s, it did little to impinge on the lives of working-class women. A number of important laws which were designed to give women a much greater equality of status were pushed through Parliament; and they served to convince the few remaining middle-class advocates of women's liberation that their day of salvation had finally come. In 1923 the Matrimonial Causes Act helped to equalise the legal causes for divorce; in 1925 women sentenced to capital punishment could gain access to the clergy; and in 1926 the Criminal Justice Act recognised that the married woman possessed a conscience. By removing the death penalty for infanticide, the Infanticide Act 1922 was simply formalising what had been happening since the late nineteenth century.[39]

In other ways that failed to attract much attention, women suffered setbacks in their long struggle for liberation from a patriarchal culture. The university scholarships which existed for women students before the war were withdrawn in the 1920s; and even prostitution – a useful index of working-class women's real status – declined as a result of the development of 'extra-marital sexual relations of a non-commercial kind'. At the same time there was also a growth of 'amateur' prostitution which defied the 'stringent supervision' of parents. In a pamphlet published by the Independent Labour

Party, prostitution was seen as a fundamental sign of capitalistic, commercial transactions and women's slavery. To Minnie Pallister the antidote was simple: 'Socialism strikes a blow at the very root of prostitution by asking from, and providing for, every woman honourable communal service, the nature of which she is free to choose.'[40]

But for working women faced with very real, practical problems in the 1920s, socialism was a distant dream. Indeed, the new spirit of militancy and self-assertion that had been seen before and during the war began to recede afterwards; and in the rural communities of England, where the farm workers' militancy had been somewhat halted, attitudes of deference were still very strong. While W.E. Carson saw the world-wide 'uprisings of the sex' in 1915 as something that was destined to gain momentum, one right-wing woman writer, in 1920, could see in 'the great mass' of working-class women 'a smouldering irrational and intemperate socialism'.[41]

Moreover, although there was a great deal of labour unrest from 1914 through to 1930, there were few strikes of working women. Driven back into the home in 1919, many working women were forced to play a restricted role in the struggle for the emancipation of their sex and class; and while some British workers played an outstanding part in supporting the miners, working-class women took up subordinate positions on the picket lines and in the committee rooms where the general strike of 1926 was fought. Throughout the 1920s working-class women were less prominent than ever; and there was a very profound sense in which the socialist movement had not only failed to mobilise working women, but had actually exerted, in the words of W.E. Carson, 'a deep influence in shaping the family to fit modern industrial conditions'.[42]

III

The decades of the 1920s and the 1930s should not, however, be lumped together without landmarks suggesting the differences and the differentiation. For example, although women played a very important role in the English labour movement immediately after the First World War, the collapse of the general strike in 1926 led to apathy and denoralisation. Marion Phillips explained the impact of the war on working-class women: 'When women became enfranchised the Labour Party was just undergoing a general re-organisation. There was a great rebirth in the labour world at that time . . . . Under these circumstances the old organisation [the Women's Labour League] was absorbed by the reconstructed Labour Party.'[43] Yet despite the setback in 1926, the revival of trade union militancy amongst women workers was already foreshadowed in 1920.

But in many ways social life and politics were quite distinctive. In the sphere of sexual politics, there was something of a counter-revolution. As C.H. Mowat put it: 'There were signs of change after 1936; even the restless younger generation was not untouched by the new social conscience. To talk or write of sex came to be in bad taste; the subject had become dull and old-fashioned. . . . Double beds returned to popularity, Victorian styles to the fashion pages. Divorce was, however, still on the increase.' In the annual report of *Criminal Statistics for England and Wales* for 1930, it was asserted that, although separation orders 'had risen rapidly between 1911 and 1928', *stability* was now returning to the lives of working-class women. However, by 1938 the number of separations with maintenance orders had reached the figure of 10,868.[44]

Although the sexual counter-revolution in the 1930s did not go quite so far among working-class as among middle- and upper-class women, wife-beating did not disappear in working-class communities. The advent of fascism in Europe helped to create a much less liberal atmosphere in England than had been evident for much of the 1920s; and, although English women did not suffer as much as their counterparts in Italy or Germany, they were not unaffected by this new development. Meanwhile, the magistrates who denied working-class men the right to 'chastise' their wives by using a stick in the 1920s had changed their minds by the early 1930s.[45]

The collective experience of English working-class women in the 1930s was complicated. Although fatalistic attitudes amongst women in working-class communities were some-

times common, there was a sort of anti-establishment counter-
culture, too. In sketching in the environmentally engendered
apathy, C.H. Mowat wrote: 'Yet it was the women who
suffered more than the men. Unemployment brought leisure
for the men, if they chose to regard it so; it brought no rest
to the wives and mothers. . . . For her [the mother] the
bitterness was unrelieved.' At the same time working-class
mothers, with the exception of the Irish-Catholics, were now
refusing to have 'big families'.[46]

Although socialist women were less prominent in the labour
movement than they had been before 1926, they did not
altogether disappear. As well as campaigning against mass
unemployment and poverty at home and fascism abroad, the
women in the Co-operative Guilds and the Women's Sections
of the Labour Party kept alive the idea of women's emancipation. As Noreen Branson and Margot Heinemann put it:
'There were still great areas of ignorance about birth control,
so that working women's organisations such as the Co-op
Guilds and Labour Women's Sections were in many areas
busy crusading to bring knowledge to the younger women as
one of the means towards female emancipation.'[47]

Despite the growing number of women's strikes in the
1930s, the question of women's emancipation was not very
prominent in the labour movement's various agitations. But
in contrast to the Communist Party, the National Council of
Labour Colleges always related the question of feminism to
the ever-present menace of fascism. And in England such
socialist women as Christine Millar saw the threat of encroaching fascism in the apathy of working-class women. In
an article on 'Feminism and Fascism' published in 1934, she
said:

> It is too often forgotten, however, by the very active socialist women that
> their big Conferences and their activities in the political and industrial
> fields are not representative of all working-class women – who have votes
> to cast. There never is an election where canvassers are not repeatedly
> told by working-class women: 'I leave politics to my husband' or 'I am
> told So-and-So is a good man but it will make no difference if he does
> not have my one vote.'

Five years later, Gordon Hosking was still making the same

observations about 'the modern girl'. Furthermore, he complained that in England a 'puritanical tradition has prevented socialists from emphasising their views on sex'.[48]

Yet despite the setbacks for English working-class women in the 1930s, they did at least make some advances in the sphere of trade union militancy. The militancy of a significant minority of working women was already foreshadowed in a major women's strike in 1929. As Allen Hutt put it: 'But with the opening months of 1929 a new tide of revolt was beginning to rise, seen in keenly-fought local strikes typified by the ten weeks' struggle of the girls at the Rego clothes factory in London for union recognition.'[49]

In a description of a typical factory in London, A.P. Jephcott said: 'Ruby said it was very noisy. The wireless was on and the forewoman was shouting all the time, "You sit down, will you! You get on there!" On the whole, however, Ruby preferred the factory to the school, although it was more tiring. She earned fourteen shillings a week and she hoped for a rise in a year's time.' At the same time, there was a very uneven awareness of trade unionism amongst English working women. As A.P. Jepcott explained:

> A Durham office girl of eighteen, daughter of a miner who is a keen member of his own union, has no idea that there is such a thing as a union for clerical workers. Her ignorance is much more common than is the knowledge of another girl who is going into a tailoring firm where her sister works, largely because the latter thinks highly of the union rates of pay and good working conditions which pertain there. 'You are for it at our place if you are not a member of the union,' says the older girl, and she will see that her young sister pays her fourpence a week and joins the National Union of Tailor and Garment Workers as soon as the child starts work.[50]

Moreover, apathy and fatalism were still apparent in many working-class communities. A significant minority of working-class women were hostile to social reform and politics. This often found an echo in the factories, mills and workshops. Furthermore, working women's sense of fatalistic apathy was frequently strengthened by employers. As Joan Beauchamp reported: 'The employers' policy of "divide and conquer" is carried out with great skill and persistence: men and women must not be seen talking together; women in one department are given different coloured overalls from those in another so that they may be spotted at once if they go into another department for the purpose of consultation and united working.'[51] Yet despite such 'divide and conquer' tactics, women's strikes did 'explode' in the midst of the most unpropitious circumstances.

In a vivid description of a women's strike in a London wireless factory in 1937, Dorothy Jacques said:

> The next week-end a quarter of the learners are paid off; and the following week-end sees another quarter go. Many of them burst into tears. This is perhaps their first insurable job and they have only eight or nine stamps on. We who are left put our heads together and talk. It seems to us that it is nothing but a 'racket'. We are taken on for an eight weeks' season, paid a learner's wage for doing a regular hand's work, and then sacked just as we are due for an increase. We talk and discuss what we can do about it. Somebody whispers: 'If only there was a Union here . . .' 'Ssh – don't you remember what the boss said last time they gave union bills out at the gate? – any girl joining the union will be instantly dismissed'.' 'Oh, shucks he did? I think we should join . . .'

In gathering together women workers throughout the factory, Jacques described how the strike developed out of a disparate labour force from Scotland, Tyneside, Wales and London:

> Hand-bills in the canteen, in the toilet, on the benches. Hand-bills tucked in beside the valves in the trays. Everybody must know about the union! There are still a few who don't. Then I get a brilliant idea. The girls who made the valve-bulbs themselves must place a bill inside each valve as they 'blow' it. The everybody will know: the public as well. 20,000 valves a day all with bills in them – we will tell all England.[52]

But in the sphere of domestic service, it was as difficult as ever before to organise women into trade unions. Although more than a million and a half women were employed in domestic service, most of them were scattered and isolated. A major handicap confronting trade union organisers was the fact that domestic servants were still in the 1930s outside the scope of the Insurance Acts. Nevertheless, the General Council of the TUC was very concerned about the virtual absence of trade unionism amongst domestic servants, and in

1937 they took the initiative in setting a new trade union for maids and 'generals'.[53]

The new light industries, particularly the electrical industry and light engineering, employed large numbers of women workers. When he addressed the annual conference of the TUC at Norwich in 1937, Ernest Bevin said:

> The position of women in industry creates a tremendous problem for this movement. It will never be solved until we can get a common acceptance by the male section in Congress that in every industry it is the common duty of men and women alike to be organised in trade unions. We have made some progress, but only the fringe of the problem has as yet been touched.

At the same time, Mrs Adamson, then chairman of the Labour Party, expressed alarm at the extreme exploitation of young women in the newer industries. As she put it: 'If you stand outside one of these factories at closing time, it almost seems as if a girls' school were being let loose. The majority of the workers are girls of 14 to 18.'[54]

Nevertheless, some of the attitudes prevalent amongst working women before the First World War were still strong. Although Lucas, one of the biggest engineering firms in Birmingham in 1937, employed over 12,000 women, less than 300 of them belonged to trade unions. In explaining the reasons for the very low percentage of women trade unionists, Joan Beauchamp said: 'Some of them don't want to join a union; they regard their work as a stop-gap before marriage and are temporarily satisfied with their wages; others would like to join but are afraid of victimisation. All sorts of rumours get around; they hear that if they join they will be the first to be fired if a trade recession develops.'[55] Yet women workers began to play an increasingly important role in English trade unions.

Indeed, from 1934 until the outbreak of the Second World War the rate of unionisation for women increased faster than it did for men. By 1934 there were 428,000 women trade unionists who belonged to organisations affiliated to the TUC. Furthermore, there were 160,000 teachers and 55,000 civil servants who belonged to non-affiliated trade unions. By 1937 more than 736,000 women belonged to trade unions affiliated to the TUC. In the very detailed study entitled *Women Who Work* published in 1937, Joan Beauchamp summed up:

> Instead of leaving the unions, more women workers are now coming in and most of the unions report increases in membership. At the same time, the spirit of militancy is becoming stronger, workers are refusing to put up with decreases of wages and new methods of speed-up, and more strikes are taking place, many of which have been successful in wringing concessions from the employers.[56]

The number of women trade unionists employed in a particular factory was not, however, a guide to their capacity for militancy. In fact, some of the sharpest struggles against employers occurred in factories where trade union organisation was often non-existent. In the Lucas factory, in Birmingham, a strike of 10,000 women and girls against the infamous Bedaux system of speed-up in 1932 led to the establishment of a strong branch of the Transport and General Workers' Union staffed by women workers.

The year 1934 was the real turning-point in the emergence of strong and active trade unionism amongst women workers. In a vivid description of some of the major strikes in 1934, Joan Beauchamp said:

> In March, 1934, 300 girls working in a carpet factory at Kidderminster defeated the employers' attempt at enforcing a wage-cut by the threat of a strike.
>
> In August, 1934, nearly 3,500 artificial silk workers went on strike at Flint, and after three days succeeded in wringing concessions from the employers with regard to rates of pay.
>
> A strike of women upholsters at the big London shops in April, 1935, which was supported by the Amalgamated Union of Upholsters, was successful in getting a 10 per cent. wage advance from the employers. These are only a few examples, it is impossible to analyse all the strikes which involved women workers in the last few years.

Furthermore, male chauvinism was on the decline in the English labour movement; and trade union officials were, in the new conditions where the newer industries were employing women, more sensitive to the agitations of women workers. As Mary Agnes Hamilton said: 'The unions which try to keep women out are today in a tiny minority. They can fairly be disregarded, since their conversion to the more general view is only a matter of time.'[57]

Many of the women's strikes in the 1930s were often characterised by the same intensity and 'spontaneity' as were evident in the 1880s and 1890s. Indeed, a common characteristic of those strikes was the role of radicals and socialists in making women workers more conscious of their right to a decent wage. Much of the work of consciousness-raising was undertaken by the TUC and the Women Workers' Group. In summing up the importance of conscious leadership in working women's struggles, Sarah Boston says: 'One of the leaflets circulated by the Women Workers Group, "To Parents", was specially addressed to parents who were trade unionists. It was part of the campaign to stress, not just to women, but to male trade unionists also, the importance of organising women.'[58]

In any case, if a growing minority of English working-class women were becoming increasingly self-assertive, most women were still the prisoners of a patriarchal society. Far from being 'emancipated' by the First World War, a growing minority of English working-class women were rediscovering the concrete *benefits* to be derived from militancy and 'spontaneous' strikes. As they found space for their struggles as a result of the growth of the newer light industries, a working-class women's movement began to develop and crystallise.

8

English Workers, Mass Unemployment and the Left, 1914–1939

I was a hero for four years once, but the War stopped. They gave me a gratuity and sent me home. . . . The next thing was the Labour Exchange where they allowed you benefit for War Services rendered. But the hero worship quickly dwindled.

Will Oxley, in 'Are you working?', 1938

Although the English workers' distinctive culture and way of life remained independent, autonomous and sometimes inward-looking, many workers began to reject the idea of unemployment. The First World War was a catalyst in transforming English workers' attitudes to state intervention, poor relief and unemployment. The process of total war did not just radicalise the English working class, although it most certainly did that. It also changed many workers' social values and political attitudes.

The most immediate consequence of the First World War was the very rapid increase in unemployment. It did not, however, last for very long, and the economic 'boom' and hunger for 'hands' or labour transformed one aspect of the social history of the English working class. In contrast to the pre-1914 workers who had accepted unemployment with a sense of fatalism, the working class – or large sections of it – now questioned the dominant *class* assumptions of English society.

Despite the socialists' protests against mass unemployment between 1883 and the outbreak of the First World War, most English workers had accepted what was seen as the inevitability of unemployment. With the growth of full employment and an unprecedented demand for labour during the war, English workers' attitudes were transformed very quickly indeed. And during the general election of 1918 the Labour Party made sure that the question of unemployment would become a major plank in their programme.

Although the pattern of unemployment varied from one part of the country to another in 1918, the labour movement was no longer prepared to accept it so uncritically as had happened before the war. But the real pinch of unemployment was not felt until October 1920. By November the number of unemployed on the register was over half a million, besides others not registered; by January 1921, over 900,000; and by February over 1,100,000. The ruling class was very sensitive to the developing problem of unemployment; and, when vacancies were registered at the Labour Exchange, ex-servicemen were given preference over those without military service.

After the First World War there was, as W.T. Colyer put it, 'a temporary change of attitude [towards the unemployed] for the better'. By the mid-1920s, however, there was a reversal of policy. Though the first 'minority' Labour Government in the interwar period treated the unemployed with relative sympathy, a particularly strong stigma was attached to unemployment between 1926 and 1939. In explaining what happened after the Great War, Colyer said: 'With astounding ease the capitalist press was able to popularise that loathsome term, "the dole", as applied to all extended benefits which had to be met out of loans or special contributions from the National Exchequer to the Unemployment Insurance Fund.'[1]

I

The Scots were much more sensitive to the threat of mass unemployment at the end of the First World War than their English counterparts. Before the war had ended the militant Scottish workers attempted to cope with the anticipated growth of mass unemployment by demanding a 40-hour week. But the Scots' sense of urgency did not, according to Helen

Vernon, the English labour historian, 'communicate itself to England'.[2] In any case, there was a longer post-war boom in England than in Scotland; and the recasting of bourgeois England resulted in a temporary sympathy for the unemployed and their families. Although W.T. Colyer, a prominent activist in the National Council of Labour Colleges, insisted that the establishment's new attitudes towards the unemployed had been engendered by a new 'humanitarianism', he had also noted that 'Even in the early days of the new administration the way was prepared – subtly and psychologically – for a return to the bad old tradition as soon as it should be safe to do so.'[3]

However, a new English working class had emerged from the process of total war between 1914 and 1918. By 1920 the rising tide of unemployment and the actual numerical growth of the trade unions and labour movement created serious problems for the establishment. Attempts were soon made to stiffen the administration of the Poor Law - a Poor Law still based in theory on the deterrent principles of the Poor Law Amendment legislation of 1834. Working-class men and women were now much less reluctant to accept relief from the Board of Guardians, and the authorities scandalised the middle class by basing scales of 'poor relief' on the amount of money necessary to maintain a family in health, not on the wages of the worst-paid labourer outside the workhouse.[4]

Although the establishment frequently pursued a dual, almost contradictory, policy after the war in recasting bourgeois England to defuse organised labour at the same time as it made certain concessions. In depicting the anti-labour aspects of a policy designed to pay relief irregularly G.D.H. Cole wrote: 'The "gap" system, well known to most of the unemployed today [1923], and many little ways of the Boards of Guardians, are examples of this form of Christian charity. And the greatest of these is the "gap" system.'[5] Nevertheless the 'gap' system itself was an historic advance on the paternalistic charity of the pre-1914 era.

Moreover, the English labour movement was in some ways much closer to the spirit, attitudes and values of the unorganised working class after the First World War than it had been beforehand. Indeed, although the left-wing Boards of Guardians elected in 1928 represented a minority of the working class, they would have been completely unthinkable in the past. They were, in fact, a reflection of new working-class attitudes towards 'poor relief' and state aid. To remedy what happened in West Ham and other recalcitrant localities the Government appointed its own nominees to replace the elected Guardians. Then in 1929 a new Act was pushed through Parliament to abolish the Boards of Guardians altogether. This new legislation transferred Poor Law administration to committees nominated by county and county borough councils on the assumption that they would be less open to popular pressure.[6]

Unemployment was much higher during the years between 1921 and 1939 than it had been during 'the Age of Empire' between 1870 and 1914. Although unemployment touched over 7 per cent during the abnormal years between 1905 and 1908, it usually range between 2.5 per cent in 1900 and 3.3 per cent in 1914. But during the period between 1921 and 1939, mass unemployment remained a *constant* problem. In depicting the human consequence of such mass unemployment Jurgen Kuczynski focused on the lack of children's clothes and shoes, the lack of funds for teachers' salaries and the bankrupt tradesmen who were forced out of business. This was, of course, inevitable in communities where the level of unemployment touched 50 per cent.[7]

What was not in doubt was the militant attitude towards poor relief in the early interwar period. Although right-wing politicians and members of the ruling class criticised 'lazy' workers who did not want to seek work throughout this period, many English workers demanded 'relief' as a democratic right. In doing so, they forced the state to provide them with aid which would have been unimaginable before the war. When the Royal Commission on Unemployment Insurance reported in the 1930s, the Commissioners admitted that since 1920 'the insurance principles on which the original scheme was based have been disregarded and benefits have been extended and made payable under less exacting conditions'.[8] This could not have happened if workers had not rejected the fatalistic passivity of the pre-1914 working class in relation to unemployment and poor relief.

Moreover, in the early 1920s the English ruling class was divided in its attitude towards the unemployed. In 1922 Sir Hall Caine sent a letter to *The Times* in which he expressed sympathy for the plight of the unemployed. What helped to eradicate ruling-class sympathy for the predicament of unemployed men and women was the measures taken by the first minority Labour Government in favour of the unemployed.[9] This was at least partly because Lord Derby expressed the hope that the second Labour Government 'would take their courage in both hands' and stamp out 'a great deal of subsidised laziness' amongst the unemployed.[10]

The unemployed workers' new hostility to the 'stigma' attached to the receipt of poor relief did not influence the leaders of the Parliamentary Labour Party in the late 1920s or early 1930s. Although W.T. Colyer attacked the bitter criticism 'leveled at the [second] Labour government for its failure to solve the unemployment problem or to provide worthy maintenance for the unemployed within the framework of capitalism', he did not convince either the Left or many of the unemployed workers themselves. Indeed, Richard W. Layman argued that the second Labour Government's lack of 'any distinctive policy' for unemployment 'alienated an unnecessarily large number of pure spirits'.[11]

While poverty remained a serious social problem in the interwar period, workers were less fatalistic than had been the case before the First World War. This was why official society increasingly criticised 'lazy' workers from the late 1920s onwards. No one had dreamt of criticising 'lazy' workers during the pre-1914 era. In surveying working-class London in *The New Survey of London Life and Labour* for the year 1929, Hubert L. Smith wrote:

> There is no doubt that in the vast majority of cases the London unemployed genuinely wish to obtain work, and a wholly misleading impression has been created by exaggerated emphasis on the comparatively smaller number of cases in which, owing perhaps to the anomalous result of some technical insurance rule, the incentive to obtain employment was reduced or removed.[12]

What was remarkable about English working-class rejection of the fatalistic acceptance of the inevitability of unemployment was the accompanying passivity and resignation of the ruling class and the Parliamentary Labour Party. In summing this up, B.G. De Montgomery wrote: 'The whole policy of the Government described here has been directed towards the relief of the unemployed, and not towards the prevention of unemployment. In the King's Speech of 15 February 1921 it was also stated that unemployment "may be alleviated but cannot be cured by legislative means".'[13] Indeed, even in the 1930s J.M. Keynes attributed unemployment to the growth of population. But many working people – and not just militant activists – increasingly argued for 'work or full maintenance' in the early interwar period.

In discussing the causes of unemployment in America, Germany and England just before the First World War, the influential *International Socialist Review* challenged the assumption that it was engendered by such things as trusts, slum life or the high cost of living. By 1923 *Plebs*, the organ of the National Council of Labour Colleges, was attacking orthodox economists who were prating on about 'the necessary surplus of labour' and 'the mysterious trade cycles which produce alternately slump and boom' without offering any real alternative socialist policies. Unemployment was, in fact, inevitable under capitalism. In A.H.D. Dickinson's words: 'The workers must organise to abolish unemployment by abolishing capitalism.' In paying tribute to the victimised shop stewards who soon 'reappeared with heroic energy as the founders of the National Unemployed Workers' Committee Movement', Ellen Wilkinson appealed for an intensification of the class struggle as the only means of alleviating the problem of mass unemployment.[14]

The real impetus acquired by the National Unemployed Workers' Movement was, however, a direct result of Labour's betrayal of the unemployed in 1929. In 1929 the Labour Party fought the general election on 'the doctrine of Work or Adequate Maintenance'. But just as James Maxton fought the battle to defend the rights of the unemployed during the period of the second 'minority' Labour Government, so did Margaret Bondfield play a major role in the Cabinet in betraying the interests of the unemployed. Furthermore, at the same time as Bondfield wanted working-class men to reduce unemployment by becoming domestic servants to the rich, so she helped J. Ramsay MacDonald to abandon unemployed men and women to a policy demanded by the bankers. The betrayal of the English unemployed began, according to John Scanlon, 'in the early part of Labour's first session as the Government of the nation' in 1929. In focusing on the role played by Bondfield and MacDonald, Scanlon said: 'At the end of two years' betrayal, it has to be recorded that none was so flagrant as the betrayal of the unemployed.'[15]

On 1 April 1930 the Boards of Guardians had ceased to exist; and the administration of the Poor Law passed into the hands of local government bodies. From now on parish relief was called public assistance; and the unemployed were henceforth given money instead of food tickets. Although the first national hunger march had been organised in 1922, it was not until the betrayal of the unemployed by the second 'minority' Labour Government that protests against mass unemployment were given a fresh impetus. Wal Hannington explained the background to the emergence of the struggles of the unemployed in the 1930s when he wrote: 'One of the burning questions amongst the unemployed when the 1929 Labour Government came in was that of mass disqualification of claimants at Labour Exchanges by the "not genuinely seeking work" clause.'[16]

II

The betrayal of the English unemployed by the second minority Labour Government in 1929 – a process culminating in the formation of J. Ramsay MacDonald's 'National' Government in 1931 – led to greater economic measures, repression and intense prolonged poverty for large numbers of workers and their families. Although it soon resulted in the hated 'means test' in 1934, the receipt of public assistance did not acquire the same stigma that had been inseparable from poor relief from the Board of Guardians before 1914. A consequence of the Unemployment Act 1934, the means test stimulated 'increased restlessness, mass demonstrations and conflict with the police'.[17]

The means test was first applied during the early months of 1935, and thousands of workers soon felt the axe. The means test was administered by the Public Assistance Board. Although the Unemployment Act 1934 was dictated to some extent by the world economic crisis provoked by the Wall Street Crash of 1929, it was also a vindictive response to the radicalisation of the English working class produced by the war. As W.T. Colyer put it: 'The Act of 1934 may be described as the legislative reaction of the "National" government to the challenge of opposition in the country.'[18]

Through a variety of means successive governments in the 1930s attempted to cow and intimidate the militant marches of the unemployed. In their introduction to *Memoirs of the Unemployed*, H.L. Beales and R.S. Lambert focused on the various responses of individual workers to the social problem of unemployment. Certainly, they supported the findings of other investigators in their establishment of the direct relationship between unemployment and the marked increase in crime. In discussing the varied responses of men and women who had had unemployment imposed on them, they said: 'Those whose interests are political will find it illuminating to collect the reflections made by these unemployed men and women on politics, or trade unions and similar bodies. They will observe the variations between disillusionment, indifference, and anger that holds a revolutionary impulse in its scope.'[19]

Perhaps the most important conclusion to emerge from *Memoirs of the Unemployed* was, however, the discovery of the extent of an independent, autonomous working class. As H.L. Beales and R.S. Lambert put it:

These *Memoirs* describe the experiences of twenty-five individuals of different age, sex, abode, occupation, and social position; and analysis reveals that these experiences have certain features in common. First of all, in the 'fed up with doing nothing' feeling. Apparently, a number of well-intentioned people heard of this, and various schemes were started to remedy it. The majority, I believe, cannot be said to have been well supported, partly because numbers of the unemployed, having been deceived on previous occasions by politicians' promises, have regarded such schemes with suspicion, some roundly asserting that gymnasiums, for instance, have only been opened to ensure the fitness of the unemployed, should they be required later on.

Furthermore, the state was no longer 'an unreal and remote abstraction' to the unemployed.[20]

The working class, and particularly the unemployed, remained very suspicious of the motives of any legislative attempts to alleviate poverty. In attacking the Government for setting up gymnasiums and social service centres, the Left did not have any problem in attracting working-class sympathy. There was no longer such a wide gulf between the labour movement and the unorganised workers, though many workers remained passive in a direct political sense. Although the Cardiff branch of the National Council of Labour Colleges supported the holiday movement inaugurated by students of British universities for the provision of holidays for unemployed workers from the Distressed Areas, the Left was usually hostile to such schemes. And so were many working-class men and women.[21]

In depicting the impact of mass unemployment in the 1930s, C.L. Mowat said: 'Industrial Lancashire was at a standstill, though not officially classified as a special area. In Wigan one man in three was on the dole. The mining villages of County Durham, the steelworks and shipyards of Tyne and Tees were derelict: Gateshead, Hebburn, Jarrow, Wallsend, Brook.' Mass unemployment radicalised many of the middle class, and this 'aroused social conscience which had been sluggish in the more hopeful twenties', according to Mowat, gave the last few years before the outbreak of the Second World War a sharp 'political intensity'. More than anything else, the Left Book Club exposed the human consequences of mass unemployment and the English workers' resilience and resistance in George Orwell's *Road to Wigan Pier* and in Ellen Wilkinson's *The Town that was Murdered*.[22]

In emphasising the fatalism induced by mass unemployment, C.L. Mowat played down the workers' resistance by focusing on the encouragement given to 'the tattle-tale and the informer, the writer of anonymous letters and the local blackmailer'. Although mass unemployment in the 1930s coincided with the escapism provided by the cinema and the growth of the pools and other forms of betting, unemployment created a bitterness and a hatred which could only be contained by state repression on many memorable occasions.

In the essay that he contributed to Jack Common's book, *Seven Shifts*, Will Oxley described one such occasion:

> Women with children in arms and in perambulators, aged parents, working-men who had no political shirt, turned out to parade their disgust at this [means test]. . . . I marvelled at them. The procession was of such huge dimension that it took three-quarters of an hour to pass a given point. Owing to factors which I could never understand there was a conflict with the police, in which batons were drawn. What followed was just hell.[23]

One Labour MP described the changes in workers' attitudes when he told A.M. Cameron, the author of *Civilisation and the Unemployed*: 'Twenty years ago a worker leaving work on Saturday midday would drop into a public-house and stand there in his dirty clothes swilling drink till late in the afternoon when he went home and subsided into a torpid slumber. Nowadays he races home, washes, shaves and changes into smart clothes and takes his wife and children to the cinema, or for a walk or a bus-ride.' Furthermore, English workers, whether employed or unemployed, were very interested in the serious radio programmes. In commenting on the higher cultural level of the workers, A.M. Cameron said that 'for those who remember the majority of the workers thirty or fifty years ago with their contented ignorance, superstition and prejudice, the change must seem a miracle'. Nevertheless, the social world of working-class England was still an 'unknown country' to most middle-class investigators and social workers. And Cameron, though hostile to the Left, admitted that the workers were suspicious of the 'unemployed clubs' set up by the authorities.[24]

Although many English communities were very prosperous in the 1930s even before the rearmament programme reduced unemployment, the better-off areas did not always escape the consequences of Government cuts in health and other social expenditure. In the study entitled *Metropolitan Man* published in 1937, Robert Sinclair chronicled the neglect of the health of the middle as well as of the working class in London. The Royal Northern Hospital had had, as he put it, 43 beds closed for three years in spite of a long waiting list. In summing up the adverse consequences of Government policy for the middle class, he said: 'The pay-beds in London hospitals, in which the "middle class" may receive the best institutional treatment for a limited number of guineas a week, number fewer than 2,000 out of those 57,000. Yet the proportions of "poor" and "middle class" potential patients are not in the ratio of twenty-eight to one; according to King Edward's Fund, which ministers to a hundred and forty-five hospitals, the ratio is about three to one. The middle classes have either to masquerade as the rich and get into debt or masquerade as the poor and get into hospital.'[25]

But the problem facing the middle class dwarfed into insignificance alongside the experience of the unemployed working class. When he spoke about the impact of mass unemployment on Stockton-on-Tees, J.B. Priestley said: 'It is like a theatre that is kept open merely for the sale of drinks in the bars and chocolates in the corridors.' He also ignored the unemployed workers' resistance to unemployment when he said: 'They have no sense whatever of waste and tragedy in themselves . . . they lived below the level of worry.'[26] Yet the unemployed protested again and again against the indignities of mass unemployment whenever opportunities presented themselves. And although the annual conference of the Trades Union Congress repeatedly refused to receive deputations from the National Unemployed Workers' Movement, the English intelligentsia was radicalised, though often sidetracked by the communists' Popular Front policy, by the spectre of mass unemployment more than any other factor. Thus in 1936 Clement Attlee, who was to become the Prime Minister in the 'majority' Labour Government in 1945, addressed a mass meeting in support of the hunger march in London.[27]

Moreover, the 1930s were characterised by resistance to evictions by greedy landlords who pushed up the rents of unemployed workers. Although resistance to evictions existed throughout England, it was particularly extensive and widespread in London. One reason for the often successful resistance against landlords in London was the support provided by the Cooperative movement as well as by Tenants' defence leagues. Even in Bristol – a city depicted by the leaders of the Trades Union Congress as free of left-wing influence – the unemployed were involved in bitter and bloody conflict with the police.[28]

III

Although the hunger marches throughout the interwar period were important in stimulating and sustaining public sympathy for the unemployed, they did not create it. Such working-class sympathy for the unemployed and their families was a by-product of the new workers' culture and attitudes engendered by the First World War. Despite the demoralising impact of prolonged unemployment on men and women, the unemployed were always potentially militant and their latent militancy quickly 'exploded' when conditions changed. In observing this trend in England in the early post-war period, Fenner Brockway said that rank-and-file workers were not 'so spiritless' as the official Labour leadership. Thus he noted that 'as soon as the trade depression began to pass, strikes broke out, and as the economic recovery proceded they grew in number'.[29]

The important studies by H.L. Beales and R.S. Lambert, Robert Sinclair, A.M. Cameron and E. Wight Bakke overlooked the unemployed workers' potential militancy by focusing on their temporary transition from 'optimism to fatalism'. Even the long-term unemployed, and particularly the women in the 1930s, were capable of engaging in strikes once new employment opportunities were provided by an expanding British economy at various moments during the interwar period. What happened in 1931, though traumatic, kept many working people hostile to the establishment social order.

Despite the electoral débâcle in 1931, many rank-and-file workers developed a belief that the Labour Party had been in the phrase of the American historian, Adam B. Ulam, 'cheated out of office and to have had its leaders kidnapped by the other side'. In any case, an increasing number of workers, including many of the unemployed, believed that the Labour Party would have stood by the English working class if it had been able to form a 'majority' Labour Government. In *The Unemployed Man* published in 1933, E. Wight Bakke noted that: 'Some still supported the Labour Party on the theory that "it never had a chance". Give it a clear majority, they thought, and the result would be different. The number who held this view were not very vocal in meetings. From the views expressed in private conversations, however, I should judge the number to be very large, particularly among the skilled workers.'[30]

Moreover, the Labour-controlled local authorities in the 1920s and 1930s often displayed fierce opposition to successive governments' measures for dealing with the unemployed. But although the example set by the West Ham and Poplar Councils in defending the rights of the unemployed caught the sympathy and imagination of popular opinion, the Parliamentary Labour leaders did not support them. Nevertheless the labour movement in the localities throughout the interwar period became increasingly aggressive and defiant of national governments. In discussing the response of Labour-controlled councils when the hated means test was introduced, W.T. Colyer said:

> Some, like the County Council of Durham, decided to refuse to do so, and subsequent local elections have shown that in their refusal they had the support of an overwhelming majority of the workers. In other areas, attempts were made to 'carry on' in the belief that a socialist authority could stand between the unemployed and the worst excesses of brutality which Government commissioners might be expected to impose. Here also, in the conditions prevailing at the time, socialist electors have accepted the judgment of their public representatives.[31]

Although the National Unemployed Workers' Movement agitated for the unemployed in the 1920s, it did not really come into its own until the introduction of the means test. It was increasingly successful because of the English workers' hostility to the existence of mass unemployment.

By 1919 workers were refusing to accept the stigma which had been attached to unemployment before the outbreak of the First World War. When the Lady Mayoress of Southport opened the annual conference of the Trades Union Congress in 1922, she said: 'Why all this unrest? What ails the workers? It seems that, in the rebound from the anxieties of the war, we are all trying to get something for nothing. Too much selfishness exists; that is the result of all the evil. We must not ask for the impossible.' The ferocity of the outcry against these right-wing sentiments was only one indication of changed and changing workers' attitudes to the problem of unemployment. By the early 1930s such right-wing sentiments were less frequently expressed in public; and there was a growth of middle-class sympathy for the plight of unemployed men and women.[32]

By exposing the social consequences of mass unemployment, the Independent Labour Party, the Communist Party, the Socialist League, the National Council of Labour Colleges and the Trades Union Congress all contributed to the creation of a more sympathetic climate of opinion amongst the English middle class than would have been conceivable before 1914. Medical officers, schoolmasters and social workers drew attention to 'the serious physical deterioration in the health standards' of the working people from 1931 onwards. Although their colleagues had already done so in the 1920s, the problems did not really assume alarming proportions until the introduction of the means test.

As a result of the hunger marches in the 1930s, the National Council of Social Services was founded to organise social life amongst the unemployed. The Prince of Wales spoke about the advantages of the social service centres as agencies 'to save the unemployed from demoralisation'. Wal Hannington and the National Unemployed Workers' Movement campaigned against these centres because they did not merely represent 'an effort to keep the unemployed quiet, but [were] also a clever move to prepare the way for a system of unpaid labour amongst the unemployed'. Outside the Left altogether, however, unemployed workers kept aloof from the the social service centres because they belonged to an alien culture.[33]

As English workers' culture merged with the oppositional left-wing movements in the early interwar period, it was clear that the recasting of bourgeois England had not cowed the potential militancy of the producers of wealth. Without ignoring the communities in which many working-class men and women were apathetic, there is a mass of evidence to document other workers' resistance to injustice, unfairness and massive inequality. In describing the contradictions and the 'dialectic' of workers' passivity and resistance within working-class communities throughout the world, Herbert G. Gutman wrote with sensitivity and perception when he observed that:

> Most of the time subordinate populations live with their exploitation. . . . Then, under certain conditions – none of them predictable – the acceptance is transformed into opposition. Chicago in the 1880s, St. Petersburg in 1905, Gdansk in the 1970s.[34]

Conclusion

The dominant motif in most historical studies of the English working class is its total subservience to the hegemony of capitalist society. With its alleged alienation from rather than hostility towards official society, the English working class with its own activities and its 'Labourist' philosophy is seen as projecting a merely negative attitude to official ideas and values. In the dominant historiography, whether of the Right or the Left, the English working class is always portrayed as a subordinate class permeated with bourgeois ideas and values. Consequently, English working-class resistance to unemployment, deskilling and authoritarian education is depicted as marginal, economistic or a backward-looking, instinctive rejection of modernity.[1]

The major reason for portraying the English working class as inherently tradition-bound, backward-looking, socially conservative and anti-socialist is a conceptual one. Because the labour process and social struggles within the wider society are so often ignored, it is usually inferred that socialism deserves no more than a footnote in the history of English labour. Instead of focusing on the historical moments when the English working class developed a fundamental challenge to class rule, the emphasis is always on the lack of English working-class resistance and dissent. By arguing in the tradition of Karl Kautsky and Vladimir Lenin that socialist ideas and sentiments could not be developed by working men and women without the intervention of socialist intellectuals, most labour historians have focused on English workers' conservative traditionalism.

In the actual history of the English working class between 1883 and 1939, resistance to *changing* bourgeois mores and values was persistent and sustained. Despite the English workers' sustained resistance to unemployment, deskilling, authoritarianism in the schools, factories and the wider society, most labour historians have focused on the workers' alleged passivity, apathy and subordination.

Moreover, while American labour historians have increasingly questioned the elitist assumptions of traditional labour historians, this important development has found little echo amongst their English counterparts.[2]

Because English labour historiography has continued to adhere to traditional assumptions in both their Liberal and Leninist forms, working-class resistance to capitalism has been largely ignored. During the period between 1883 and 1939 most socialist activists' barometers for registering social tensions were restricted to Parliamentary elections and institutional conflict. Outside these institutionalised conflicts, social tensions were expressed in a variety of ways socialists had not envisaged. Rather than questioning the assumptions and evaluations of socialists who were active in those years, most labour historians have echoed the elitist views of such socialists as H.M. Hyndman.

By focusing on the conservative traditionalism rather than the anti-capitalist sentiments of English men and women, the memory of socialism in English history has been almost exorcised from contemporary consciousness. This view is expressed by Victor Kiernan: 'But whatever the defects of leadership or programme, it would seem that *socialist consciousness* has always been restricted to a *very few*, and that the bulk of the working class (as of every other, it may be) is inert except when activated by some direct material stimulus. This in turn would imply that most collective conduct is "behaviouristic", and most of history mechanically determined, with little room for dialectical subtlety of combination and change except at corners and fringes.'[3] In spite of his immense learning and erudition, Kiernan's devaluation of the role of socialism in English history is determined by a failure to look at what was happening in the wider society.

In insisting on the alleged insignificance of English socialism, Kiernan reflects the epistemology of traditional labour historiography. But although his conceptualisation of English working-class history is shaped by certain philosophical assumptions, it can only be sustained by ignoring the labour processes and the wider social struggles in English history. Before looking at the relationship between the labour process and the growth of socialist sentiments, it is worthwhile quoting what Dale Tomich and Anson Rabibach have to say about traditional labour historiography: 'As an epistemology, traditional labour history was characterised by a restrictive definition of socialism as leaders, parties and ideologies, which ignored social and cultural experiences and reduced history to an expression of power.'[4] In breaking out of this traditional historiography and in focusing on English workers' anti-capitalist resistance, Richard Price argues that:

> The thing to be explained, of course, is the failure of those traditions to translate into a coherent political presence. I do not think it correct to explain this in terms of their marginality, economicism or predominance of subordination, not only because the struggle over the labour process can generate a shifting political consciousness, but also for two other reasons. In the first place, in the informal behaviour of labour, one can detect certain themes that do suggest pre-figurative, alternative systems of authority and hierarchy and which occasionally receive quasi-ideological expression. Such themes as rank-and-file control over negotiations, opposition to the priorities and tendencies of bureaucratised union policies, and suspicion of unrecalled leaders, suggest the roots of a decidedly un-Leninist ideology and action. In the second place, the hegemony of official Labour Party socialism has never been unproblematic; it has constantly been challenged by alternative policies which lie closest to the logic of labour action than do many official policies. Stephen Yeo's religion of socialism represents the first such challenge; Bennism the latest.[5]

Moreover, there is an innate relationship between the English socialist intelligentsia's elitist contempt for working men and women and the lack of an adequate historiography of the working-class politics of anti-capitalist resistance. Richard Price touches on this problem when he argues that 'The inability to force a space within the dominant themes of national culture is illustrated by the failure of the discussion of syndicalism, guild socialism or workers' control, that bracketed the First World War, to throw up any major theorist.'[6] By exaggerating the influence of bourgeois ideas in English working-class communities, the dominant leadership of the Social Democratic Federation (SDF), the Fabians and the Independent Labour Party (ILP) preferred to ignore the concrete evidence of the anti-capitalist struggles of English working men, women and children.[7]

In looking at the actual functioning of the dominant educated elites within the labour movement and their hostile attitude to the spontaneous self-activity of working people, it is clear that H.M. Hyndman, Ernest Belford Bax, J. Hunter Watts, Harry Quelch and Herbert Burrows were out of touch with the culture, values and sentiments of the 'uneducated' dissidents. But if they were out of touch with the English workers, it was because they were often contemptuous of them. Instead of attempting to canalise the strong class feelings of the sort expressed by miners' poaching, schoolchildren's strikes and resistance to deskilling and unemployment, the dominant socialist intelligentsia were either hostile or indifferent.[8]

In most accounts of the history of the English working class, there is no account of working-class activity outside of the factories, coal mines and shipyards.[9] Because of the restricted definition of socialism as consisting solely of leaders, parties and ideologies, it is usually assumed that socialist consciousness was confined to a few working men and women. Far from the evidence of the anti-capitalist sentiments against state interference being seen as something positive, it is dismissed. Workers' opposition to the Liberals' social welfare legislation has been described as a 'rearguard action, or burying heads in the sand, or clinging to a bad old past'.[10] This serious conceptual problem is rooted in traditional labour historiography; and it inhibits an understanding of the widespread class resentment of the state.

In looking at English working-class community life, it is clear that the social and emotional needs of working men, women and children were satisfied within their own circles without much help from the state. As a result of massive state intervention in workers' lives between 1906 and 1914, working-class resentment against interference with old habits and private life, dislike of the compulsory medical inspection of schoolchildren, exclusion of children from pubs and the intensification of the hatred of the police and temperence reformers led to widespread riots and outbursts of violence. Although the riots against the Liberals' social welfare legislation preceded the labour unrest which erupted in 1910, the two agitations merged and gave a new edge to anti-capitalist sentiments.

The English workers' hatred of the state preceded their agitation against the Liberals' legislation. But the workers' agitation against interventionalist social welfare legislation was soon accompanied by a concerted resistance to the new attempts to discipline the labour force through the creation of Labour Exchanges and national insurance schemes. Although a general working-class hatred of the state's representatives antedated the spate of social welfare legislation, the coalesence of the workers' resentment against interference in their social lives with the labour unrest produced a new anti-capitalist outlook. Whilst this, together with a challenge to bourgeois cultural hegemony, was evident in the 'new unionism' which emerged in the 1880s, it attracted much greater support during the decade before the outbreak of the First World War.

There were persistent anti-capitalist sentiments expressed in the factories, coal mines and shipyards as well as in the wider society outside. This was seen, for example, in the spontaneous strikes of the children in the state schools against brutality, authoritarian teachers and indoctrination. But although there were repeated children's strikes in England from 1883 onwards, they did not articulate distinctive socialist demands until the children's strikes of 1911.[11] With their elitist assumptions about what motivated the protests of the workers' children in the state schools, the spokespersons for the middle class attributed the children's strikes to copycatting. As Arnold Freeman put it: 'It has been conjectured that the "school-boys' strikes" of 1911 were directly caused by the exhibition of films of the strike-scenes in the various parts of the country.'[12] But the socialists' demands for democratising the state schools probably followed rather than preceded the demands of the children. In a children's strike in 1913, for example, the strikers in one city put forward a comprehensive programme of demands: 'Shorter school hours, a half-holiday on Wednesday in addition to the Saturday half-holiday, school books to be supplied free, the abolition of corporal punishment, and no writing on copybooks made by any firm involved in trade disputes.'[13] A small section of the British Socialist Party began to agitate for a similar programme in 1914.[14]

In arguing that the English workers articulated a hatred of capitalism as well as of elementary reforms like compulsory medical inspection of schoolchildren and compulsory national insurance, I shall be criticised for trying to combine mutually exclusive approaches. Just as the dominant socialist intelligentsia in the SDF rejected the possibility of socialism from below (as distinct from socialism from above), so many labour historians will argue that even a socialist government would have been compelled to impose the same reforms on a recalcitrant working class. However, the English workers were not so much opposed to reforms as suspicious of the motives of those who were attempting to impose them. As Jeremy Seabrook has argued: 'It is not that they object to the principle of State pensions for doctrinaire reasons. They simply fear that if they accept the allowance some secret and undisclosed obligation may later be made known, some unacceptable condition come to light.'[15]

English workers' culture was inimical to the acquisitive individualism of capitalist society. A prominent aspect of the culture of the English working class was its network of mutual aid. To prevent men and women from being buried in a dreaded pauper's grave, '"friendly leads" (or street collections) were organised to defray the costs of a funeral' were organised in many working-class communities.[16] Jack Metzga's description of Johnstown, a contemporary American working-class community, could be an accurate description of a typical English working-class community between 1883 and 1914:

> It's when one's needs are completely satisfied within this circle that one is most happy. Conversely, having to seek help or guidance from the church or State (or even doctors and hospitals) gives people a sense of losing control of their lives. Even the trade union is viewed as a foreign entity: a particular grievance man or a friend in a union office is drawn

upon as an individual, not as a representative of a class institution. This is not individualism (though often working people themselves describe it as such), but a nearly absolute reliance on those people one knows in a daily face-to-face context and a nearly total distrust of institutions. In such a culture, a working-class person really trusts only that which is somehow provided though the extended network of family and friends: working-class people will oblige themselves among peers where possible, rather than submit themselves to impersonal mechanisms, whether bureaucracies or the cash nexus, which are dominated by other classes.[17]

In pre-1914 working-class England the suspicion of doctors and hospitals was a *class* suspicion of the 'other class'.[18]

In sketching a picture of English 'workers' notions about all such things beyond the narrow horizons of daily life' as 'hazy and unstable', Victor Kiernan sees little except a conservative traditionalism.[19] Standish Meacham, a more right-wing labour historian, argues that the English working class did not display any evidence of class consciousness between 1890 and 1914: 'Confused by the challenge to traditions they had relied upon, working-class men and women were not at all sure what to do. Some contented themselves with doing little or nothing. Those who did something did many apparently contradictory things at once; they sent unions their dues and resisted their union's leadership; they hid from the State while collecting its pensions; they voted Labour and agreed that Labour accomplished nothing.'[20] In their shared condescension towards the English working class, Kiernan and Meacham deny working men and women any consciousness of their own as distinct from a 'behaviouristic' response to the accumulation of capital.

In the face of foreign competition and the serious social problems revealed by socialist propaganda, English capitalism was undergoing important changes. Some working men and women were cowed and intimidated. But because many working men and women were not simply automata, they resisted changes in the labour process and the state's response to working-class rebellion. In doing so, they often displayed a socialist consciousness – but one not institutionalised or codified. Instead of trying to identify the rhyme and reason in these changing working-class responses, Standish Meacham focuses on what he depicts as an almost mindless traditional-ism. In the reality of working-class life consciousness was more evident than mindlessness.

With sudden leaps, somersaults, dramatic leaps and re-verses, consciousness was at the centre of the dynamic of English working-class history. In recovering the hidden history of the cultural class struggle as a part of the relative autonomy of social change, it is useful to focus on the labour process. As Richard Price has explained:

> The new machines and methods, the resultant unemployment or de-skilling were not seen from a narrow economist perspective, but as interconnected forces that portended untrammelled subordination. The sense of being faced with larger forces than traditional union action could control was, of course, reinforced by the participation of the unions themselves in the agencies of subordination. Thus the reluctance of official unionism to abandon procedures led through rank-and-file militancy to political questions: 'What could arbitration do about the ever-increasing number of men displace by machinery?', asked a London shoemaker in 1895. 'He repeated that their only hope lay in the direction of getting control of the industries themselves'. Precisely the same connections were to play a critical role in the radicalisation of the railwaymen ten years later.
>
> The point is that these kind of issues opened the space into which socialism could enter as a means of comprehending what was going on and to become a vocabulary of change. This was true incidentally throughout the whole period until the early 1920s: the emergent quasi-corporatist relationship between labour, the State and industry in the pre-1914 period. . . . But in the 1890s socialist sentiments developed most strongly in those trades where control over the labour process was sharpest – as a glance at the early affiliations to the Labour Representa-tion Committee reveal.[21]

But in a few working-class communities such as Norwich where trade unionism was relatively weak, socialism was 'powerful enough to return one of the two members in the Parliamentary representation of the city'.[22]

What was critical in the growth of the 'new unionism' of the unprivileged in the period between 1883 and 1914 was the existence of autonomous agencies of mutual aid. But although the 'new unionism' ultimately eschewed the friendly benefit activities of the 'old unions', the pressures exerted by capitalist society soon forced them to adopt the self-help approach of the 'old unions'. In the labour unrest before the First World War, many trade unions reverted to the socialist approach of the 1880s. As C.M. Lloyd explained: 'The revolt against the excessive friendly activities of the older unions began with the "new unionism" of the 1880s, and there is a growing aversion today among the more militant section from what is called "the glorified goose and coffin club" idea.'[23] Moreover, a trade union official complained that 'there is a growing feeling that all that is necessary is to go on strike and the workers can have anything they ask for, and if only the trade union officers would get out of the way the workers would do things'.[24]

Underneath the official Labourist definition of socialism, many English workers developed a discernible socialist counter-culture. Within English Labourism there was a constant tension between official 'socialism' and the counter-culture of many rank-and-file workers. But official Labourism could only function as an agency for incorporating workers into the existing social order by adopting a militant socialist rhetoric. As an ILP trade union official wrote in 1893: 'The battle cry of the future must be, not Liberalism v. Toryism, but Labourism v. Capitalism'.[25] In identifying the tensions within the labour movement after 1900, Joseph Clayton argued: 'By placing in positions of responsibility and authority an increasing number of the ablest working-class leaders, the army of revolutionary insurrection found its advocates diminished. The very electoral successes of the ILP dampened down the fires of socialism.'[26] But in the labour unrest between 1906 and 1914 the fires of socialism were rekindled.

Karl Marx and Frederick Engels always repudiated the view that socialism could only come to the working class from the outside. Even when the English working class was 'a class in itself' rather than 'a class for itself', they could perceive what they described as its 'unconscious socialism'. In a comment on the May Day celebrations in London in 1890, Engels wrote about 'the English proletariat, newly awakened from its forty-year sleep'. In a new preface to *The Condition of the Working Class in England in 1844* written and published in 1892, Engels returned to the theme of 'unconscious socialism':

Needless to say that today there is indeed 'Socialism again in England', and plenty of it – socialism of all shades: socialism conscious and unconscious, socialism prosaic and poetic: socialism of the working class and socialism of the middle class. . .. At the same time, we have no reason to grumble at the symptom itself.[27]

The most concrete evidence of this 'unconscious socialism' was the development of the 'new unionism'. Engels summed up thus: 'The "new unions" were founded at a time when the faith in the eternity of the wages system was severely shaken; their founders and the supporters were socialists either consciously or by feeling; the masses were entirely free from the inherited "respectable" bourgeois prejudices which hampered the brains of the better situated "old" unionists.'[28]

The classical Marxist concept of 'unconscious' working-class socialism was inimical to Lenin's notion of the role of the 'vanguard' socialist party. Without underestimating the role of socialist parties and organisations in diffusing enlightenment about the nature of exploitation and mystification in capitalist society, Marx and Engels did not believe that socialist consciousness could come to working people from 'without'. In a direct reference to the English working class in the late nineteenth century, Engels wrote: 'Now without noticing it themselves, they are approaching the theoretically right track; they drift into it, and the movement is so strong that I believe it will survive the inevitable blunders and their consequences.'[29]

Although the major phases of conscious, articulate English working-class socialism during the years between 1883 and 1939 were episodic, they nevertheless left a permanent imprint on the workers' consciousness. When the space was opened up at particular historical moments before being stifled by the apparatus of official Labourism, the 'unconscious socialism' of working men and women was transformed into conscious, articulate socialism. An important moment in the conscious socialism of English working people coincided with the advent of the 'new unionism'. Another such moment was seen during the general strike in 1926.

By the mid-1890s the leaders of the 'new unions' were attempting to impose friendly benefits and temperance on their members. This was one of the contributory factors in the decline of union membership. The insistence on temperance in the ILP branches and branches of the 'new unions' integrated some workers into the existing social order and alienated other workers from the labour movement.[30] The mass of the unskilled workers in most working-class communities were hostile to temperance propaganda.[31] In some chemical works and factories unskilled workers needed drink to tolerate the harsh conditions of their employment. In summing up the attitudes of workers in chemical works and factories who were victimised for joining trade unions anyway, R.H. Sherard spoke for the voiceless: 'Let the temperance reformers legislate against the things which make for drunkenness, and do away with the factories where as Dr. Bellew of St. Helens said, "the men cannot work unless they are half-drunk".'[32]

In the periods when official Labourism attempted to stifle the 'unconscious socialism' of English working men and women, there was a constant cultural class struggle waged by the voiceless. In the agricultural communities the farm labourers described the gentry, farmers, the local doctors, corn merchants and the schoolmasters as 'Them as ought to know'. The poor in the great cities including 'many of the most superior' expressed their dislike of 'inspectors, foremen, etc.',[33] and in the communities where the London dockers lived there was 'an unconquerable hatred of government'.[34] When the space opened up for unskilled and semi-skilled workers to identify with socialism from below, the 'underground' cultural class struggle erupted. During the labour unrest between 1910 and 1914, this cultural class struggle merged with conscious socialist sentiments. In contrast to the periods when official Labourism allowed the employers to prevent trade union members from wearing union buttons at work, a number of strikes flared up during the labour unrest over the issue of union buttons.

It is also somewhat ironic to observe the differing attitudes of working men and women and the middle-class socialists within the educated elite of the SDF.[35] As Eduard Bernstein explained: 'A large percentage of English working-class socialists are total abstainers, while the majority of middle-class socialists do not despise the delights of beer, wine or whisky.'[36] Temperance advocacy was very unpopular in working men's clubs;[37] and the ILP 'gathered its converts not from people who used the public-house as a club'.[38] But though working-class responses to socialists who advocated temperance were often hostile, some trade unionists were alienated because they had to 'attend meetings in pubs'.[39] In 1904 the Labour Party's programme on temperance included a proposal to reduce the number of pubs in England. This alienated many workers from the labour movement. In discussing this problem, Edward Parry wrote: 'Labour leaders short-sightedly favour the puritans' views. Certainly, our public-houses being what they are, it is choice of evils to keep out of them.'[40]

During the historical phases of 'unconscious socialism', many of the voiceless adhered to anti-capitalist attitudes. There was a dialectical relationship between the moments of apparent quiescence and the moments of open class struggle. In his essay on 'Rethinking Labour History', Richard Price shows that open class struggle could not 'explode' without the existence of an oppositional working-class culture:

> To understand this it is necessary to appreciate that resistance and subordination are neither mutually exclusive, nor autonomously separable from the other. Within working-class culture as a whole, there is a constant and uneasy tension between acquiescence and dissent. At different times and within different levels of experience, one may predominate over another, but both are constantly present not as a predetermined, static relationship, but as a constantly changing and shifting dynamic.[41]

The phases of comparative acquiescence and apparent subordination contained social tensions which were managed by official Labourism.

The decade between 1885 and 1895 was marked by the merging of the 'unconscious' working-class socialism with the socialism of a militant middle-class intelligentsia. As Stephen Yeo has argued:

> For a time there was a convergence between important parts of middle-class social consciousness and important parts of working-class social consciousness. One point of intersection (blurred though it was), was

'socialism'. This produced a distinctive phase in the history of the idea of socialism, a phase of revolutionary evangelicalism – a temper which was not just the aberration of a few eccentrics who had not yet 'matured' enough to divest themselves of religious language, but which is central to an understanding of those who called themselves socialists c.1885–1895'.[42]

During such moments in the history of English socialism some of the hitherto passive elements of the working class were drawn into the class struggle.[43] Although the police were recruited from 'the ultra-conformist section of the working class' and broke up trade union and socialist meetings, they were also influenced by socialist agitation in the early 1890s. For example, in London the police came out on strike with the dockers, postmen and the soldiers.[44]

But although the socialist intelligentsia between 1883 and 1939 were often very conservative in their day-to-day practice, socialism did make an enormous impact on English society whenever a genuine, though unrepresentative, socialist intelligentsia merged with spontaneous working-class revolt against capitalist social values. There were three such phases when authentic middle-class socialist intellectuals came together with the spontaneous struggles of working-class militants: first, there was the phase between 1885 and 1895 identified and discussed by Stephen Yeo; secondly, there was the phase between 1906 and 1914; and thirdly, there was the phase between 1917 and 1926.

Moreover, the socialist intelligentsia were not always allowed to play a conservative role by trying to integrate the workers into the existing social order. At various phases in the social history of socialism, the socialist intelligentsia were sometimes able to merge with spontaneous working-class militancy. For example, workers' spontaneous feelings between 1906 and 1914 merged with a new anti-capitalist critique. Before looking at the latter phases in the social history of the socialist idea, it is worth considering Stephen Yeo's 'revisionist' comments on what happened between 1885 and 1895.

In this critical decade official Labourism was struggling to create a 'machine' for imposing its dominance over the English working class. As Stephen Yeo puts it:

> Socialism in that period had not yet become the prisoner of a particular, elaborate party machine – a machine which would come to associate its own well-being with the prospects for socialism. One of the most important (and unwritten) parts of the history of the mid-1890s is precisely the shaping of the ILP into such a machine against much resistance from below . . . it was financially difficult to keep typical 1885–1895 associations going and the difficulty pervades the records, but the difficulty took a little time to warp the associations themselves. . . . Furthermore, socialism had not yet been faced with a distorted reflection of itself in the mirror of 'social politics' and welfare legislation, and a rapidly enlarging State. Nor had it become the ideology of administrative and academic engineers; socialism had not yet become confused with the superior understanding of the experts of what the working class 'needed'.[45]

In opposing the superior understanding of the experts, English working men and women were preserving their own 'socialism'. Through its 'unconscious socialism', the working class constituted a barrier in the path of the encroaching 'Servile State'.

During the ten years before 1895, official Labourism was already crystallising. In the years between 1895 and 1906, the 'unconscious socialism' of the English working class was again struggling to free itself from official Labourism. What made the articulation of 'unconscious' into conscious socialism a possibility after 1895 was the survival and appearance of new socialist intellectuals who refused to be drawn into the electoral machinery of official Labourism or the quiescence of the SDF. In discussing the important role of one such English socialist intellectual, Sheila Rowbotham has written:

> In the changed context of the 1900s Edward Carpenter became estranged from old friends like Bruce Glasier who had become preoccupied with the beginnings of a labour Parliamentary machine. His political sympathies went towards new movements at odds with this Parliamentary Labourism. The militancy of the Syndicalists and the Suffragettes awakened memories of the 1880s more than any Parliamentary manoeuvring. He was excited by Victor Grayson's victory in the Colne Valley by-election in 1907. Grayson's moral enthusiasm, his refusal to reduce socialism to immediate tactical priorities echoed the hopes of the 1880s.[46]

Moreover, the SDF also helped to reinforce the forces of official Labourism before 1907 by criticising spontaneous working-class revolt and expressions of libertarian socialism.

With the SDF's transformation into the British Socialist Party (BSP) in 1911, it seemed that the pattern described by Stephen Yeo between 1885 and 1895 was again beginning to assert itself. Sections of what had been a hitherto conservative socialist intelligentsia were, of course, radicalised by the labour unrest. The emergence of the BSP in 1911 was a response to the spontaneous militancy of English working men and women. During the years between 1910 and 1914 most members of the ILP were critical of 'the overt electoral and Parliamentary alliance' with the Liberals. Indeed, a number of ILP branches broke away in 1911 to help form the BSP.[47] In identifying with the demands of the children involved in the school strikes, the most militant elements of the BSP (though in a minority) moved to the Left. They were not, however, typical of the socialist intelligentsia as a whole. In its most fundamental attitudes to the workers' actual struggles, the BSP shared Labourism's preoccupation with defending the status quo. As Andráe Tridon wrote in 1913:

> The BSP has watched the growth of the New Unionism with the same concern which the American Socialist Party has expressed over the development of the Industrial Workers of the World. While the British socialists have not as yet pronounced against the Syndicalist as definite a sentence of excommunication as the Americans, the executive committee of the BSP has felt called upon to define its attitude by means of a manifesto. . . . The manifesto ends by appealing to all members not to let themselves be forced into committing errors by the appeals of the direct actionists in the present critical period.[48]

Although I am identifying with the arguments of such socialist historians as Richard Price and Stephen Yeo, I am not trying to romanticise the way of life of English working people. But just as I am not attempting to romanticise workers' behaviour, so I do not want to ignore the existence of the significant minority who supported capitalist society out of deep conviction in the midst of indescribable poverty. Furthermore, working-class men who articulated a sympathy for socialist ideas could also be very unsympathetic towards their own women. Nevertheless working-class Tories were not agents of social change: the socialist workers, whether men or women, were agents of change and they initiated a process of ameliorating the harsh conditions of working-class life.

The most important changes in factory and community life before the First World War were often achieved by socialists who were not incorporated into the machinery of official Labourism. In fostering new attitudes towards birth control and the dignity of women, many of the uninstitutionalised socialists played an important role in raising the status of women. One index of this development was seen in the quite significant growth of trade unionism amongst women workers. Moreover, in the London dockers' strike in 1889, the socialists took advantage of the opportunities to address strikers' meetings by appealing to them to give up their traditional practice of beating their wives.[49] In the North of England in the early 1890s, there were two strikes conducted by the mixed trade unions against foremen who had sexually assaulted women factory workers.[50]

Moreover, working-class women played a crucial role in the labour unrest between 1910 and 1914. The strike of the women chain-makers at Cradley Heath was a landmark in the development of women's trade unionism. When they sent a deputation to the Trades Union Congress in 1910, the President, James O'Grady, gave them uncritical support.[51] In Bermondsey the national transport strike caught the imagination of the women workers in London, and every factory employing women was soon emptied.[52]

In focusing on the historical moments when sharp class conflict at the point of production merged with a socialist critique of capitalism unhindered by the electoral preoccupations of official Labourism, Richard Price argues that: 'These forces provided the vocabulary which could move into the social space opened up by the material forces pressing on labour during these years, and in doing so, of course, they ensured the predominantly Labourist definition of socialism. But it is important to note that from the very beginning there was a distinct tension between the logic of contests at the labour process and the political ideology articulated by official Labourism.'[53] But although he does not actually ignore the importance of the labour process in English working-class history, Standish Meacham focuses on workers' traditionalism: 'Evidence about the English working class before the

First World War tells us with remarkable persistence that men, women and children depended upon habit and custom to help them live their own lives. Women as they moved from house to neighbourhood; men as they geared their existence to the patterns imposed by the factories; children as they repeated and played the games others had played before them, all took comfort in the familiar and set great store by it.'[54]

In the dominant labour historiography, whether of the Right or the Left, there is no recognition of the elements of working-class socialisation which allows men, women and children to resist economic change and the role assigned to them by a triumphant capitalism. One result is that such historians either have to ignore the schoolchildren's strikes or account for their motivation in terms of copycatting. But in criticising orthodox Marxist historiography, Stanley Aronowitz argues that:

> Contrary to the reflexive model posited by orthodox Marxism in which all institutions other than the economic base merely copy the requirements of that base, the family, the school, mass culture, etc., are absolutely necessary for the production of the economic institutions. . . . The importance of the socialising institutions is that they make unnecessary the use of force, because workers in their earliest experiences find themselves at the bottom of a pyramidal structure within these institutions and come to expect all social institutions will assign to them the same position.[55]

But although Aronowitz is concerned with the history of the American working class, some of his insights are applicable to the history of the English working class.

Stanley Aronowitz argues that the roots of working-class resistance at the point of production can be seen in the socialisation of workers' children:

> Most child's play has embedded within it elements of non-hierarchical and non-authoritarian relationships. For example, the purest form in which these elements constitute the prevailing mode of the game is 'ring around a rosy'. Significantly, the circle is the most universal form of child's play, transcending cultures and social systems. The participants join hands and move in a circle, a form of sheer equality. The circle is broken when all fall down, whereupon the process is re-created in precisely the same form indefinitely. There are no winners and no losers.[56]

Although that early stage of childhood is followed by a second stage in which games become more hierarchical in structure, Aronowitz concludes: 'The distinction herein described, nevertheless, constitutes a kind of nostalgia and resistance that we shall see is never quite purged in later life from either institutional or non-institutional social relationships.'[57] Seen in this light, the English workers' anti-capitalist sentiments were much more socialistic than orthodox labour historiography has allowed for.

What helped to make the labour unrest between 1910 and 1914 so *explicitly* socialistic was the existence of an oppositionalist socialist intelligentsia. The English workers' resistance to change in the labour process was inseparable from their own 'unconscious socialism'. It also received more attention from official society than the workers did between 1896 and 1906 after the temporary 'triumph' of official Labourism. As Richard Price argues: 'For the first time since Chartism, labour process issues were concordant with a wider cultural debate which was largely concerned with the nature of liberty and freedom, the basis of authority in morals, literature and the arts and, especially, about the proper organisation of society.'[58] Although official Labourism kept its 'dominance' with the perhaps unwitting assistance of the SDF, oppositional socialism existed, too. As William Orton argued: 'Guild socialism – one of the many important contributions of the *New Age* to social history – was moving towards its place as a recognised policy from 1908 onwards. At a critical moment the reaction against Fabian collectivism was reinforced by Hilaire Belloc's brilliant attack on the "Servile State".'[59]

Because of the unprecedented militancy expressed in the labour unrest between 1910 and 1914, it is ironic that the most permanent legacy of those years should now reside in Robert Tressell's classic, *The Ragged Trousered Philanthropists*. Although David Smith insists that Tressell (or Noonan) assumed that the English working class 'must make the specific effort for their own emancipation', this is simply not true.[60] In identifying the 'two souls of socialism' in the international labour movement before the advent of Marxism, Hal Draper has made a vital distinction between socialism from below and socialism from above. *The Ragged Trousered*

Philanthropists is, in fact, permeated with the spirit of socialism from above from beginning to end.

The reason why Robert Tressell denigrates the English working class is because of an elitist commitment to socialism from above. In characteristic phrases, Tressell speaks about the workers being 'the real enemy' and 'the real oppressors'. In case there should be any misunderstanding about Tressell's superior attitude, he must be allowed to speak for himself: 'No wonder the rich despised them and looked upon them as dirt. They were despicable. They were dirt. They admitted it and gloried in it.'[61]

Despite the re-emergence of the workers' self-assertiveness and expressions of sympathy for socialism between 1917 and 1921, Robert Tressell's novel, *The Ragged Trousered Philanthropists*, continued to enjoy great popularity in the labour movement. First published in an abridged edition in 1914 and not published in full until after the Second World War, it has enjoyed an unrivalled popularity to the present day. But Tressell's popularity was fostered by a variety of socialists – and for a variety of motives – before the introduction of elitist Leninist ideas into the English labour movement. Although I focus on the reasons for the popularity of *The Ragged Trousered Philanthropists* among the English communists elsewhere, I want to stress that Tressell also provided the pre-1917 generation of elitist socialists with a validation for their world-view.

In criticising Perry Anderson and Tom Nairn for denying 'the presence of a counter-ideology amongst the working class', Richard Price insists that 'From the very moment of its inception, official Labourism has been challenged by policies and programmes that lie much closer to the self-activity of the working class.' Price also explains why there has been such a vast gap between the militant self-activity of the English workers and the comparative absence of their socialism in the dominant labour historiography: 'The logic of the Leninist position that working-class self-activity is relatively insignificant has fitted well with the dominant cultural (and institutional) traditions in Britain. . . . Conceptualising labour history requires that we move the self-activity of the working class to the centre of the stage and proceed from there, rather than arrive at that activity with a bundle of Webbian and Leninist or Labourist categories and expectations into which it is then placed and judged.'[62]

Although the social distance between working-class men and women and the labour movement was narrowed between 1910 and 1924 as a result of the 'labour unrest', it did not disappear. What happened after the First World War was a growth of the Labour leaders' tolerance for the cultural *peculiarities* of the English workers' distinctive way of life. Yet despite the narrowing of the social distance between them, the workers' cultural values remained relatively independent. But in contrast to the pre-First World War behaviour of English socialists towards the unorganised, concessions were forced upon the socialists afterwards. In 1921, for example, Shaw Desmond complained about 'one prominent Labour paper, edited and partly, I believe, controlled by a deeply religious and entirely genuine man, reduced to the straits of giving racing "selections" upon its posters.'[63]

Yet the English Labour leaders remained very puritanical in the interwar period. Although he exaggerated the point when he asserted that 'English Labour and its leaders were essentially Puritan', Egon Wertheimer was not altogether inaccurate. The mistake he made was to lump the culture of the English workers together with that of the Labour leaders who had certainly been shaped by their national 'Nonconformist prejudices'. Undoubtedly, though, 'the Labour Party in cultural questions' was 'neutral, not to say conservative'.[64]

When Margaret Bondfield was interviewed in 1924, she had become remote and somewhat isolated from the English working class. In explaining why the leaders of the Trades Union Congress and the Labour Party supported local option rather than prohibition as a means of dealing with the problems of drunkenness, she said: 'What we have got and what we have had for years in the trade union movement is a temperance fellowship – a fellowship of trade union officials who take a pledge never to take intoxicating liquors during the time they are on trade union business and not to hold meetings in public houses. That has had a good influence.'[65]

Yet in this respect at least, the English socialist leaders were copying the attitudes and behaviour of the European socialists.

Unlike the European socialists, however, the English did not adopt a distinctive attitude towards sport. In fact Egon Wertheimer lamented the failure of English socialists to recognise the class dimension in sport. As he put it: 'That sport, for instance, can be a matter of class division is an idea foreign to the average English socialist.' Furthermore, despite the closing of the social distance between English workers and Labour leaders and socialists after the First World War, it sometimes re-emerged.[66]

In the sphere of education, the majority of the unorganised working-class men and women had not been deeply influenced by the Labour leaders' new emphasis on the need for a higher level of education for working-class children. Although trade union and Labour officials became increasingly sympathetic to the education provided by the National Council of Labour Colleges and the Workers' Educational Association, the unorganised workers had less ambitious educational aspirations for their children than their American counterparts.[67]

And despite the important changes in the outlook of many English working people, social conservatism remained an obstacle in the way of the socialists' agitations. Nevertheless advances were made. With the foundation of the Teachers' Labour League in 1925, ruling-class assumptions in history books were challenged. Furthermore, in communities where Labour was the dominant political force, the observance of Empire Day was ignored.[68]

But although the English tradition was against working-class children 'going far in school unless they were unusually brilliant', workers were more sympathetic to the socialists' attempts to develop a left-wing, counter-culture.[69] Although fewer local and national newspapers were now being published, the socialists began to publish papers of their own. During the 1930s there was a growth of left-wing newspapers, and in 1936 the Left Book Club's *Left News* had 'assumed an important role and an impressive circulation'.[70]

The English working class was much less conservative with a small 'c' in the interwar period than it had been during 1883 and 1914. Yet social conservatism remained a strong feature of working-class life. In reflecting the *national* culture in which it had evolved historically, the English workers were less interested than their Continental counterparts in agitating for the co-education of both sexes and the removal of the stigma of illegitimacy. Unlike the European socialists, too, the English labour movement did not ask for any changes in 'questions of contraception, interruption of pregnancy and revision of medieval legislation on homosexuality.'[71]

Nevertheless the English workers' social outlook had been transformed by the experience of the First World War. In their attitudes to sex, poor relief, unemployment, and so on, they were more enlightened and radical than ever before. Despite the very real social conservatism that existed in the 1920s and 1930s, the *progressive* changes engendered by the war and the workers' responses to war and militarism have not always been recognised by labour historians.

A major weakness in the essays and books of many left-wing historians is the tacit assumption that there has always been an identity of interests and sympathies between the labour movement and the unorganised majority of working-class men and women. Thus in a powerful critique of Richard Hoggart's portrayal of the history of the English working class in the 1930s, Peter Worsley said:

> But it is not good enough to give a mere two or three pages out of 282 to the 'minority' who built the unions, Labour Party and the co-operative movement. All social groups are led by minorities, by tiny elites whose energy (whatever their motivating drive-pelf, altruism, love of power, etc.) enables them to inspire, drive, delude or dragoon the mass membership. . . . To omit this minority, however, is to omit the yeast from working-class society. And when it is presented within a framework of working-class cultural activities in which *reading* is taken as the key index, the general effect is to heavily overweight frivolity and aimlessness. For the same 'average' man who does little beyond read the *Mirror* and drink his pint is the same man who voted Labour, and who had played such an important part in developing working-class political bodies to their present high pitch of organisation.[72]

What Peter Worsley overlooked, however, was the militancy of English workers in times and circumstances where a *coercive* educated socialist elite was absent. By assuming that the socialist intellectuals always constitute the working-class 'vanguard', such scholars contribute to the process of concealing the *real* history of working men and women. With great perception, Ferdynand Zweig wrote about the unorganised workers' environmentally-induced class-consciousness as follows: 'It is produced by common experiences, common attitudes, behaviour, and common environment. When any member of the class is attacked from the outside, all at once the other members are up in arms in common defence. The class consciousness sleeps but it is at all times present.' And in refuting the assumptions that socialist ideas came from the 'outside' rather than as a 'genuine internal growth arising from their own needs, interests and feelings', he could have been describing English working-class culture in the 1920s or 1930s as well as in the 1940s.[73]

Notes

Introduction

1. Peter Worsley, 'Britain: Unknown Country', *The New Reasoner,* Summer 1958, pp. 53-64; *Working-Class Culture,* ed. John Clarke, Chas Critcher and Richard Johnson (London, 1979), especially pp. 41-71; Karl Kautsky, *The Social Revolution* (Chicago, 1902), p. 102.
2. James D. Young, 'Totalitarianism, Democracy and the British Labour Movement before 1917', *Survey,* No. 1, Vol. 90, 1974, p. 140; J.M. Kennedy, 'What the Workmen Think', *Nineteenth Century,* October 1913, p. 695.
3. Robert Barltrop, *The Monument. The Story of the Socialist Party of Great Britain* (London, 1975, p. 87; Arnold Freeman, *Boy Life and Labour* (London, 1914), p. 151; James A. Little and Charles Watney, *The Workers' Daily Round* (London, 1913), p. 277; L.T. Hobhouse, *The Labour Movement* (London, 1912), pp. 126-41.
4. John Stevenson, *British Society, 1914–1945* (Harmondsworth, 1984), pp. 82, 96; Fenner Brockway, 'Bloomsbury Socialism and Coalfield Socialism', *New Leader,* 19 April 1929; Mass Observation, *Britain* (Harmondsworth, 1939), p. 169.
5. Egon Wertheimer, *Portrait of the Labour Party* (New York, 1929), p. 91.
6. Ralph Miliband, *Capitalist Democracy in Britain* (Oxford, 1984), pp. 89-90; James D. Young, 'Elitism, Authoritarianism and Western Socialism: A Critical Comment', *Bulletin of the Society for the Study of Labour History,* No. 25, 1972.
7. Ross Terrill, *R.H. Tawney and His Times* (London, 1974), p. 173; Interview with Bob Selkirk, 3 April 1971; Stephen Reynolds, *Seems So! A Working-Class View of Politics* (London, 1911), pp. 26-9; James D. Young, 'The Problem and Progress of the Social History of the British Working Class', *Labor History,* Vol. 18, No. 2, 1977, pp. 257-66.
8. Ross McKibbin, 'Why was there no Marxism in Great Britain?', *English Historical Review,* April 1984, p. 325.
9. Ian Britain, *Fabianism and Culture* (Cambridge, 1982), pp. 223-9;

234

James D. Young, 'Militancy, English Socialism and The Ragged Trousered Philanthropists', *Journal of Contemporary History,* Vol. 20, No. 2, 1985, pp. 283-304.

10. Stuart Macintyre, *A Proletarian Science. Marxism in Britain 1917–1933* (London, 1980), p. 38; Fred Henderson, *The Labour Unrest* (London, 1911), pp. 148-55; James D. Young, 'Totalitarianism, Democracy and the British Labour Movement before 1917', *Survey: A Journal of East and West Studies,* Vol. 20, No. 1, 1974, pp. 132-53.

11. G. Braunthal, *In Search of the Millennium* (London, 1945), p. 319.

12. Ellen Wilkinson, *The Town That Was Murdered* (London, 1939), p. 197.

13. McKibbin, op. cit., p. 325.

14. Ibid., p. 309; R.H. Sherard, *The White Slaves of England* (London, 1897), pp. 109-20; Charles Watney and James A. Little, *Industrial Warfare* (London, 1912), passim.

15. Stephen Humphries, *Hooligans or Rebels* (Oxford, 1981), p. 54; R.H. Best, W.J. Davies and C. Perks, *The Brassworkers of Berlin and of Birmingham* (London, 1905), p. 27; Olive C. Malvery, *The Soul Market* (London, 1906), p. 192; F.W. Head, *The Heart of the Empire* (London, 1907), p. 267.

16. Joseph Toole, *Fighting Through Life* (London, 1935), p. 10; Stephen Reynolds, *The Lower Deck* (London, 1912), p. 29; Arthur Shadwell, *Industrial Efficiency* (London, 1906), p. 409.

17. R.E. Hughes, *The Making of the Citizens* (London, 1903), p. 15.

18. Dave Marson, *Children's Strikes in 1911* (History Workshop, Oxford, 1973).

19. Humphries, *Hooligans or Rebels* (Oxford, 1981), p. 54.

20. Toole, op. cit., p. 5.

21. Michael Blanch, 'Imperialism, Nationalism and Organised Youth' in *Working-Class Culture,* ed. op. cit., p. 104; Thomas Holmes, *London's Underworld* (London, 1912), pp. 168-71; Herbert Morrison, *An Autobiography* (London, 1960), p. 11.

22. J.W. Brown, *So Far . . .* (London, 1943), p. 25.

23. Ben Tillet, *Memories and Reflections* (London, 1931), pp. 89-90; Bart Kennedy, *Slavery* (London, 1905), p. 196; Edward Cadbury, *Women's Work and Wages* (London, 1907), p. 191; Edward Parry, *The Law and the Poor* (London, 1914), pp. 149, 215.

24. David Robinson, *World Cinema* (London, 1973), p. 73.

25. Paul Wild, 'Recreation in Rochdale 1900–1940', in *Working-Class Culture,* op. cit., p. 155.

26. Allen Hutt, *The Condition of the Working Class in Britain* (London, 1922), p. 177.

27. Charles Watney and James A. Little, *Industrial Warfare* (London, 1912), p. 2.

28. Noreen Branson and Margot Neineman, *The Nineteen Thirties* (St Albans, Herts, 1973), p. 277.

29. Lord Snell, *Men, Movements and Myself* (London, 1936), p. 138; R.M. Fox, *The Triumphant Machine* (London, 1928), pp. 59-60; Mary

Hamilton, *Mary Macarthur* (London, 1925), p. 101; R.A. Woods, *English Social Movements* (London, 1895), p. 31.
30. D. Craig, *The Real Foundations* (London, 1973), passim.
31. James Sexton, *Sir James Sexton, Agitator* (London, 1936), p. 114; 'Masked Clerks', *Morning Post*, 15 September 1913; Jack London, *The People of the Abyss* (London, 1902), p. 100.
32. Will Thorne, *My Life's Battles* (London, 1925), p. 126.
33. C.M. Lloyd, *Trade Unionism* (London, 1921), p. 127.
34. Fenner Brockway, *Socialism Over Sixty Years* (London, 1946), p. 28.
35. R.A. Woods, *English Social Movements* (London, 1895), p. 20.
36. Frederick Verinder, 'The Agricultural Labourer', *Workers on their Industries*, ed. F. Galton (London, 1896), p. 162.
37. Dan Finn, Neil Grant and Richard Johnson, 'Social Democracy, Education and the Crisis', *On Ideology*, ed. Bill Schwarz (London, 1977), p. 148.
38. Ralph Miliband, 'A State of De-Subordination', *British Journal of Sociology*, Vol. 29, No. 4, 1978, p. 402.
39. H.A. Mess, *History of Factory Legislation* (London, 1936), passim.
40. Wilkinson, op. cit., pp. 196, 192.

1   The Labour Movement and 'the Poor', 1833–1914

1. James D. Young, 'Totalitarianism, Democracy and the British Labour Movement before 1917', *Survey*, No. 1, Vol. 90, 1974, pp. 132-6.
2. *Socialism and the Intelligentsia, 1880–1914*, ed. Carl Levy (London, 1987), pp. 14, 17.
3. J. Hunter Watts, 'Signs of the Times', *Justice*, 13 August 1889.
4. H. Quelch, 'Social Democracy and Trade Unionism', ibid., 22 May 1887.
5. R.A. Woods, *English Social Movement* (London, 1895), p. 40.
6. Fred Henderson, *The Labour Unrest* (London, 1911), pp. 154-6.
7. *Socialism and the Intelligentsia, 1880–1914*, op. cit., p. 148.
8. Ellen Wilkinson, *The Town That Was Murdered* (London, 1939), p. 112.
9. Paul Thompson, *Socialists, Liberals and Labour, the Struggle for London, 1885–1914* (London, 1975), p. 239.
10. James D. Young, 'Class Consciousness, the Class Struggle, and International Labour History', *Internationale Tagung der Historiker der Arbeiterbewegung, Sanderkonferenz 1983*, ed. Brigitte Galande (Vienna, 1984), p. 239.
11. Robert Roberts, *The Classic Slum* (Harmondsworth, 1973), p. 42.
12. M. Loane, *From Their Point of View* (London, 1908); idem, *The Next Street But One* (London, 1907), pp. 85-7.
13. M.L. Eyles, *The Woman in the Little House* (London, 1922), p. 87.
14. *Justice*, 11 March 1905.
15. Ibid., 18 March 1905.

16. 'In sum the Socialist Parties as they developed their institutions from the 1890s could absorb much of the energy and much of the leisure time of the workers, who, for whatever reason, felt alone in a hostile world. This was undoubtedly one of their chief attractions but it may also have curtailed the revolutionary fervour of potentially radical workers.' Peter N. Stearns, in Harvey Mitchell and Peter N. Stearns, *The European Labour Movement, the Working Classes, and the Origins of Social Democracy* (Ithaca, 1971), p. 207.

17. Henry Pelling, *The Origins of the Labour Party* (Oxford, 1966), p. 21.

18. H.M. Hyndman, *The Record of an Adventurous Life* (London, 1911), p. 432.

19. There is not much evidence for Irving Howe's view that there was no conflict in pre-1917 European social democracy between voluntarism and their acquiescence in the status quo by ceding socialism to the automatic laws of history'. I. Howe, 'Sweet and Sour Notes: On Workers and Intellectuals', *Dissent*, Winter 1972, p. 265.

20. A.P. Hazell, 'Social Degradation of the Worker', *Justice*, 11 July 1885.

21. Professor Eric Hobsbawm is in the SDF tradition when he says: 'It is not the working class itself which takes power and exercises hegemony, but the working-class movement or party, and (short of taking an anarchist view) it is difficult to see how it could be otehwise.' E.J. Hobsbawm, 'Class Consciousness in History', *Aspects of History and Class Consciousness*, ed. I. Howe, (London, 1971), p. 17.

22. *The Clarion*, 2 August 1899.

23. Eugene D. Genovese, *Roll, Jordan, Roll: The World the Slaves Made* (New York, 1976), p. 201.

24. 'Economic forms, I repeat, are ready. Intelligence and class discipline are lacking.' H.M. Hyndman, 'The Need for a British Republic', *Justice*, 5 April 1917.

25. Socialist League Archives, Miscellaneous file, International Institute of Social History, Amsterdam.

26. Robert Tressell, *The Ragged Trousered Philanthropists* (Harmondsworth, 1941), p. 235.

27. 'I have often thanked my stars or forebears that I was not born a working man. Very likely if I had been I should have grown up just such another as the majority of my "intelligent" working men countrymen around me. I have no delusions on that head.' H.M. Hyndman, 'Trade Unions and Progress', *Justice*, 8 September 1900.

28. James D. Young, 'Individualism and Individuality: A Forgotten Chapter in Socialist History, 1880–1939', *Internationale Tagund der Historiker der Arbeiterbewegund, Linzer Konferenz 1985*, ed. Helmut Konrad (Vienna, 1985), pp. 480-500.

29. J. Hunter Watts, 'Political Arena', *Justice*, 12 April 1890.

30. Herbert Burrows, 'Without Haste – Without Rest', ibid., 29 September 1888.

31. H. Collins 'The Marxism of the Social Democratic Federation', *Essays in Labour History*, ed. Asa Briggs and John Saville (London, 1971), p. 57.

32. James D. Young, 'Elitism, Authoritarianism and Western Socialism: A Critical Comment', *Bulletin of the Society for the Study of Labour History*, No. 25, 1972.
33. Frederick Engels, *Condition of the Working Class in England in 1844* (London, 1892), p. 125.
34. Ibid., p. 297.
35. James D. Young, 'Karl Marx: Moralist, Reformist and Utopian', *New Politics*, No. 1, 1972.
36. Engels, op. cit., p. 290.
37. James D. Young, 'Militancy, English Socialism and The Ragged Trousered Philanthropists', *Journal of Contemporary History*, Vol. 20, No. 2, 1985.
38. Ernest Belford Bax, *The Religion of Socialism* (London, 1901), p. 119.
39. Karl Marx and Frederick Engels, *Selected Correspondence* (Moscow, 1935), p. 379.
40. Stuart Macintyre, *A Proletarian Science: Marxism in Britain, 1917–1933* (Cambridge, 1908), p. 207.
41. H.W. Lee and E. Archbold, *Social Democracy in Britain* (London, 1935), p. 146.
42. G.P., 'Socialism and Pluck', *The Vanguard*, July 1913.
43. Arthur Shadwell, *Industrial Efficiency* (London, 1906), p. 277.
44. *Socialism and the Intelligentsia*, op. cit., p. 165.
45. Ernest Duckershoff, *How the English Workman Lives* (London, 1899), pp. 66-8.
46. Edward Cadbury, *Women's Work and Wages* (London, 1907), p. 198; 'The Question of Football', *Lancet*, 11 November 1905.
47. Karl Kautsky, *The Social Revolution* (Chicago, 1892), p. 106.
48. W. Booth, *In Darkest England* (London, 1890), p. 34; E. Andrews, *A Woman's Work is Never Done* (Ystrad, 1948), p. 4.
49. Ibid., pp. 6-11.
50. Roberts, op. cit., p. 21; *Report of Commission on the Housing of the Poor in Relation to their Social Condition* (Glasgow, 1891), p. 8.
51. R.H. Sherard, *The White Slaves of England* (London, 1897), p. 62; Charles Booth, *Life and Labour of the People of London* (London, 1902), Vol. 2, p. 128.
52. Booth, *In Darkest England*, op. cit., p. 170.
53. Booth, *Life and Labour of the People of London*, Vol. 1, op. cit., p. 249.
54. Fred Willis, *101 Jubilee Road, London, S.E.* (London, 1941), pp. 14-15.
55. Sherard, op. cit., p. 134.
56. George Bernard Shaw, 'The Death of an Old Revolutionary Hero', *The Clarion*, 24 March 1905.
57. Tressell, op. cit., p. 33.
58. Royden Harrison in his Afterword to the most recent edition of Samuel Smiles, *Self-Help* (London, 1968), p. 170; H.V. Emy, *Liberals, Radicals and Social Policies, 1892–1914* (Cambridge, 1971), passim; Eduard Bernstein, *My Years of Exile* (London, 1921), p. 260; *Workman's Times*, 6 March 1891; John Burns, *The Man with the Red Flag* (London,

1889), p. 5.
59. H. Pelling, *Popular Politics and Society in Late Victorian Britain* (London, 1968), pp. 37-61; Dan Irving, 'Some Thoughts on the Labour Movement', *Justice*, 28 January 1893; J. Hunter Watts, 'The Unemployed', ibid., 24 September 1887.
60. Quoted in Z. Bauman, *Between Class and Elite* (Manchester, 1972), p. 78; Lee and Archbold, op. cit., p. 83; G. Howell, *Trade Unionism, Old and New* (London, 1892), p. 83.
61. Quoted in H. Pelling, *A History of British Trade Unionism* (London, 1963), p. 94.
62. T.R. Threlfall, the Lib-Lab Secretary of the Labour Electoral Association. *Annual Report of the British TUC*, 1885 and quoted in Woods, *English Social Movements*, op. cit., p. 21.
63. *Justice*, 11 April 1898.
64. *Pall Mall Gazette*, 9 February 1886; Gareth Stedman Jones, *Outcast London* (Oxford, 1971), p. 295.
65. *Letters of Stephen Reynolds*, ed. Harold Wright (London, 1923), p. 118; F.W. Tickner, *Women in English Economic History* (London, 1923), p. 157; B.S. Rowntree and B. Lasker, *Unemployment: A Study* (London, 1911), p. 230.
66. Sidney and Beatrice Webb, *History of Trade Unionism* (London, 1920), p. 374; W. Graham, *Socialism Old and New* (London, 1890), p. xiv; F.J.C. Hearnshaw, *A Survey of Socialism* (London, 1929), p. 5.
67. Ernest Belford Bax, *Essays in Socialism Old and New* (London, 1906), p. 36; Sidney and Beatrice Webb, *Industrial Democracy* (London, 1897), p. 36; H.G. Wells, *The Great State* (London, 1913), p. 48.
68. Sidney Webb, *The Progress of Socialism* (London, 1888), p. 18 and *Webb: Diaries 1912–1924*, ed. Margaret Cole (London, 1952), p. 18.
69. *Justice*, 12 April 1912.

2   Racism, the Working Class and English Socialism, 1883–1914

1. Robert Tressell, *The Ragged Trousered Philanthropists* (Harmondsworth, 1940), passim.
2. Rozima Visram, *Ayahs, Lascars and Princes* (London, 1986), pp. 237, 53.
3. Tom Nairn, 'The Anatomy of the Labour Party', *New Left Review*, No. 27, 1962, p. 50.
4. E.P. Thompson, *The Poverty of Theory* (London, 1978), p. 68.
5. Edward Tupper, *Seaman's Torch* (London, 1938), p. 89.
6. Quoted in François Bédarida, *A Social History of England, 1851–1945* (London, 1979), p. 147.
7. Ernest Belford Bax, *Essays in Socialism Old and New* (London, 1907), p. 95.
8. Robert Roberts, *The Classic Slum* (Harmondsworth, 1971), p. 143.
9. Bédarida, op. cit., p. 145.
10. Roberts, op. cit., p. 143.

11. Hugh Cunningham, 'The Language of Patriotism', *History Workshop,* No. 12, 1981, p. 25.
12. Bédarida, op. cit., p. 146.
13. Peter Stearns, 'Working-Class Women in Britain, 1890–1914', *Suffer and Be Still,* ed. Martha Vicinus (Bloomington, 1971), p. 113.
14. Hugh Cunningham, 'Jingoism and the Working Classes', *Bulletin of the Society for the Study of Labour History,* No. 19, 1968, p. 8.
15. Henry Pelling, *Popular Politics and Society in Late Victorian Britain* (London, 1968), p. 86.
16. Bédarida, op. cit., p. 146.
17. Richard Price, *An Imperial War and the British Working Class* (London, 1974), pp. 241, 234.
18. P.D. Curtin, '"Scientific" Racism and the British Theory of the Empire', *Journal of the History Society of Nigeria,* Vol. 2, No. 1, 1960, p. 50.
19. Ibid., p. 48.
20. Raphael Samuel, 'Sources of Marxist History', *New Left Review,* No. 20, p. 41.
21. Bédarida, op. cit., p. 147.
22. A.L. Morton and George Tate, *The British Labour Movement* (London, 1956), p. 41.
23. Thompson, op. cit., p. 67.
24. Frederick J. Gould, *Hyndman, Prophet of Democracy* (London, 1928), p. 134.
25. James Walvin, *Black and White. The Negro and English Society, 1555–1945* (London, 1973), p. 202.
26. Ernest Belford Bax, *The Religion of Socialism* (London, 1901), p. 126.
27. Tingfur F. Tsiang, *Labor and Empire. A Study of the Reaction of British Labor, Mainly as Represented in Parliament to British Imperialism since 1880* (New York, 1923), p. 95.
28. Ibid., p. 96.
29. J.R. Widdup, 'Socialism and Colonial Development', *The Social Democrat,* June 1896, p. 211.
30. George Bernard Shaw, *Fabianism and the Empire* (London, 1900), pp. 4, 30.
31. J.A. Hobson, *The Psychology of Jingoism* (London, 1900), p. 33.
32. John George Godard, *Racial Superiority. Being Studies in Imperialism* (London, 1905), p. 13.
33. Curtin, op. cit., p. 50.
34. Ibid., p. 42.
35. 'In a giveaway aside, Hobson wrote: "Did Great Britain seek to thrust the English language at the sword's point on the Boers? The conveniences and the merits of our tongue need no championing."' J.A. Hobson, *The War in South Africa* (London, 1901), p. 47.
36. Alexander Davis, *The Native Problem in South Africa* (London, 1903), p. 19.
37. H.R. Fox Bourne, *The Aborigines' Protection Society: Chapters in its History* (London, 1895), p. 46.
38. Major C.T. Dawkins, *Precis of Information concerning Southern*

Rhodesia. Compiled in the Intelligence Division of the War Office, (London, 1899), p. 12.
39. Davis, op. cit., p. 66.
40. P.D. Curtis, *The Image of Africa* (London, 1977), p. 98.
41. Peter Fryer, *Staying Power: The History of Black Britain* (London, 1984), p. 185.
42. George Lichtheim, *A Short History of Socialism* (London, 1970), p. 182.
43. Morton and Tate, op cit., p. 141.
44. Quoted in Victor Bernard, *British Imperialism and Commercial Supremacy* (London, 1906), p. 231.
45. Quoted in ibid., p. 231.
46. *The New Age,* 22 February 1911.
47. *The Crisis,* August 1911 and Duse Mohamed Ali, 'White Women and Coloured Men', *The New Age,* 21 August 1909.
48. Julius Branthal, *A History of the International, 1864–1914* (London, 1966), p. 139.
49. H.R. Fox Bourne, 'Bechuana Rebels', *The Social Democrat,* December 1897, p. 1101.
50. Fox Bourne, *The Aborigines' Protection Society* op. cit., pp. 47, 45.
51. Godard, op. cit., p. 226.
52. Davis, op. cit., p. 67.
53. H.R. Fox Bourne, *Blacks and Whites in South Africa* (London, 1908), p. 77.
54. Davis, op. cit., p. 98.
55. J.A. Hobson, *Imperialism: A Study* (London, 1905), pp. 8, 216, 214.
56. Dudley Kidd, *Karif Socialism* (London, 1908), pp. 137, 185.
57. Davis, op. cit., pp. 95-9.
58. Hobson, *Imperialism,* op. cit., p. 304.
59. Hobson, *The War in South Africa,* p. 208.
60. Trevor Lloyd, 'Africa and Hobson's Imperialism', *Past and Present,* May 1972, p. 130.
61. Robin Cohen, Jean Copans and Peter C.W. Gutkin, 'Introduction', *African Labour History* (London, 1978), p. 8.
62. Raymond C. Buell, *The Native Problem in Africa* (New York, 1928), Vol. 2, p. 329.
63. Kidd, op. cit., p. 3.
64. C.L.R. James, *A History of Negro Revolt* (London, 1938), p. 37.
65. Andre Sik, *The History of Black Africa* (Budapest, 1966), Vol. 2, p. 49.
66. Victor Kiernan, *The Lords of Human Kind* (London, 1969), p. 235.
67. *Justice,* 20 July 1901.
68. F. Colebrook, 'Hobson's "The War in South Africa"', ibid., 24 March 1900.
69. H.W. Brailsford, *The Life Work of J.A Hobson* (London, 1948), p. 25.
70. F. Colebrook, "The Annual Conference of the S.D.F.', *Justice,* 11 May 1900.
71. Davis, op. cit., p. 154.
72. Eddie and Win Roux, *Rebel Pity* (London 1970), p. 15.

3 English Working-Class Women and the Labour Movement, 1883–1914

1. Dr G. Von Schulz-Gaevernitz, *Social Peace* (London, 1893), p. 277; Anna Stafford, *A Match to Fire the Thames* (London, 1961), pp. 64-5.
2. Sylvia Anthony, *Woman's Place in Industry and Home* (London, 1932), p. 116; *The Times,* 23 July 1888.
3. H.L. Smith and V. Nash, *The Story of the Dockers' Strike* (London, 1889), p. 103; *The Scotsman,* 2 October 1894.
4. E.A. Pratt, *Pioneer Women in Victoria's Reign* (London, 1897), pp. 1-2; T.G. Spyers, *The Labour Question* (London, 1984), p. 113; Mrs Bernard Bosanquet, *Rich and Poor* (London, 1896), p. 116.
5. Catherine Webb, *The Woman with the Basket* (Manchester, 1927), pp. 23-4.
6. Matilda J. Gage, *Woman, Church and State* (New York, 1893), p. 440.
7. Bosanquet, op. cit., p. 107.
8. *Pall Mall Gazette,* 20 October 1882; *South Wales Daily News,* 2 May 1882.
9. Smith and Nash, op. cit., p. 82.
10. Gage, op. cit., p. 438.
11. Isabella O. Ford, 'Woman's Wages', *Cruelties of Civilisation,* ed. Henry S. Salt (London, 1892), p. 13.
12. Report of the Trades Union Congress, 1888, p. 43.
13. Karl Pearson, *The Ethic of Freethought* (London, 1888), p. 236.
14. Samson Bryher, *An Account of the Labour and Socialist Movement in Bristol* (Bristol, 1929), p. 33.
15. *Justice,* 28 December 1895; ibid., 4 January 1896; ibid., 28 November 1896; ibid., 9 May 1896.
16. Thomas W. Higginson, *Common Sense about Women* (London, 1896), p. 183.
17. Ethel B. Harrison, *The Freedom of Women* (London, 1908), p. 44; Clara E. *Educating Working Women* (London, 1902), p. 128.
18. Robert Roberts, *The Classic Slum* (Harmondsworth, 1973), passim; Olive C. Malvery, *The Soul Market* (London, 1906), p. 33.
19. Joseph Clayton, *Trade Unions* (London, [n.d.], 1912?), p. 85.
20. *Maternity. Letters from Working Women, Collected by the Women's Co-operative Guild* (London, 1915), pp. 5-6; Dora B. Montefiore, *The Position of Women in the Socialist Movement* (London, 1909), p. 3.
21. Ibid., p. 8.
22. Cecil Chapman, *Marriage and Divorce* (London, 1911), p. 48; Edward Jenks, *Husband and Wife in the Law* (London, 1909), p. 48; Elizabeth S. Chesser, *Woman, Marriage and Motherhood* (London, 1913), p. 41; W.H. Stuart, *Children and the Law* (London, 1911), p. 2.
23. Chesser, op. cit., p. 33; *Woman's Trade Union Review,* April 1914.
24. C.G. Hartley, *The Truth about Women* (London, 1914), p. 279; Margaret Bondfield, *A Life's Work* (London, 1948), p. 38; Annie Abram, 'Newcastle', *Married Women's Work,* ed. Clementina Black

(London, 1915), p. 195.
25. Christabel Pankhurst, *The Great Scourge and How to End It* (London, 1913), p. 120; Lily H. Montage, 'The Girl in the Background', *Studies in Boy Life,* ed. E.J. Urwick (london, 1904), p. 242; C.B. Hawkins, *Norwich: A Social Study* (London, 1910), p. 43.
26. Mrs Archibald Colquhoun, *The Vocation of Woman* (London, 1913), p. 149; A.M. Anderson, *Woman in the Factory* (London, 1922), p. 161.
27. Edward Cadbury, *Women's Work and Wages* (London, 1907), p. 212; *Social Conditions in Provincial Towns,* ed. Mrs Bernard Bosanquet (London, 1912), p. 40; *Our Freedom and Its Results,* ed. Ray Strachey (London, 1936), p. 143.
28. Margaret McCarthy, *Generation in Revolt* (London, 1953), p. 18; A.M.B. Meakin, *Woman in Transition* (London, 1907), p. 74.
29. Annual Report of the Principal Lady Inspector of Factories for 1904, *Parliamentary Papers,* Vol. X, 1905, p. 239; Annual Report of the Principal Lady Inspector of Factories for 1907, *Parliamentary Papers,* Vol. XII, 1908, p. 151; Dora B. Montefiore, *Some Words to Socialist Women* (London, 1907), p. 11.
30 Annual Report of the Principal Lady Inspector of Factories, *Parliamentary Papers,* Vol. XII, 1908, p. 152.
31. Cited in Anonymous, *Ancilla's Share* (London, 1924), p. 146.
32. W.C. Sullivan, *Alcoholism* (London, 1906), p. 159; J.F. Sutherland, *Britain's Blot* (Edinburgh, 1908), p. 30; David Dewar, *The Children's Act* (London, 1910), p. 16.
33. Lady MacLaren, *The Woman's Charter of Rights and Liberties* (London, 1909), p. 36.
34. Malvery, op. cit., p. 134; Meakin, op. cit., p. 218.
35. A. Beatrice Wallis Chapman, *The Status of Women under English Law* (London, 1909), p. 62.
36. *The Case for Women's Suffrage,* ed. Brougham Villers (London, 1907), p. 95; Hartley, op. cit., p. 356; Jane J. Christie, *The Advance of Women* (Philadelphia, 1912), p. 179.
37. C.V. Drysdale, *The Smaller Family System* (London, 1913), p. 98; Chapman, op. cit., p. 79; Chesser, op. cit., p. 77.
38. *Working Women and Divorce. An Account of the Evidence Given on Behalf of the Women's Co-operative Guild before the Royal Commission on Divorce* (London, 1911), pp. 4, 39.
39. Alexander Paterson, *Across the Bridges* (London, 1911), p. 203.
40. T.F. Thiselton-Dyer, *Folk-Lore of Women* (London, 1905), p. 148.
41. Ethel Snowden, *The Feminist Movement* (London [n.d.], 1914?), p. 147.
42. Marion Holmes, *The ABC of Votes for Women* (London [n.d.], 1910?), p. 7; C.W. Saleeby, *Woman and Womanhood* (London, 1912), p. 292.
43. Alfred C. Plowden, *Grain or Chaff. The Autobiography of a Police Magistrate* (London [n.d.], 1914?), pp. 276, 278.
44. J. Johnston, *Wastage of Child Life* (London, 1909), p. 29.
45. Mrs H.M. Swanwick, *The Future of the Women's Movement* (London,

1913), p. 81.
46. Hargrave L. Adam, *Woman and Crime* (London, 1911), p. 5.
47. Holmes, op. cit., p. 7; Malvery, op. cit., p. 47; A. Davies Edwards, *Children of the Poor* (London, 1909), p. 7.
48. Chapman, op. cit., p. 47.
49. Ethel Snowden, *The Woman Socialist* (London, 1907), p. 15.
50. Jack London, *The People of the Abyss* (London, 1915), p. 292; W.E. Carson, *The Marriage Revolt* (London, 1915), p. 292; James D. Young, 'Totalitarianism, Democracy and the British Labour Movement before 1917', *Survey,* No. 90, 1974.
51. H.G. Wells, *Socialism and the Family* (London, 1907), p. 29.
52. A.J.P. Taylor, *English History, 1914–1945* (Oxford, 1965), p. 165; Arthur Sherwell, *Life in West London* (London, 1897), p. 124; Mary Higgs, *Glimpses into the Abyss* (London, 1906), p. 231.
53. Bondfield, op. cit., p. 42.
54. Margaret Sanger, *My Fight for Birth Control* (London, 1932), p. 97.
55. Caroline Nelson, 'The Control of Child Bearing', *International Socialist Review,* March 1914; Roberts, op. cit., p. 127.
56. *The Declining Birth Rate: Its Causes and Effects. Being the Report and the Chief Evidence taken by the National Council of Public Morals* (London, 1916), p. 304; Peter Stearns, *Lives of Labour* (London, 1975), p. 272; Stephen Reynolds, *Seems So! A Working-Class View of Politics* (London, 1911), p. 266; John Peel, 'Birth Control and the British Working-class Movement', *Bulletin of the Society for the Study of Labour History,* No. 7, 1962, p. 19.
57. Wells, op. cit., p. 51; Pell, op. cit., passim; Stearns, op. cit., p. 270.
58. David Heron, *On the Relation of Fertility in Man to Social Status and on Changes in this Relation that have taken place during the past fifty years* (London, 1906), p. 19; Elderton, op. cit., p. 23; Lady Bell, *At the Works* (London, 1911), p. 273.
59. *The Declining Birth Rate,* op. cit., p. 139; *Maternity: Letters from Working Women,* op. cit., p. 15.
60. *The Declining Birth Rate,* op. cit., p. 279.
61. G.S. Hughes, *Mothers in Industry* (New York, 1910), p. 28.
62. Karl Pearson, *Nature and Nurture* (London, 1913), p. 28.
63. Chesser, op. cit., p. 317.
64. Elderton, op. cit., p. 188.
65. Chesser, op. cit., p. 166.
66. Elderton, op. cit., pp. 181, 105, 121.
67. Olive Schreiner, *Women and Labour* (London, 1911), p. 124; Olive Malvery, *Baby Toiler* (London, 1907), p. 60.
68. Cadbury, op. cit., p. 137.
69. Robert G. Sherard, *The Child Slaves of Britain* (London, 1905), p. 234.
70. Ellen Key, *The Woman Movement* (New York, 1912), p. 37.
71. Andrew Rosen, *Rise Up Women* (London, 1974), p. 50; R.S. Neale, *Class and Ideology in the Nineteenth Century* (London, 1972), p. 156.
72. Villiers, op. cit., p. 52.
73. Helen Blackburn, *Women's Suffrage* (London, 1902), p. 215; Richard

Bell, *Trade Unionism* (London, 1907), p. 82; Ray Strachey, *The Cause. A Short History of the Women's Movement in Great Britain* (London, 1928), p. 290.

74. *Minutes of the East London Federation of Suffragettes,* 27 January 1914, International Institute of Social History, Amsterdam, Holland.
75. M.G. Fawcett, *What I Remember* (London, 1925), p. 183; Dora B. Montefiore, *From a Victorian to a Modern* (London, 1927), p. 52; Millicent G. Fawcett, *Women's Suffrage* (London, 1912), p. 63; *International Council of Women,* edited by the Countess of Aberdeen (Rome, 1914), p. 429.
76. E.T. Hiller, *The Strike* (Chicago, 1928), p. 11.
77. Gertrude M. Tuckwell, (ed.), *Women in Industry from Seven Points of View* (London, 1908), p. 72.
78. W.L. Blease, *The Emancipation of English Women* (London, 1910), p. 86; *Plebs,* Vol. 5, No. 9, 1913, p. 195; W.A. Anderson, *Women in the Factory* (London, 1922), p. 32.
79. Barbara Drake, *Women in the Trade Unions* (London, 1921), p. 42.
80. Snowden, *The Feminist Movement,* op. cit., p. 192.
81. Charles Watney and James A. Little, *Industrial Warfare* (London, 1912), p. 198.
82. Drake, op. cit., p. 50.
83. Mary A. Hamilton, *Mary Macarthur* (London, 1925), p. 57; Drake, op. cit., p. 34; Arthur Gleason and Paul U. Kellogg, *British Labor and the War* (New York, 1919), p. 141.
84. Hamilton, op. cit., p. 148.
85. Chapman, op. cit., p. 213; Tuckwell, op. cit., p. 81.
86. *Woman Worker,* 28 August 1908.
87. Reynolds, op. cit., p. xix.
88. *Letters of Stanley Reynolds,* ed. Harold Wright (London, 1923), p. 118.
89. *The Socialist,* April 1906.
90. Hamilton, op. cit., pp. 88, 96, 99.
91. *Annual Report of the Trades Union Congress,* 1910, p. 122.
92. Meakin, op. cit., p. 209.
93. *Woman's Trade Union Review,* July 1912; Christopher Holdenby, *Folk of the Furrow* (London, 1913), p. 144.
94. B.L. Hutchins, *Women in Modern Industry* (London, 1915), p. 134.
95. Bridget Adam, 'Scheme for Training Working Women', *Plebs,* Vol. IV, No. 7, 1912; *Woman's Trade Union Review,* April 1914.

4   English Working-Class Attitudes to State Intervention and the 'Labour Unrest', 1883—1914

1. John Foster, *Class Struggle and Industrial Revolution* (London, 1974), p. 238.
2. A.L. Bowley, *The Measurement and the Purpose of the Measurement of Social Phenomena* (London, 1915), p. 93; James D. Young, 'The

Problems and Progress of the Social History of the British Working Classes', *Labor History*, Vol. 18, No. 2, 1977; James D. Young, 'Totalitarianism, Democracy and the British Labour Movement before 1917', *Survey*, No. 1, Vol. 90, 1974.

3. J.M. Kennedy, 'What the Workers Think', *Nineteenth Century*, October 1913.
4. A.P. Hazell, 'The Cussedness of the Working Class', *Justice*, 21 April, 1888.
5. J. Hunter Watts, 'The Unemployed', ibid., 24 September 1887; Dan Irving, 'Some Thoughts on the Labour Movement', ibid., 28 January 1893.
6. Royden Harrison, 'Afterword' to Samuel Smiles, *Self-Help* (London, 1968), p. 269.
7. Socialist League Archives, K.2449/1, International Institute of Social History, Amsterdam, Holland.
8. E.P. Thompson, 'Homage to Tom Maguire', *Essays in Labour History*, ed. Asa Briggs and John Saville (London, 1967), pp. 276-316; Robert Roberts, *The Classic Slum* (Harmondsworth, 1973), p. 28.
9. Joseph Toole, *Fighting Through Life* (London, 1935), p. 5.
10. William Booth, *In Darkest England* (London, 1890), p. 192. Socialist League Archives, L.3545.
11. E.W. Brabrook, *Provident Societies and Industrial Welfare* (London, 1898), p. 80; *Essays in Anti-Labour History*, ed. K.D. Brown (London, 1974), pp. 2-3; 'Insurance and Infant Mortality, *Lancet*, 7 January 1889. 'In taking charge of the lives of the incapable, State socialism finds it proper work, and by doing it completely, would relieve us of a serious danger.' Charles Booth, *Life and Labour of the People of London* (London, 1889), p. 167. First series, *Poverty*, Part 1.
12. J.M. Budish and George Soule, *The New Unionism* (New York, 1920), p. 134; Louis Cazamian, *Modern England* (London, 1911), p. 213.
13. Walter Besant, (ed.), *The Poor in Great Cities* (London, 1896), pp. 261-2; J.R. Clynes, *Memoirs* (London, 1937), p. 47.
14. Peter Gordon, *The Victorian School Manager* (London, 1974), p. 116.
15. Ibid., p. 100; George Haw, *No Room to Live* (London, 1899), p. 113; R.E. Hughes, *The Making of Citizens* (London, 1903), p. 15.
16. Toole, op. cit., p. 10; Flora Thompson, *Lark Rise to Candleford* (London, 1948), p. 462.
17. Frank Hodges, *My Adventures as a Labour Leader* (London [n.d.]), p. 24; Jack Lawson, *A Man's Life* (London, 1924), p. 92; Toole, op. cit., p. 79.
18. C. Violet Butler, *Social Conditions in Oxford* (London, 1912), p. 243; Ben Turner, *About Myself* (London, 1930), p. 74; *The Nursing Record*, 11 August 1892.
19. R.E. Hughes, *The Making of Citizens* (London [n.d.], 1905?), p. 24.
20. G. Lowes Dickinson, *Justice and Liberty* (London, 1908), p. 208.
21. Richard Hyman, *Strikes* (London, 1972), p. 149.
22. Bob Holton, *British Syndicalism 1900-1914* (London, 1976), p. 203.
23. Pat Thane, 'The Working Class and State "Welfare", 1880-1914',

Bulletin of the Society for the Study of Labour History, No. 31, 1975, p. 8; Henry Pelling, *Popular Politics and Society in Late Victorian Britain* (London, 1968), p. 164.

24. M. Loane, *From Their Point of View* (London, 1908), p. 64; *Christianity and the Working Classes,* ed. George Haw (London, 1906), pp. 74, 196.

25. Alfred Marshall, *Elements of the Economics of Industry* (London, 1909), Vol. 1, pp. 390-1; Richard Bell, *Trade Unionism* (London, 1907), p. 76; Robert Roberts, *The Classic Slum* (Harmondsworth, 1973), p. 57.

26. C.M. Lloyd, *Trade Unionism* (London, 1914), p. 129; Thomas Holmes, *London's Underworld* (London, 1912), p. 195.

27. Charles Watney and James A. Little, *Industrial Warfare* (London, 1912), p. 244; L. Bowley, *The Measurement and the Purpose of the Measurement of Social Phenomena* (London, 1915), p. 92; Christopher Holdenby, *Folk of the Furrow* (London, 1913), p. 222; Stephen Reynolds and Bob and Tom Woolley, *Seems So! A Working-Class View of Politics* (London, 1911), p. xv; Mrs Carl Meyer and Clementina Black, *Makers of Our Clothes* (London, 1909); Alexander Paterson, *Across the Bridges* (London, 1911), p. 38.

28. Harry Quelch, 'Riot and Revolution', *The British Socialist,* Vol. 1, No. 4, 1912, p. 146; Ben Tillet, *Memories and Reflections* (London, 1931), p. 238; *Falkirk Herald,* 16 July 1904.

29. Arthur Shadwell, *Industrial Efficiency* (London, 1906), p. 409; Oliver C. Malvery, *The Soul Market* (London, 1906), p. 192; Stephen Reynolds, *The Lower Deck* (London, 1912), p. 29; Gertrude M. Tuckwell and Constance Smith, *The Worker's Handbook* (London, 1912), p. 31; Reynolds, *Seems So,* op. cit., pp. 27-8; Holdenby, op. cit., p. 156; Edward Cadbury, M.C. Catheson and George Shann, *Women's Work and Wages* (London, 1907), p. 197; W.C. Sullivan, *Alcoholism* (London, 1906), p. 94.

30. Reynolds, *Seems So,* op. cit., p. 118; Malvery, op. cit., p. 76; *Social Conditions in Provincial Towns,* ed. Mrs Bernard Bosanquet (London, 1912), p. 45.

31. Bart Kennedy, *The Hunger Line* (London, 1908), pp. 16, 19; George Bourne, *Change in the Village* (London, 1966), p. 117; Bart Kennedy, *Slavery* (London, 1905), pp. 98, 136; Lady Bell, *At the Works* (London, 1911), p. 352; Reynolds, *Seems So,* op. cit., p. 86; W.J. Brown, *So far . . .* (London, 1943), p. 25.

32. Bourne, op. cit., p. 173; M. Loane, *The Queen's Poor* (London, 1910), p. 127; Bell, op. cit., p. 175; Reynolds, *Seems So,* op. cit., p. 183.

33. *Lancet,* 11 November 1905; Stephen Reynolds, *A Poor Man's House* (London, 1908), p. 188; J. Johnston, *Wastage of Child Life* (London, 1909), p. 23; *Lancet,* 11 November 1905 and 8 August 1908.

34. Frank Hodges, *My Adventures as a Labour Leader* (London [n.d.]), p. 24; Joseph Toole, *Fighting Through Life* (London, 1935), p. 79; Roberts, *The Classic Slum,* op. cit., p. 28; F.G. Masterman, *The Heart of the Empire* (London, 1907), p. 5; Jack Lawson, *A Man's Life* (London, 1920), p. 92.

35. Anna Martin, *The Married Working Woman* (London, 1911), p. 41; *The Declining Birth-Rate. Its Causes and Effects* (National Council of Public Morals, London, 1916), p. 312; J.M. Winter, *Socialism and the Challenge of War* (London, 1974), p. 77; J.M. Kennedy, 'What the Workmen Think', *Nineteenth Century*, October 1913, p. 695.

36. A.H. Hogarth, *Medical Inspection of Schools* (London, 1909), pp. 44, 175; Margaret Alden, *Child Life and Labour* (London, 1908), p. 81; G.A.N. Lowndes, *The Silent Social Revolution* (Oxford, 1937), p. 227; Reynolds, *Seems So,* op. cit., p. 82.

37. *Fife Free Press,* 13 February 1904; M. Loane, *The Next Street But One* (London, 1907), p. 86; John Gorst, *The Children of the Nation* (London, 1907), p. 6; Roberts, *The Classic Slum,* op. cit., p. 73; T.N. Kelynack, *Medical Examination of Schools and Scholars* (London, 1910), p. 268; *Report of the City of Oxford Education Committee, 1909–1910,* p. 38; and *Durham County Advertiser,* 24 Jaunary 1913.

38. 'I once had a conversation with a French lady, the wife of a well-known sociologist and professor. She severely criticised the dress of the English working classes, whose Sunday clothes, she said, were cheap and shoddy imitations of the richer fashionable people. We had a very pretty discussion in which I maintained that the English idea was more democratic. I said it proved the English workman, at bottom, believed himself to be as good as his fellow countryman of the wealthier classes.' Henry Stelle, *The Working Classes in France* (London, 1904), p. 43; *Lancet,* 20 June 1914; *British Journal of Nursing,* 23 January 1926; *The Times.* 27 July 1911; *Falkirk Mail,* 14 July 1914.

39. F.W. Tickner, *Women in English Economic History* (London, 1923), p. 86; Olive C. Malvery, *Baby Toilers* (London, 1907), p. 61; A.J. Wilson, *The Business of Insurance* (London, 1904), p. 27; *New Statesman,* 13 March 1915; Martin, op. cit., p. 41; Reynolds, *Seems So,* op. cit., p. 31. *Letters of Stephen Reynolds,* ed. Harold Wright (London, 1923), p. 130.

40. L. Marion Springall, *Labouring Life in Norfolk Villages, 1834–1914* (London, 1936), p. 131; *Working Days,* ed. Margaret A. Pollock (London, 1926), p. 128; Onlooker, *Hitherto* (London, 1930), p. 78; Holdenby, op. cit., pp. 159-60.

41. Wright, op. cit., p. 133; 'The crowd of a town in a moment flashes into a delirious mob, and, swept away on a torrent of excitement and reckless of appearance, plunges into acts of unmitigated folly. The invention of the new term "Mafficking" is alone sufficient to indicate the extent of the transformation.' R.A. Bray, *The Town Child* (London, 1907), p. 145.

42. Mary A, Hamilton, *Mary Macarthur* (London, 1925), p. 102; Arnold Freeman, *Boy Life and Labour* (London, 1914), pp. 41, 135; C.B. Hawkins, *A Social Study* (London, 1910), p. 311; James A. Little and Charles Watney, *The Worker's Daily Round* (London, 1913), p. 277; idem *Industrial Warfare,* op. cit., p. 2.

43. Joseph Claydon, *Trade Unions* (London [n.d.], 1912?), p. 85; Watney and Little, *Industrial Warfare,* op. cit., p. 262; Bray, op. cit., p. 136;

Karl Kautsky, *The Social Revolution* (Chicago, 1902), p. 100.
44. *Woman Worker,* 28 August 1908; Gorst, op. cit., p. 88; Little and Watney, *Daily Round,* op. cit., p. 240; Roberts, op. cit., p. 88; William Savage, *Rural Housing* (London, 1915), p. 144; B.L. Hutchins, *Women in Modern Industry* (London, 1915), p. 105; George Edwards, *From Crow-Scaring to Westminster* (London, 1922), p. 144; Cadbury *et al.,* op. cit., p. 257; H.A. Mess, *Factory Legislation and its Administration, 1891–1924* (London, 1926), p. 164.
45. L.T. Hobhouse, *The Labour Movement* (London, 1912), p. 4; *Socialist,* July 1910; R. Page Arnot, *South Wales Miners* (London, 1967), p. 75; Hodges, op. cit., p. 23; Joseph and Ethel Wedgwood, *The Road to Freedom* (London, 1913), pp. 41-2.
46. Reynolds, *Seems So,* op. cit., p. xix.
47. Basil Thomson, *Queer People* (London, 1922), p. 265.
48. Fred Henderson, *The Labour Unrest* (London, 1911), p. 139; B. Seebohm Rowntree, 'The Industrial Unrest', *Contemporary Review,* October 1911, p. 464; David Evans, *Labour Strife in the South Wales Coalfield, 1910–1911* (Cardiff, 1911), p. 2; J.M. Budish and George Soule, *The New Unionism* (New York, 1920), p. 5.
49. Henry Clay, *The Problem of Industrial Relations* (London, 1929), p. 211; Lord Askwith, *Industrial Problems and Disputes* (London, 1920), p. 357.
50. Watney and Little, *Industrial Warfare,* op. cit., p. 247; Hamilton, op. cit., p. 101.
51. F.E. Green, *The Tyranny of the Countryside* (London, 1913), p. 15. Ernest Selley, *Village Trade Unionists in Two Centuries* (London, 1919), and F.E. Green, *A History of the English Agricultural Worker* (London, 1927), pp. 197, 263.
52. Selley, op. cit.; and Edward Tupper, *Seamen's Torch* (London, 1938), p. 70.
53. Quoted in G. Stone, *A History of Labour* (London, 1921), p. 240.
54. Robert Wiliams, *The New Labour Outlook* (London, 1921), p. 135; C.L. Goodrich, *The Frontier of Control* (London, 1920), p. 109.
55. Peter Stearns, *Lives of Labour* (London, 1975), p. 329; Clay, op. cit., p. 8; Goodrich, op. cit., p. 108.

5   The First World War and the Recasting of Bourgeois England

1. Ross McKibbin, 'Labour and Politics in the Great War', *Bulletin of the Society for the Study of Labour History,* No. 34, 1977, p. 4.
2. E. Sylvia Pankhurst, *The Home Front* (London, 1932), p. 369.
3. Rowland Kenny, *Westering* (London, 1939), p. 186.
4. Raymond Challinor, *The Origins of British Bolshevism* (London, 1977), passim.
5. Wiliam Orton, *Labour in Transition* (London, 1921), p. 40.
6. Arthur Gleason, *What the Workers Want* (New York, 1921), p. 472.

7. Whitling Wiliams, *Full Up and Fed Up. The Worker's Mind in Crowded Britain* (New York, 1921), p. 135.
8. Victor Kiernan, 'After Empire', *New Edinburgh Review,* No. 37, 1977.
9. R.H. Sherard, *The White Slaves of England* (London, 1897), p. 21.
10. Geoffrey Drage, *The Labour Problem* (London, 1896), pp. 224-5.
11. Lewis L. Lorwin, *The International Labor Movement* (Westport, Connecticut, 1977), p. 61.
12. Keith Hutchison, *Labour and Politics* (London, 1925), pp. 99-100.
13. A. Creech Jones, *Trade Unionism Today* (London, 1928), p. 10.
14. Orton, op. cit., p. 88.
15. J.J. Mallon and C.T. Lascelles, *Poverty: Yesterday and Today* (London, 1930), p. 82.
16. Paul Kellogg and Arthur Gleason, *British Labor and the War* (New York, 1919), p. 149.
17. McKibbin, op. cit., p. 3.
18. David Kynaston, *King Labour. The British Working Class, 1850–1914* (London, 1976), p. 119.
19. David Smith, *Socialist Propaganda in the Twentieth-Century Novel* (London, 1978), p. 39.
20. Gleason, op. cit., pp. 10, 7-8.
21. C.F.G. Masterman, *The New Liberalism* (London, 1920), p. 198.
22. E. Llewelyn Lewis, *The Children of the Unskilled* (London, 1924), p. 105.
23. Ben Turner, *Heavy Woollen District Textile Workers' Union* (Huddersfield, 1917), p. 123.
24. Will Thorne, 'Preface' to Jack Jones, MP, *His Book* (London, 1924), p. 6.
25. *Labour and Capital after the War,* ed. S.J. Chapman (London, 1918), p. 129.
26. Arnold Freeman, *How to Avoid Revolution* (London, 1919), p. 13.
27. Charles S. Maier, *Recasting Bourgeois Europe* (Princeton, NJ, 1975), pp. 41-3.
28. Robert Williams, *The New Labour Outlook* (London, 1921), p. 100.
29. Kellogg and Gleason, op. cit., p. 44.
30. Herman Mannheim, *Social Aspects of Crime in England between the Wars* (London, 1940), p. 156.
31. Williams, op. cit., pp. 98-9.
32. Stephen R. Graubard, *British Labour and the Russian Revolution, 1917–1924* (London, 1956), pp. 11-12.
33. Williams, op. cit., p. 127.
34. Margaret L. Eyles, *The Woman in the Little House* (London, 1922), pp. 101, 9.
35. Lady Bell, *At the Works* (London, 1911), p. 175.
36. Hubert L. Smith, *The Unemployed Man* (London, 1933), p. 15.
37. John G. Sinclair, *Easingden* (Oxford, 1926), p. 49.
38. Ibid., p. 29.
39. Olive Malvery, *The Soul Market* (London, 1906), p. 74; H.E., 'Colliery Surface-Man', *Working Days,* ed. Margaret Pollock (London, 1926), p.

73; H.A. Mess, *The Message of the C.O.P.E.C.* (London, 1924), p. 47.
40. Eyles, op. cit., pp. 27-8.
41. Hubert L. Smith, *The New Survey of London Life and Labour* (London, 1935), Vol. IX, p. 268; and H.A. Mess, *The Facts of Poverty* (London, 1920), pp. 96, 41.
42. George Lansbury, *My Life* (London, 1928), pp. 64, 168; Sylvia Pankhurst, op. cit., passim.
43. Gilbert McAllister, *James Maxton* (London, 1935), p. 95; W.J. Brown, *So Far*. . . (London, 1943), p. 25; Sir Wyndham Childs, *Episodes and Reflections* (London, 1930), p. 265.
44. *Annual Report of the Medical Officer of the London County Council,* 1922, pp. 40-5.
45. *Lancet,* 11 November 1905.
46. *Studies in Boy Life,* ed. E.J. Urwick (London, 1904), pp. 82-3; Alexander Paterson, *Across the Bridges* (London, 1911), p. 210.
47. Mess, op. cit., p. 39; Anon. *Ancillia's Share* (London, 1924), p. 302.
48. Mary A. Hamilton, *Remembering My Good Friends* (London, 1944), p. 175.
49. W. Eagar and H.A. Secretan, *Unemployment Among Boys* (London, 1924), p. 11.
50. Freeman, op. cit., p. 25.
51. Before developing this analysis, she quoted the remark 'a certain Colonel' made to her in early 1924: 'If you educate everybody alike, where are the working people to come from?' Margaret Pollock, *These Things Considered* (London, 1924), p. 182.
52. 'Socialism and the Education Bill', *Socialist,* December 1902.
53. *The School Bell,* September 1921.
54. Jack Common, *The Freedom of the Streets* (London, 1938), pp. 61-3.
55. William Booth, *In Darkest England* (London, 1890), p. 34; James A. Little and Charles Watney, *The Worker's Daily Round* (London, 1913), p. 240.
56. A. Creech Jones, 'The Condition of the Port Workers', *Working Days,* op. cit., p. 190.
57. Pollock, op. cit., p. 122.
58. Ernest Selley, *Village Trade Unionism in Two Centuries* (London, 1919), p. 158 and S.L.B., 'One Union for Agriculture', *New Statesman,* 9 October 1920.
59. Christopher Holdenby, *Folk of the Furrow* (London, 1913), p. 183; F.E. Green, *The Tyranny of the Countryside* (London, 1913), p. 203.
60. W.J. Shingfield, 'The Work of Farm Labourers', *Working Days,* op. cit., p. 124.
61. J.W. Robertson, *England's Green and Pleasant Land* (London, 1925), p. 90.
62. Holdenby, op. cit., p. 133; Eyles, op. cit., p. 18.
63. Report of the Chief Inspector of Factories and Workshops, *Parliamentary Papers,* Vol. XX, 1892, p. 30.
64. 'Notes on the Coal Industry', *Working Days,* op. cit., p. 82.
65. Sinclair, op. cit., p. 5.

66. J. Johnston, *Wastage of Child Life* (London, 1909), p. 23.
67. H. Stanley Jevons, *The British Coal Trade* (Newton Abbot, 1969), p. 620.
68. H.M. Swanwick, *I Have Been Young* (London, 1935), pp. 200-1.
69. Lawrence Weaver, *The 'Country Life' Book of Cottages* (London, 1919), p. 30.
70. Eyles, op. cit., p. 52.
71. See the various essays in *Women and the Labour Party*, ed. Marion Philips (London, 1919).
72. Theodore C. Taylor, 'The Labour Crisis', *Contemporary Review*, May 1922.
73. Maier, op. cit., p. 44.
74. Arthur Greenwood, 'The Labour Crisis: A Labour View', *Contemporary Review*, July 1922, p. 39.
75. W.T. Colyer, *An Outline History of Unemployment* (London [n.d.], 1937?), p. 35.
76. Irene Osgood and Margaret A. Hobbs, *Economic Effects of the War on Women and Children in Great Britain* (New York, 1921), pp. 201, 9.
77. G.A. Gardiner, *England Today* (London, 1921), p. 55.
78. Williams, op. cit., p. 208.
79. Quoted in Osgood and Hobbs, op. cit., p. 158.
80. Ibid., pp. 159-60.
81. E. Sylvia Pankhurst, *The Suffragette* (London, 1911), p. 9; John J. Clarke, *The Housing Problem* (London, 1920), p. 158.
82. H.A. Secretan, *London Below the Bridges* (London, 1931), p. 50.
83. Eleanor Rathbone, *The Disinherited Family* (London, 1924), pp. 42-3.
84. Lewis, op. cit., p. 92.
85. Thomas Holmes, *London's Underworld* (London, 1912), p. 195; Eyles, op. cit., p. 49.
86. 'About two-fifths of the working classes would rather starve than go to a pawnshop.' Ibid., p. 61.
87. Will Thorne, *My Life's Battles* (London, 1925), p. 217; Harry Gosling, *Up and Down Stream* (London, 1935), p. 186.
88. Leslie Bailey, *Scrapbook for the Twenties* (London, 1959), p. 89.
89. Eugene A. Heckner, *A Short History of Women's Rights* (New York, 1910), p. 260.
90. Leonora Eyles, *(Women's Problems of Today* (London, 1926), p. 63.
91. Ibid., pp. 88, 73, 79.
92. C.F.G. Masterman, 'The Coalition, Liberalism and Labour', *Contemporary Review*, May 1921.
93. Beverley Nichols, *The Sweet and Twenties* (London, 1958), p. 24.
94. Eyles, op. cit., p. 84.
95. John Saville, 'Notes on Ideology and the Miners before World War I', *Bulletin of the Society for the Study of Labour History*, No. 23, 1971, pp. 25-7.
96. Royden Harrison, 'Afterword', to Samuel Smiles, *Self-Help* (London, 1968), p. 269.
97. *Infancy of Labour*, Vol. 1, in the Library of the London School of

Economics and Political Science.
98. A.L. Morton and George Tate, *The British Labour Movement, 1770–1920* (London, 1956), p. 274.
99. *Socialist,* December 1917.
100. Iconoclast [Mary A. Hamilton], *Fit to Govern* (London, 1924), p. 9.
101. Adolf Sturmthal, *The Tragedy of European Labor, 1918–1938* (New York, 1943), p. 104.
102. Frank Budgen, *Myselves When Young* (London, 1970), p. 209.
103. James D. Young, 'Daniel De Leon and Anglo-American Socialism', *Labor History,* Vol. 17, No. 3, 1976, pp. 329-50.
104. John Scanlon, *Decline and Fall of the Labour Party* (London, 1933), p. 45.
105. Quoted in Catherine Ann Cline, *Recruits to Labour* (Syracuse, 1965), p. 141.
106. Scanlon, op. cit., p. 44; Richard W. Layman, *The First Labour Government* (London, 1957), p. 219.
107. Egon Wertheimer, *Portrait of the Labour Party* (New York, 1929), p. 81; Layman, pp. 279, 240.

6   Racism, the Working Class and English Socialism, 1914–1939

1. James Walvin, *Black and White. The Negro and English Society, 1555–1945* (London, 1973), p. 202.
2. Sylvia Pankhurst, *The Home Front* (London, 1932), passim.
3. Hugh Cunningham, 'The Language of Patriotism', *History Workshop,* No. 12, 1981, p. 25.
4. Walvin, op. cit., pp. 205-6.
5. Elsie M. Lang, *Women in the Twentieth Century* (London, 1929), p. 183.
6. James Marley, 'The Colour-Bar in England', *The Socialist Review,* December 1929, p. 78.
7. Whitling Williams, *Full Up and Fed Up. The Worker's Mind in Crowded Britain* (New York, 1921), p. 20.
8. Peter O. Esedebe, A History of the Pan-African Movement in Britain 1900–1948, PhD thesis, University of London, 1968, pp. 112, 115.
9. Ernest Marke, *Old Man Trouble* (London, 1975), pp. 28, 51, 61.
10. R. Palme Dutt, 'The British Empire', *Labour Monthly,* October 1923.
11. Ralph Fox, *Colonial Policy of British Imperialism* (London, 1938), p. 109.
12. Palme Dutt, op. cit., p. 207.
13. P.D. Curtis, '"Scientific Racism" and the British Theory of Empire', *Journal of the Historical Society of Nigeria,* Vol. 2, No. 1, 1960, p. 46.
14. Leonora Eyles, *Women's Problems of Today* (London, 1926), p. 75.
15. P.O. O'Mara, *The Autobiography of a Liverpool Slummy* (London,

1934), p. 74.

16. Logie Barrow, 'The Origins of Robert Blatchford's Social Imperialism', *Bulletin of the Society for the Study of Labour History*, No. 19, 1969.
17. Fenner Brockway, *How to End War. The ILP View on Imperialism and Internationalism* (London, 1926), p. 11.
18. J.M. Winter, *Socialism and the Challenge of War* (London, 1974), p. 64.
19. David Vaughan, *Negro Victory. The Life Story of Dr. Harold Moody* (London, 1950), p. 47.
20. Ibid., p. 48.
21. Letter from the late Dr Archie Lamond to the author, 28 April 1982.
22. *New Leader,* 10 June 1927. For conflicting accounts of racism in Scotland in the interwar period, see James Drawbell, *Scotland: Bitter-Sweet* (London, 1972), p. 23; A.S. Neill, *Neill, Neill, Orange Peel* (New York, 1970), p. 127.
23. M.E. Fletcher, *Report on an Investigation into the Colour Problem in Liverpool and other Ports* (Liverpool, 1930), p. 7.
24. Ibid., p. 8.
25. Ibid., p. 17.
26. Esedebe, op. cit., pp. 113-14.
27. Ibid., p. 112.
28. Quoted in *Negro Anthology,* ed. Nancy Cunard (London, 1934), p. 538.
29. *Negro Worker,* June 1931.
30. 'Blacks Not Wanted', ibid., May 1932.
31. A. Dde Ademola, 'Colour-bar Notoriety in Great Britain', in Cunard, op. cit., p. 556.
32. Special Correspondent, 'The Jubilee is Over', *New Leader,* 10 May 1935; Interview with Harry McShane, 3 April 1980.
33. Interview with the late Tom Murray, 20 March 1982.
34. Ras Makonnen, *Pan-Africanism from Within,* recorded and edited by Kenneth King (Oxford, 1973), p. 97.
35. 'Internationalist', 'The Coloured Line', *Plebs,* April 1929.
36. *Negro Worker,* April–May 1933; Kenneth King, *Negroes in Britain* (London, 1956), p. 62.
37. *Negro Worker,* August 1934.
38. 'Smash the Attack on Colonial Seamen', ibid., July 1934; *The Keys,* October–December 1935.
39. *Daily Worker,* 17 May 1934; An Indian Comrade, 'The Anti-Imperialist Struggles in Britain', *Communist Review,* July 1934; Little, op. cit., p. 77.
40. *Negro Worker,* July 1934; *New Leader,* 24 July 1934.
41. Walvin, op. cit., p. 290; George Padmore, 'Race Prejudice in England', *Negro Worker,* March 1932.
42. 'Democracy in the British Empire', *Plebs,* July 1934.
43. Cecil Lewis, 'Cardiff Report', *The Keys,* October–December 1935; 'Coloured Seamen on the Beach', ibid., January–March 1937.
44. 'Britain's Coloured Seamen', ibid., July–September 1937.
45. 'Coloured Seamen', ibid., July–September 1937; Makonnen, op. cit.,

p. 129.
46. Ibid., p. 130.
47. *Negro Worker,* March 1933.
48. George Padmore, *Pan Africanism or Communism?* (London, 1956), p. 329.
49. Vaughan, op. cit., p. 59.
50. *The Keys. The Official Organ of the League of Coloured Peoples,* with an Introductory Essay by Roderick J. MacDonald (New York, 1976), p. 7.
51. *Negro Worker,* August 1934; 'African: A Confused Argument', *Labour Monthly,* September 1937; George Padmore, *How Britain Rules Africa* (London, 1936), p. 396.
52. P.S. Gupta, *Imperialism and the British Labour Movement, 1914–1964* (London, 1975), p. 128; C.S. Samson, The British Labour Movement and South Africa, 1918–1955. Labourism and the Imperial Tradition, PhD thesis, Birmingham, 1981, p. 43.
53. Gilbert Murray's 'Introduction' to Norman Leys, *Kenya* (London, 1924), p. 4; *Justice,* 28 February 1924.
54. Leys, op. cit., p. 29.
55. Fox, op. cit., p. 115.
56. James D. Young, 'A Letter from George Orwell to Charlie Doran', *Bulletin of the Society for the Study of Labour History,* Vol. 51, Part I, 1986.
57. C.L.R. James, 'The Negro Question', *Socialist Appeal,* 25 August 1939.

7 English Working-Class Women and Organised Labour, 1914–1939

1. Charlotte Luetkens, *Women and a New Society* (London, 1946); E.M. White, *Women in World History* (London, 1924), p. 284.
2. *Palgrave's Dictionary of Political Economy,* ed. Henry Higgs (London, 1926), Vol. 2, p. 855; Millicent G. Fawcett, *The Women's Victory and After* (London, 1920), p. 106; Mrs Alex Tweedie, *Women and Soldiers* (London, 1918), p. 104; Mary R. MacArthur, 'The Women Trade Unionists' Point of View', *Women and the Labour Party,* ed. Marion Phillips (London, 1919), p. 18.
3. Leslie Baily, *Scrapbook for the Twenties* (London, 1959), p. 28; John Collier and Iain Lang, *Just the Other Day* (London, 1932), p. 201.
4. Arthur Marwick, *The Deluge* (London, 1965), p. 107; Collier and Lang, op. cit., p. 210.
5. Francis W. Hirst, *The Consequences of the War to Great Britain* (Oxford, 1923), p. 107.
6. *Letters of Stanley Reynolds,* ed. H. Wright (London, 1923), p. 272; Helen Fraser, *Women and War Work* (New York, 1918), pp. 269-70;

Minutes of the East London Federation of Suffragettes, 1 May 1916; International Institute of Social History, Amsterdam; ibid., 17 January 1916; Richard Bennett, *A Picture of the Twenties* (London, 1961), p. 16; Vera Brittain, *Women's Work in Modern England* (London, 1928), p. 11.

7. Ibid., pp. 11-12; Mary A. Hamilton, *Margaret Bondfield* (London, 1924), pp. 114-15; Meyrick Booth, *Women and Society* (London, 1929), p. 53.

8. Irene O. Andrews, *Economic Effects of the World War Upon Women and Children in Great Britain* (New York, 1921), p. 218.

9. *Annual Report of the Chief Inspector of Factories,* Parliamentary Papers, Vol. XII, 1921, p. 16; ibid., Vol. IX, 1924, p. 45; A.M. Anderson, *Women in the Factory* (London, 1922), pp. 15-16; J. Blainey, *The Woman Worker and Restrictive Legislation* (London, 1928), p. 50; Arthur Gleason, *What the Workers Want* (London, 1920), p. 227.

10. Barbara Drake, *Women in Trade Unions* (London, 1921), p. 111; Hamilton, op. cit.; Brittain, op. cit., p. 12; Gladys Boone, *The Women's Trade Union League in Great Britain and the United States of America* (New York, 1942), p. 40.

11. 'Notes on Women in Industry', *Working Days,* ed. Margaret A. Pollock (London, 1926), p. 248; G.D.H. Cole, *An Introduction to Trade Unionism* (London, 1918), p. 17; Drake, op. cit., p. 220.

12. *Women in the Class Struggle* (London [n.d.] 1925?), p. 4.

13. *The Plebs,* November 1925; Leonora Eyles, *Women's Problems of Today* (London, 1926), p. 10; I owe this information to Mary Docherty, a veteran communist, who still lives in Cowdenbeath, Fife, where she was born. Interview, 14 June 1973; Eyles, op. cit., p. 40.

14. J.G. Sinclair, *Easingden* (Oxford, 1926), p. 28.

15. Eleanor F. Rathbone, *The Disinherited Family* (London, 1924), pp. 42-3.

16. E. Llewelyn Lewis, *The Children of the Unskilled* (London, 1924), p. 92; Hubert L. Smith, *The New Survey of London Life and Labour* (London, 1932), Vol. 3, p. 175; Lewis, op. cit., p. 96; ibid., p. 100; 'The Cotton Operatives', *Clarion,* 11 February 1921; A.L. Bowley and M.H. Hogg, *Has Poverty Diminished?* (London, 1925), p. 23; Baily, op. cit., p. 152; Marion Phillips, *Women and the Miners' Lock-Out* (London, 1927), p. 78; Roger Dataller, *From a Pitman's Note Book* (London, 1925), pp. 73-5.

17. Sinclair, op. cit., pp. 31-3; Dataller, op. cit., p. 29; Sinclair, op. cit., p. 14; ibid., pp. 95-6.

18. G.W. Johnson, *The Evolution of Woman* (London, 1926), p. 193; B. Seebohm Rowntree, *The Responsibility of Women Workers for Dependants* (Oxford, 1921), p. 31.

19. *The Plebs,* April 1929; Sir Thomas Oliver, *The Health of the Workers* (London, 1925), p. 53; Vera Brittain, *Women's Work in Modern Britain* (London, 1928), p. 197; *Manchester Guardian,* 18 October 1927; *International Council of Women,* ed. Marchioness of Aberdeen

(London, 1925), p. 356; Bowley and Hogg, op. cit., p. 152; Charlotte Haldane, *Motherhood and Its Enemies* (London, 1927), p. 32.

20. Civil and Judicial Statistics for England and Wales, Parliamentary Papers, 1929–30, Vol. XXX, p. xi; Charles J. Tarring, *The State and Sexual Morality* (London, 1920), p. 28.

21. Annual Report of the Chief Inspector of Factories and Workshops, Parliamentary Papers, 1923, Vol. XI, p. 49; F.W. Tickner, *Women in English Economic History* (London, 1923), p. 222; Margaret Eyles, *The Women in the Little House* (London, 1922), pp. 93-4; Annual Report of the Chief Inspector of Factories and Workshops, Parliamentary Papers, 1922, Vol. VII, p. 91; R.M. Fox, *The Triumphant Machine* (London, 1928), p. 32.

22. S.B., 'Textile Workers', in *Working Days*, ed. Margaret Pollock (London, 1926), p. 237; H.A. Mess, *The Facts of Poverty* (London, 1920), p. 97; Constance Williams, *How Women Can Help in Political Work* (London, 1920), p. 25; Eyles, *The Women in the Little House*, op. cit., p. 19.

23. Noreen Branson, *Britain in the Nineteen Twenties* (London, 1975), p. 20; W.G. Clarke, *In Breckland Wilds* (London, 1925), p. 171; *Working Days*, op. cit., pp. 65-6; Sinclair, op. cit., p. 5; Dataller, op. cit., pp. 245-6.

24. Arnold Bennett, *Our Women* (London, 1923), p. 160; Norah March's Preface to *Woman in the Little House*, op. cit., p. 9; ibid., p. 10; Rathbone, op. cit., p. 9; Hubert L. Smith, *The Unemployed Man* (London, 1933), p. 15; J.J. Astor, *The Third Winter of Unemployment* (London, 1922), p. 80; ibid., pp. 173-4; H.A. Secretan, *London Below the Bridges* (London, 1931), p. 14.

25. Lewis, op. cit., p. 105; *Working Days*, op. cit., p. 73; Mess, op. cit., p. 165; Sinclair, op. cit., p. 79; Eyles, *Woman in the Little House*, op. cit., p. 49; C.F.G. Masterman, *How England is Governed* (London, 1921), p. 155; *Working Days*, op. cit., p. 128.

26. Beverley Nichols, *The Sweet and Twenties* (London, 1958), p. 25; John Montgomery, *The Twenties* (London, 1957), p. 57; Smith, *The New Survey of London Life and Labour*, Vol. 1, op. cit., p. 50; Bennett, op. cit., pp. 115-16; Hamilton Fyfe, *The Revolt of Women* (London, 1933), p. 271.

27. Eyles, *Women's Problems of Today*, op. cit., p. 36; Rathbone, op. cit., pp. 88-9; Eyles, *The Woman in the Little House*, op. cit., p. 141; Fyfe, op. cit., p. 101; Sheila Rowbotham, *Hidden from History* (London, 1974), p. 142.

28. Haldane, op. cit., p. 277; Fyfe, op. cit., p. 122.

29. Gerald Heard, *These Hurrying Years* (London, 1934), p. 266; Margaret Sanger, *An Autobiography* (London, 1939), pp. 267-9.

30. Marie C. Stopes, *'Wise Parenthood* (London, 1912), p. 18; ibid., p. 38; Fyfe, op. cit., p. 118.

31. Guy Aldred, *No Traitor's Gait* (Glasgow, 1963), Vol. III, No. 1, p. 23; John Peel, 'Birth Control and the British Working-Class Movement', *Bulletin of the Society for the Study of Labour History*, No. 7, 1963;

Worker's Dreadnought, 10 March 1923.

32. Marie C. Stopes, *Married Love* (London, 1918), p. 90; Montgomery, op. cit., p. 165.

33. Fyfe, op. cit., p. 261; Eyles, *The Woman in the Little House,* op. cit., p. 159; *Civil and Judicial Statistics for England and Wales,* Parliamentary Papers, 1929–1930, Vol. XXX, p. xi; Alex Craig, *Sex and Revolution* (London, 1934), p. 80; Helena Normanton, *Everyday Law for Women* (London, 1932), pp. 386-9.

34. Bennett, *Our Women,* op. cit., p. 162.

35. Smith, *The New Survey of London Life and Labour,* Vol. 1, op. cit., p. 397; Mess, op. cit., p. 91; Report of the Royal Commission on Licensing, *Parliamentary Papers,* 1929–1930, p. 139.

36. Dr Herman Mannheim, *Social Aspects of Crime in England between the Wars* (London, 1940), pp. 170-7; *Civil and Judicial Statistics for England and Wales,* Accounts and Papers, Parliamentary Papers, 1929–1930, Vol. XXX, p. 1i.

37. Lewis, op. cit., p. 54; ibid., p. 59; *The Proceedings of C.O.P.E.C. Being a Report of the Meetings of the Conference on Christian Politics, Economics and Citizenship* (London, 1924), pp. 140-1; Marie Stopes, *Mother England* (London, 1929), pp. 174-5; Henry T. Waddy, *The Police Court and Its Work* (London, 1925), pp. 102-4; Alfred Fellows, *The Case Against the English Divorce Law* (London, 1932), p. 118.

38. Elizabeth S. Chesser, *Woman, Marriage and Motherhood* (London, 1915), p. 7.

39. Ray Strachey, *The Cause: A Short History of the Women's Movement in Great Britain* (London, 1928), p. 44; Maud I. Crofts, *Woman under the England Law* (London, 1923), p. 45; Strachey, op. cit., p. 383; Crofts, op. cit., p. 39.

40. G.S.M. Ellis, *The Poor Student and the University* (London, 1925), p. 33; Smith, *The New Survey of London Life and Labour,* Vol. IX, op. cit., p. 33; Haldane, op. cit., p. 196; Minnie Pallister, *Socialism for Women* (London, 1929), p. 23.

41. B.L. Hutchins, *Women in Modern Industry* (London, 1915), p. 189; J.W. Robertson Scott, *England's Green and Pleasant Land* (London, 1925), p. 90; W.E. Carson, *The Marriage Revolt* (London, 1915), p. 42; Arabella Kenealty, *Feminism and Sex-Extinction* (London, 1920), pp. 283-4.

42. Robert Rayner, *The Story of Trade Unionism* (London, 1929), pp. 256-8; Carson, op. cit., p. 88.

43. Dr Marion Phillips, 'Organisation of Women', in *British Labor Speaks,* ed. Richard Hogue (New York, 1924), p. 114.

44. C.H. Mowat, *Britain between the Wars* (London, 1950), p. 522; *Criminal Statistics for England and Wales,* Parliamentary Papers, Vol. XXVI, 1931–1932; *Criminal Statistics for England and Wales,* Parliamentary Papers, Vol. XXV, 1938–1939, p. 72.

45. Elsie M. Lang, *British Women in the Twentieth Century* (London, 1929), p. 177; Fellows, op. cit., p. 118.

46. Mowat, op. cit., p. 487; Noreen Branson and Margot Heinemann,

Britain in the Nineteen Thirties (London, 1971), p. 181.
47. Branson and Heinemann, op. cit., p. 182.
48. Christine Millar, 'Feminism and Fascism', *The Plebs,* August 1934; Gordon Hosking, 'Socialism and the Modern Girl', ibid., December 1939.
49. Allen Hutt, *British Trade Unionism* (London, 1941), p. 37.
50. A.P. Jephcott, *Girls Growing Up* (London, 1942), pp. 72, 95.
51. Maud Royden, *Women's Partnership in the New World* (London, 1941), p. 50; Joan Beauchamp, *Women Who Work* (London, 1937), p. 28.
52. Dorothy Jacques, 'Women Workers in a Wireless Factory', *Labour Monthly,* December 1937.
53. Mary Agnes Hamilton, *Women at Work* (London, 1941), p. 18.
54. Ibid., p. 19; Beauchamp, op. cit., p. 53.
55. Ibid., p. 27.
56. Hamilton, op. cit., pp. 31-4; Beauchamp. op. cit., p. 99.
57. Beauchamp, op. cit., pp. 101-2.
58. Sarah Boston, *Women Workers and the Trade Unions* (London, 1980), p. 156.

8   English Workers, Mass Unemployment and the Left, 1914–1939

1   W.T. Colyer, *An Outline History of Unemployment* (London [n.d.], 1935?), pp. 35-6.
2. Helen Vernon, The Socialist Labour Party and the Working-Class Movement on the Clyde, 1901–1921, M. Phil. thesis, University of Leeds, 1967, p. 226.
3. Colyer, op. cit., p. 35.
4. A.W. Kirkaldy, *British Labour* (London, 1921), pp. 198-209.
5. G.D.H. Cole, *Out of Work* (London, 1923), p. 71.
6. Peter Kingsford, *The Hunger Marchers in Britain, 1920–1940* (London, 1982), p. 80.
7. Jurgen Kuczynski, *A Short History of Labour Conditions under Capitalism* (London, 1942), pp. 110, 109.
8. Colyer, op. cit., pp. 34-5.
9. *The Times,* 22 November 1922.
10. Quoted in Colyer, p. 37.
11. Ibid., p. 30; Richard W. Layman, *The First Labour Government* (London, 1957), p. 281.
12. Allen Hutt, *The Condition of the Working Class in Britain* (London, 1933), pp. 154-7; and Hubert L. Smith, *The New Survey of London Life and Labour* (London, 1932), Vol. 3, p. 177.
13. B.G. De Montgomery, *British and Continental Labour Policy* (London, 1922), p. 437.

14. G. Ritenskamp, 'Unemployment and the Six-Hour Day', *International Socialist Review*, January 1914; Pleb, 'An Open Letter to the Out-of-Work', *The Plebs*, February 1923; H.D. Dickenson, 'The History of Unemployment', ibid., February 1923; Ellen Wilkinson, 'Trade Unionism since the War', ibid., January 1925.
15. John Scanlon, *Decline and Fall of the Labour Party* (London, 1933), pp. 133-46.
16. Will Oxley, 'Are you Working?', in *Seven Shifts*, ed. Jack Common (London, 1938), p. 121; Wal Hannington, *My Life and Struggles amongst the Unemployed* (London, 1936), p. 202.
17. Oxley, op. cit., p. 120.
18. Colyer, op. cit., p. 45.
19. H.L. Beales and R.S. Lambert, *Memoirs of the Unemployed* (London, 1934), p. 46.
20. Ibid., pp. 25-6, 48.
21. E.H. Follis, 'The Unemployed Get a Break', *The Plebs*, November 1937.
22. C.L. Mowat, *Britain Between the Wars, 1918–1940* (London, 1955), pp. 480-2.
23. Ibid., pp. 484, 500; Oxley, op. cit., p. 133.
24. A.M. Cameron, *Civilisation and the Unemployed* (London, 1934), pp. 15, 19.
25. Robert Sinclair, *Metropolitan Man* (London, 1937), pp. 206-9.
26. J.B. Priestley, *English Journey* (London, 1937), p. 306.
27. Allen Hutt, *British Trade Unionism* (London, 1938), p. 122.
28. Hutt, *The Condition of the Working Class in Britain*, op. cit., pp. 180, 199.
29. Fenner Brockway, *Workers' Front* (London, 1938), p. 23.
30. Adam B. Ulam, *Philosophical Foundations of English Socialism* (Cambridge, Mass.), p. 151; and E. Wight Bakke, *The Unemployed Man* (London, 1933), p. 233.
31. Colyer, op. cit., p. 41.
32. Hannington, op. cit., p. 79.
33. Ibid., pp. 272-81.
34. 'Herbert G. Gutman', in *Visions of History*, ed. Henry Abelove (New York, 1983), p. 202.

Conclusion

1. 'Indeed, marxism has always found this activity a difficult matter to handle because of the failure of historians really to question either the subsumptionist view of the labour process or the reductionism of Leninist views of trade union consciousness. Within British culture, this failure has been compounded by the absence of any firmly entrenched intellectual traditions to accommodate the politics of resistance. In this

context, the supremacy of Labourism is perfectly comprehensible as providing the closest fit between the material situation of the working class and the expressions of that situation within a political vocabulary.' Richard Price, 'The Labour Process and Labour History', *Social History*, Vol. 8, No. 1, 1983, p. 73; Cliff Slaughter, 'The English Working Class', *Labour Review*, Spring 1985; Theodore Rothstein, *From Chartism to Labourism* (London, 1929), passim.

2. For example, David Montgomery, *Worker's Control in America* (Cambridge, 1979); Jeremy Brecher, *Strike* (San Francisco, 1972).

3. Victor Kiernan, 'Labour and Literate in Nineteenth-Century Britain', *Ideology and the Labour Movement*, ed. David Martin (London, 1979), p. 59. My emphasis; Tom Nairn, 'The English Working Class', *New Left Review*, No. 24, 1964. For a brilliant counter-attack on Nairn, see E.P. Thompson, *The Poverty of Theory* (London, 1978), pp. 35-88.

4. Dale Tomich and Anson G. Rabinach, 'George Haup, 1928–1978, *International Labor and Working Class History"*, No. 14, 1979, p. 3.

5. Price, op. cit., p. 73.

6. Ibid., p. 74.

7. An exaggeration of the domination of bourgeois ideas on workers' consciousness may, in the idiom of Ralph Miliband, 'lead to a quite inadequate account being taken of the many-sided and permanent challenge which is directed at the ideological predominance of the "ruling class", and of the fact that this challenge, notwithstanding all difficulties and disadvantages, produces a steady erosion of that predominance'. Ralph Miliband, *Marxism and Politics* (Oxford, 1978), p. 52.; Rowland Kenney, *Men and Rails* (London, 1913), p. 179; George Stone, *A History of Labour* (London, 1921), p. 240; *Short History of the Modern British Working-Class Movement* (London, 1919), pp. 62-9.

8. 'In any case, poaching was not generally regarded as anti-social behaviour. The result was a sort of guerilla warfare'. Henry Pelling, *Popular Politics and Society in Late Victorian Britain* (London, 1968), p. 70.

9. Although he seems to underestimate what he calls 'anti-capitalist cultural resistance', Bob Holton acknowledges that 'An area of State social control was the social welfare programme enacted by the Liberals between 1906 and 1914. Whatever their progressive "Welfare State" reputation, such policies were designed to discipline labour and make it more efficient.' But he makes no attempt to look at the English workers' resistance to the Liberals' social welfare legislation. Bob Holton, *British Syndicalism, 1900–1914* (London, 1976), pp. 203, 35.

10. In a critical evaluation of my draft chapter, 'English Working-Class Attitudes to State Intervention and the Labour Unrest, 1883–1914', Victor Kiernan used those words to describe working-class opposition to the Liberals' social welfare legislation. Letter to the author, 9 March, 1979. Though I disagree with his conceptualisation of English working-class history, I thank him for offering his critical comments. Robert Williams, *The New Labour Outlook* (London, 1921), pp. 134-7; B.L.

Hutchins, *Woman in Modern Industry* (London, 1915), pp. 128-31.
11. For an account of the children's strikes, see Dave Marson, *The Children's Strikes of 1911* (Oxford, 1972); James D. Young, *John Maclean* (Glasgow, 1988), pp. 12-33.
12. Arnold Freeman, *Boy Life and Labour* (London, 1914), p. 135.
13. *Morning Post,* 19 September, 1913.
14. *Justice,* 9 July, 1914.
15. Jeremy Seabrook, *The Unprivileged* (Harmondsworth, 1973), p. 65; T.E. Kebbel, *The Agricultural Labourer* (London, 1893), p. 230; Thomas Holmes, *London's Underworld* (London, 1912), p. 192.
16. *New Statesman,* 13 March, 1915; John E. Gorst, *The Children of the Nation* (London, 1907), p.6; Olive C. Malvery, *The Soul Market* (London, 1906), p. 191.
17. Jack Metzgan, 'Plant Shutdown and Workers Response: The Case of Johnstown', *Socialist Review,* No. 53, 1980, p. 37.
18. English working people accused doctors of 'running after the rich and cutting about the poor'. Stephen Reynolds, *A Poor Man's House* (London, 1908), p. 188.
19. Victor Kiernan, 'Working Class and Nation in Nineteenth-Century Britain', *Rebels and Their Causes,* ed. Maurice Cornforth (London, 1978), p. 127.
20. Standish Meacham, *A Life Apart. The English Working Class 1890–1914* (London, 1977), p. 219.
21. Price, op. cit., p. 69.
22. C.B. Hawkins, *Norwich. A Social Study* (London, 1910), p. 287.
23. C.M.Lloyd, *Trade Unionism* (London, 1914), p. 129.
24. Quoted in Charles Watney and James A. Little, *Industrial Warfare* (London, 1913), p. 247; Edward Tupper, *Seamen's Torch* (London, 1938), p. 70; N.S. Rowntree, *The Human Needs of Labour* (London, 1918), p. 165; C.L. Goodrich, *The Frontier of Control* (London, 1918), p. 109.
25. Leonard Hall, *The Old and the New Unionism* (Manchester, 1893), p. 9.
26. Joseph Clayton, *The Rise and Decline of Socialism in Great Britain 1844–1924* (London, 1926), p. 109.
27. Quoted in George Rude, *Ideology and Popular Protest* (New York), 1980, p. 163.
28. Frederick Engels, *The Condition of the Working-Class in England in 1844* (London, 1892), p. xviii.
29. Karl Marx and Frederick Engels, *Letters to Americans, 1848–1895* (New York, 1953), p. 224.
30. 'They have to recognise, for instance, the marked effect which the temperate lives of the leaders of the new unionism have upon the rank-and-file.' R.A. Woods, *English Social Movements* (London, 1895), p. 228; A.M. Bulley and M. Whitlet, *Women's Work* (London, 1894), p. 83; L.T. Hobhouse, *The Labour Movement* (London, 1912), p. 92; F.E. Green, *The Tyranny of the Countryside* (London, 1913), p. 15.
31. C. Violet Butler, *Social Conditions in Oxford* (London, 1912), p. 220.
32. R.H. Sherard, *The White Slaves of England* (London, 1897), p. 34.

33. Christopher Holdenby, *Folk of the Furrow* (London, 1913), p. 222;
    M. Loane, *The Queen's Poor* (London, 1910), p. 127.
34. Walter Besant, *The Poor in Great Cities* (London, 1896), p. 261.
35. Sir William Not-Bower, *Fifty-Two Years A Policeman* (London, 1926),
    p. 159.
36. Edward Bernstein, *My Years of Exile* (London, 1921), p. 209.
37. Peter Gordon, *The Victorian School* (London, 1974), p. 115.
38. Clayton, op. cit., p. 116.
39. Walter Bateson, *The Way We Came* (Bradford, 1928), p. 116.
40. *Infancy of Labour*, 29 March 1904, Vol 1, p. 236. Library of the London
    School of Economics; Edward A. Parry, *The Law and the Poor*
    (London, 1914), p. 308.
41. Richard Price, 'Rethinking Labour History: The Importance of Work',
    Social Conflict and the Political Order in Modern Britain (London,
    1982), ed. James Cronin, p. 198.
42. Stephen Yeo, 'A Phase in the Social History of Socialism,
    c.1885–c.1895', *Bulletin of the Society for the Study of Labour
    History*, No. 22, 1971, p. 6.
43. Robert Roberts, *The Classic Slum* (Harmondsworth, 1973), p. 100; Will
    Thorne, *My Life's Battles* (London, 1925), p. 134; Jack Jones, *His Book*
    (London, 1924), p. 13; Charles Watney and James A. Little, *Industrial
    Warfare* (London, 1912), pp. 2-10; William Paul, *The State* (Glasgow,
    1918), pp. 178-81; R. Page Arnot, *South Wales Miners* (London, 1967),
    p. 70.
44. Woods, op. cit., p. 10.
45. Stephen Yeo, 'A New Life: The Religion of Socialism', *History
    Workshop*, No. 4, 1977, p. 31; T.G. Spyers, *The Labour Question*
    (London, 1984), p. 22; H.A. Mess, *Factory Legislation and its
    Administration* (London, 1926), pp. 162-9.
46. Sheila Rowbotham and Jeffrey Weeks, *Socialism and the New Life*
    (London, 1977), pp. 103-4.
47. R.E. Dowse, *Left in the Centre* (London, 1966), pp. 17-18.
48. André Tridon, *The New Unionism* (New York, 1915), p. 148. Emphasis
    in original.
49. H.L. Smith and V. Nash, *The Story of the Dockers' Strike* (London,
    1889), p. 82; Karl Pearson, *The Chances of Death* (London, 1897), Vol.
    1, p. 237; Barbara Drake, *Women in Trade Unions* (London, 1921), p.
    47.
50. A.A. Bulley and M. Whitley, *Women's Work* (London, 1894), pp.
    99-100.
51. *Annual Report of the Trades Union Congress*, 1910, p. 122.
52. Mary A. Hamilton, *Mary Macarthur* (London, 1925), p. 102.
53. Price, 'The Labour Process and Labour History', op. cit., p. 70.
54. Meacham, op. cit., p. 194.
55. Stanley Aronowitz, *False Promises: The Shaping of American Working
    Class Consciousness* (New York, 1973), p. 58.
56. Ibid., p. 62.
57. Ibid., p. 65.

58. Price, 'The Labour Process and Labour History', op. cit., p. 70.
59. William Aykott Orton, *Labour in Transition* (London, 1921), pp. xxii-xxiii,
60. David Smith, *Socialist Propaganda in the Twentieth-Century British Novel* (London, 1978), p. 29.
61. Robert Tressell, *The Ragged Trousered Philanthropists* (London, 1965), p. 46.
62. Price, 'The Labour Process and Labour History', op. cit., p. 79.
63. Shaw Desmond, *Labour: The Giant with the Feet of Clay* (London, 1921), p. 145; Flora Thompson, *From Lark Rise to Candleford* (London, 1948), p. 462; Arthur Gleason and Paul U. Kellogg, *British Labor and the War* (New York, 1919), passim; *Woman's Trade Union Review*, April 1923.
64. Egon Wertheimer, *Portrait of the Labour Party* (New York, 1929), pp. 94-5.
65. *British Labor Speaks*, ed. W. Hogue (New York, 1924), p. 67.
66. Wertheimer, op. cit., p. 117.
67. Paul Blanshard, *An Outline of the British Labor Movement* (New York, 1923), pp. 91-100.
68. Mark Starr, *Lies and Hate in Education* (London, 1929), pp. 68-70.
69. Blanshard, op. cit., p. 188.
70. Herbert Tracey, *The British Press* (London, 1929), p. 95; Dean E. McHenry, *The Labour Party in Transition, 1931–1938* (London, 1938), pp. 70-8.
71. Wertheimer, op. cit., p. 90.
72. Peter Worsley, 'Britain — Unknown Country', *The New Reasoner*, No. 5, 1958, p. 59.
73. Ferdynand Zweig, *The British Worker* (Harmondsworth, 1952), pp. 188, 201.

Index

This book is

Exmouth

INTER-SITE LOAN
Cancelled

University of Plymouth Library

Subject to status this item may be renewed
via your Voyager account

http://voyager.plymouth.ac.uk

Exeter tel: (01392) 475049
Exmouth tel: (01395) 255331
Plymouth tel: (01752) 232323